Grace grew up in Scotland and has lived in Australia for over two decades. Her professional life has been spent as a theatre director and playwright and she has written two books on musical theatre: *Her Turn on Stage: The Role of Women in Musical Theatre (*McFarland 2015) and *National Identity and the British Musical: From Blood Brothers to Cinderella* (Methuen Drama 2022). Grace has a PhD from the University of Technology Sydney. Grace loves to swim at Wylie's Baths.

For Mum, who loved to swim.

Grace Barnes

IN SEARCH OF MINA WYLIE

AUSTIN MACAULEY PUBLISHERS™

LONDON * CAMBRIDGE * NEW YORK * SHARJAH

ISBN 9781398437715 (Paperback)
ISBN 9781398437722 (ePub e-book)

www.austinmacauley.com

First Published 2023
Austin Macauley Publishers Ltd®
1 Canada Square
Canary Wharf
London
E14 5AA

Throughout this process, a number of people were extremely helpful and generous with their time. I would like to take this opportunity to acknowledge the following people for their guidance and for sharing their knowledge.

The staff in the Special Collections at the Mitchell Library. Georgina Keep, Local Studies Librarian at Randwick City Council, based in the Bowen Library. Joy England and Katrina Corcoran at Pymble Ladies College. Marion Washburn, archivist in the Henning Library at the International Swimming Hall of Fame in Fort Lauderdale. Also, Bruce Wigo, CEO at the ISHOF, for his enthusiasm concerning this project.

Eileen Slarke, Courtney Tallon and Tony Cousins at Wylie's Baths, Coogee.

Jo Thompson, daughter of Vivian Chalwin, who granted me access to personal photographs and papers concerning her father and Chalwin Castle.

My sincere thanks to you all.

Introduction

Many older homes rest upon a dark and airless void that signifies the end of the building foundations and the beginning of the house itself. An empty space filled with the imagination of children and the occasional feral creature. It is the forgotten room, rarely entered and fit only for storing lawn mowers or rusty bicycles. In a space exactly like this, beneath a family home in the Sydney beach suburb of Coogee, a secret lay undiscovered for almost a decade. Protected from the outside world by the instability of memory and a layer of sand blown in from the nearby beach.

This secret belonged to Wilhelmina Wylie, one of the greatest swimmers Australia ever produced. Born on 27 June 1891, Wilhelmina—always known as Mina—was one of two swimmers who were the first women to represent Australia at an Olympic Games in 1912. When she retired from competition after a career spanning an incredible two decades, Mina Wylie had won more state and national titles than any other Australian swimmer, male or female, and also held more world records in more strokes than any other female swimmer worldwide. What makes her success even more extraordinary is the fact that it occurred against a backdrop of virulent opposition against women engaging in all forms of sport.

Mina was one of the first female sporting celebrities—not just within Australia—and at one point she was so well known that a letter addressed only to 'Miss Mina Wylie, Coogee' was delivered to her home. Yet, whenever I tell anyone I am writing about her, I am invariably met with a blank stare and the response, 'Who?' In a nation that judges its international standing by sporting success, it could be the fact that the majority of Mina's triumphs took place on home soil, which reduced their long-term impact. Equally likely is the fact that she was a woman in an arena with an indisputable male bias. How likely is it, after all, that a male swimmer with her credentials would disappear so quickly and so completely in a country styling itself as the Sporting Nation?

While the country that produced Dawn Fraser, Shane Gould and Ian Thorpe may have forgotten the unequalled achievements of this early swimming pioneer,

Mina Wylie had an acute sense of her own importance within the sporting history of the nation. Throughout her career she saved programmes, posters, ticket stubs, autographs, medals, postcards, race position labels, newspaper cuttings, photographs … in fact, anything which bore witness to her time in the sun. She hoarded this trove for over five decades, until the inevitable reckoning which accompanies old age could be postponed no longer.

Sometime in the late 1970s, Mina, now in her mid-eighties, contemplated the piles of scraps left over from a life. She made decisions on what to keep and what to throw away, what was relevant and what was not. She read her mother's handwriting and longed for the security of childhood again. She held her father's swimming certificates and placed them carefully alongside her own. She gazed at the photograph of the three 1912 Olympic medallists from the inaugural 100m ladies freestyle in Stockholm, and she smiled at her youthful, defiant self. She pondered on how easy it was to see the physical deterioration of a vigorous body over the years and wondered if the fighting spirit also gradually eroded with time. Frightening, the now elderly swimmer mused, on how we go from that to this.

I have no way of knowing how many hours, or even days, it took for Mina to sift through the bundles of keepsakes from her past life as a champion swimmer. Neither do I know what exactly prompted her decision to methodically pack her chosen possessions into thirteen individual boxes and place them in a large airtight metal chest, hidden in the dark and dusty space beneath the Coogee house she had lived in for over fifty years. What I know is that she told no one of the existence of the treasure chest when she moved to a nearby nursing home, leaving it to chance that it might be discovered and the contents brought back into the light. As incredible as it may seem, Mina appears to have locked the lid of the metal chest containing the evidence of her glorious career, gone back upstairs into the house and forgotten her own life.

If I step back and picture the scene which took place in that forgotten space, I see an elderly woman kneeling in the sand, secretly squirrelling her life away for safe-keeping. And I find the clandestine of nature of the task she has set herself, agonising. Alone and utilising secrecy to avoid the scorn ignited by sentimental attachment to water-stained shipboard menus and illegible postcards. I see an image shrouded in loneliness. Or at least, isolation. The long-distance swimmer adrift from the pilot boat with only the distant cliffs to guide her.

But perhaps I am wrong. Perhaps this scene played out in a stuffy basement was Mina's last act of defiance against the ongoing view of female athletes as irrelevant. I have come to believe that when she selected artefacts and concealed the boxes, she did so in the unswerving belief that someone else would appreciate the significance of an autograph album from 1912, and a signed photograph of the American freestyling sensation, Ethelda Bleibtrey. Someone, Mina was convinced, at some point, would understand the meaning of all of this.

Someone would hold her breath as she held the Olympic medal in her hand, would recognise the camaraderie between team mates laughing in photographs, and would be so intrigued by what she found in these boxes that she would look further afield, even travelling abroad, in her search for a forgotten champion. Someone, someday, would thank Mina Wylie for having the foresight to preserve this cache in a safe place.

Someone like me.

In which case, the scene beneath the house in Neptune Street is neither sad nor poignant, but glorious in its boldness. If the boxes were not forgotten in the confusion of old age, but deliberately hidden, then the image I have conjured up of an elderly woman ensuring that her deeds are remembered is, in its own way, joyous. A demand that women's lives are not ignored or dismissed but brought out of storage and placed alongside the acts of the lofty 'great men' so often accorded gratuitous praise for lesser feats.

Mina Wylie calls to me across the century because I was a child who had the reply, 'an Olympic swimmer', ready for the parade of adults enquiring as to what I would be when I grew up. I competed from the age of nine and my high school years were dominated by early morning training sessions and a preoccupation with cutting a fraction of a second off my personal best in the 100m freestyle.

I was the youngest member of the county team and somewhere at the back of a rarely opened drawer, are the medals and certificates I won during this time. They tarnish and fade more with each year that I do not get around to having them framed. Why do I keep these mementoes from almost four decades ago when they are of no value to anyone other than myself? Why did Mina hold onto swimming carnival programmes when she was the only person left alive who could put faces to the names listed inside? Because these artefacts defined her. This poster, this newspaper report, this medal, this is how she saw herself. More importantly, this is how she wanted to be remembered.

Mina died in 1984, aged either 86 or 93, depending which obituary one chooses to believe. The family home in Neptune Street was sold to local resident Meredith Clark, and it was she who discovered the boxes containing the swimming memorabilia and personal items belonging to Mina and to her father Henry, also a champion swimmer. Meredith Clark was astute enough to realise the historical value of her find and offered the archive to the Mitchell Library in Sydney, which took possession of it in 1986.

The version of Mina's life that I have ended up telling is inspired by what is now named the Mina Wylie Collection[1] housed in the Special Collections at the Mitchell. I cannot claim that my version of events is the definitive one, or even one hundred percent factually correct. As with all personal collections, there are gaps and missing years which are too tantalising to leave empty. This is my interpretation of the contents of the hidden boxes and at times, the temptation to succumb to imagination has proved hard to resist. It might not, of course, have been Mina herself who assembled the collection and stored it in the metal chest, but for the purpose of this narrative I am assuming that it was. My version of Mina's life admittedly has elements of fiction, but it is fiction inspired by the traces she left behind.

As I began my investigation, I realised that my perception of Mina as a former champion who was dismissed as having passed her sell-by date was not entirely correct. Her status as 'one of the first' women to swim for Australia at an Olympic Games has ensured her inclusion in sporting history, and her association with Wylie's Baths in Coogee is proudly noted by the local community. Indeed, a three-sided bronze statue of Mina is the first thing visitors encounter when they pass through the gates of the ocean pool built by Mina's father, Henry, in 1907.[2] One side of the statue greets the visitors as they arrive, another watches the swimmers in the pool below and the third side looks towards Randwick Cemetery where Mina is buried.

It did not take me long to reach the conclusion that three sides were nowhere near enough to do justice to this woman who so intrigued me. A woman who, I was to discover, is enveloped—and indeed surrounded herself—in a myriad of fictions and half-truths. For although Mina may not be completely forgotten amongst certain circles, she is misremembered. Over time, her image has been reconstructed and manipulated to suit the prevailing mood and to offer up a much-needed sporting heroine in a land of aggressively masculine heroes.

The myths attached to Mina have subsequently been enshrined as fact, and the truth overlooked in favour of a better story. A story in which the principal character is a feminist advocate and a sporting pioneer who 'battled' chauvinistic authorities to claim her right to compete. The fact that this tale is not true only added to my fascination.

Extracting Mina's life from the scraps she concealed and the myths she encouraged seems to me to mirror the process employed by women in Mina's era who engaged in the decorative art of decoupage. I select an object, trim it to suit my requirements and carefully paste it down within the frame. I then arrange a complementary item designed to illuminate the first and bestow depth on the whole, and I repeat the process.

Again and again and again. Choosing, rearranging, varnishing ... until an image begins to emerge, ultimately coalescing into an intricate mosaic. I do this because I know that Mina refused to accept the fact that she might disappear. She held onto the proof of her glory years not because she was in love with her younger Olympian self, but because she had an idea, maybe only the vaguest of notions, of her importance within the history of women athletes in Australia.

Many pieces, one whole.

Three sides, one person.

When Mina first began competing in the early 1900s, society viewed the female swimmer as immodest and lacking in the Victorian virtues of decorum and ladylike femininity. Her behaviour—flaunting her body and engaging in strenuous physical activity—repulsed and infuriated large sections of conventional society. Women who swam, or indeed took part in any form of sport, were derided for being in possession of a competitive spirit, regarded as an innately masculine quality. These attitudes ensured that women's sport was either dismissed as abhorrent or viewed as a trivial addendum to the real business of men's sport. Consequently, few visual or written records of women's sporting achievements were maintained. This makes Mina's trove valuable beyond the personal as it fills one tiny corner of the gaping space where the early women athletes should be. Those rebellious young women who abandoned corsets and restrictive frills, careered through country lanes on bicycles, rowed down the Brisbane river and raced each other in ocean pools. Those women, like Mina Wylie, who shrugged off the disapproval, ignored the taunts and revelled in their new-found physical freedom. In doing so, they redefined femininity for the new, modern era.

When I study the photographs taken of Mina around various swimming pools, it is her stance that convinces me that here is someone I instinctively know well. Her head is high, her shoulders back and her eyes coolly return the gaze of the camera, as if issuing a challenge. Mina strikes me as a woman who saw no reason to conform and lived life on her own terms. That appeals to me. I want to be in those sepia photographs with her. I want to swim laps with her at her father's pool in Coogee and discuss our stroke technique on the boardwalk above. I long to have blazed a trail and to have been alive to thrill at the triumphs of the first women to fly planes, swim the English Channel, drive racing cars, explore new lands, race horses, organise unions …

I know I would have thrived amongst those committed women demanding their place in the polling booths, on the playing field and in the Universities.

I see myself as Mina's team mate, pacing her over endless laps at Wylie's Baths. I am the swimmer who closes the gap against the Americans in the third lap of the relay, enabling Mina to bring home gold in the final one hundred. We do this together. As one.

Some forty years ago, an elderly woman who had once been a champion picked out a photograph from a pile and studied the image of a young swimmer. Dressed in a swimsuit cut higher on the thigh and lower in the neck than regulations allowed, the woman's hands rested boldly on her hips.

Her hair fell over her shoulders in waves and a gold bangle shone on one wrist. Her eyes issued a dare to the onlooker: just try and stop me. Try. The elderly woman smiled.

'I knew you were in there somewhere.'

Decades after the former champion had stopped swimming for good, a middle-aged woman with an insatiable need to know lifted the lid of a box in a hushed library. And she too smiled.

'There you are,' she breathed. 'There you are.'

Items from the Mina Wylie collection, Mitchell Library, Sydney.

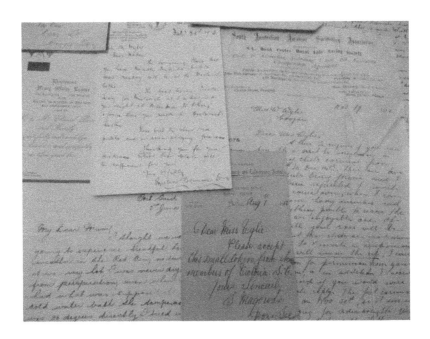

Letters contained in the Mina Wylie collection, Mitchell Library, Sydney.

Programmes from the swimming competition, 1912 Olympic Games in Stockholm. Mina Wylie collection, Mitchell Library, Sydney.

Chapter 1
The Grand Old Lady of Australian Swimming

The fact that Mina Wylie is remembered at all in contemporary culture is remarkable given the lack of recording of women's swimming events in the early days of competition and the male bias in sporting history. Her rediscovery amidst a blaze of front-page publicity in 1975 seems an appropriate coda for such a remarkable life: the last glowing sunbeam before the inevitable rise of the moon. Following her retirement in 1924, Mina lived with her father, Henry, and her brother, Harry, in the family home in Coogee, their days, as ever, revolving around the operation of the family business—Wylie's Baths.

In 1928, she joined the staff of Pymble Ladies College (PLC) on Sydney's north shore as a swimming teacher and remained there for over forty years. She attended the 1956 Olympics in Melbourne as a VIP guest and appears in grainy film footage of a charity event held at the private home of sporting official Vivian Chalwin in 1957. But apart from those two occasions, she left behind few traces of her life beyond the competitive swimming circuit. Had she not been selected for induction into the International Swimming Hall of Fame (ISHOF) in Florida in 1975, it is highly likely Mina would have disappeared into the footnotes of Australia's sporting history. As it was, the controversy that erupted when the Federal government refused to contribute funds to enable her to attend her induction ceremony transformed her from a long-forgotten champion into headline news and, inadvertently, a feminist advocate.

In 1975, young Australian swimming fans basked in the Olympic glory of Shane Gould, Beverley Whitfield and Gail Neal, who had brought home five gold medals from the Munich competition three years previously. The parents of this generation still recalled the triumphant 1956 Melbourne Olympics and the extraordinary clean sweep by Australian swimmers Dawn Fraser, Lorraine Crapp, Faith Leach, Jon Hendricks, John Devitt and Gary Chapman in their respective 100m freestyle finals. Australia was a swimming nation to be reckoned with, of that there was no doubt, but beyond the swimming circuit itself there were few who had an awareness of just how far back this history stretched. And only two members of the triumphant 1912 Olympic team were left alive to tell the tale: 86-year-old Les Boardman, who had won gold alongside Cecil Healy, Malcolm Champion and Harold Hardwick in the 4 x 200m freestyle relay, and Mina Wylie.

A handful of Coogee residents were aware they had a former champion living in their midst and curious children pointed out the grey-haired portly woman in a shapeless flowery dress passing through the turnstiles of what had once been Wylie's Baths.

'She won an Olympic medal.'

'No, she didn't.'

But by and large, Mina Wylie and her grinning team mates from the harbour pool in Stockholm now languished in forgotten photograph albums. The Sporting Nation had moved on to televised competitions, electronic timing and younger and faster swimmers. Two world wars and twelve Olympic games had passed since Mina and team mate, Fanny Durack, first gave Australian women a reason to celebrate their potential physical prowess. Henry had been dead for almost sixty years and Mina, in her 80s in 1975, whiled away the days swimming her regular laps, reading detective novels and playing the occasional game of cards with Harry. She had been a champion, she retired, and the nation looked elsewhere. End of story.

Except it was not the end of the story.

In 1974, Mina had received a letter from Buck Dawson, the executive director of the International Swimming Hall of Fame in Fort Lauderdale, Florida, informing her that she had been selected as an Honoree and would be inducted into the Hall of Champions at a ceremony the following year. This was a huge honour as it placed Mina alongside the greats of world swimming, including Australians Dawn Fraser, Murray Rose, Boy Charlton and Fanny Durack. It was both an assurance that she was not forgotten and validation that she was still relevant to the international swimming community. Mina dusted off her Olympic team blazer and eagerly anticipated the trip, blithely assuming that the government would offer financial assistance.

In early May 1975, however, she told a reporter that she would be unable to attend the Florida ceremony later that month due to the refusal of the Federal government to pay her fare despite having done so three years previously for the legendary Dawn Fraser. The media smelt blood. Here was the perfect opportunity to both shame the Federal government and champion the archetypal Aussie Battler with a story saturated in populist appeal. Then 83 years old, Mina was cast as the hard done by and overlooked heroine of Australian swimming. The plucky youngster who had brought glory to the fledgling nation, now spurned by unsympathetic authorities who refused to be swayed either by her age or her claims of financial hardship. This, in the land that prided itself on a 'fair go'. The fact that a week earlier these same journalists had never heard of her, was neither here nor there.

Into the growing controversy galloped a knight in shining armour in the guise of NSW MP, Neil Pickard. He quickly became the driving force behind the escalating media call for the government to pay for Mina to travel to Florida, although why he took up her cause with such enthusiasm is not clear given that he was not her local MP. When his request for funding from the Federal Government was refused, Pickard established a public fund for donations and contributed $100 of his own money. Being an MP, he naturally made this expansive gesture in front of a group of assembled journalists, ensuring that the Sydney newspapers carried the story of the appeal in the following morning editions.

It may have been Mina's age that touched a nerve with readers, or outrage at the 'un-Australian' attitude from the government towards a former sporting star. It may even have been a collective sense of guilt at having allowed this early pioneer to slip from national memory. Whatever it was, the Sydney public responded to Pickard's appeal for donations in a way no one had foreseen. Within twenty-four hours, enough money had been raised to cover the cost of both Mina and her brother Harry to fly to Florida to be present at her induction ceremony into the International Swimming Hall of Fame.

Mina's self-effacing remark, 'I'm surprised anybody still cared. I thought people would have forgotten about me by now' was quoted in the *Daily Mirror*[3] on 13 May and carried an undeniable aura of truth. She had been retired from competitive swimming for over fifty years and the populace had indeed forgotten about her. But Neil Pickard and his fund ignited public imagination. As did the knowledge that the first woman to represent Australia in swimming at an Olympic Games was alive and well and swimming in Coogee.

On 14 May 1975, the front page of the *Sydney Morning Herald* carried the headlines, 'Swim star wins trip to the US', above a large image of a beaming

Mina holding aloft her newly acquired passport and Neil Pickard benignly looking on. A copy of this photograph is amongst Mina's items held by the Mitchell Library and what makes this fact interesting is that the image was donated by Mina herself in 1976. So, far from being ignored, as I had initially (and self-righteously) assumed, a respected archival institution had recognised Mina's value as a historical subject a full ten years before her memorabilia had been discovered. In other words, she was already on their radar.

Whether it was Mina who approached the Mitchell Library in 1976 with an offer to donate photographs, or vice versa, is less relevant than the fact that the institution was willing to accommodate her alongside comparable 'great' luminaries. And it is highly likely that this was a direct result of the row over Florida played out in on the front pages of the Sydney newspapers. If the Federal government had simply agreed to pay Mina's fare to the USA, there is a good chance the media would have been interested in the story only as an aside: three or four lines buried in the weekend sporting section focusing on 'Australia's Oldest Olympian'.

But in an ironic twist, it was the obduracy of the Federal Minister for tourism and recreation at the time, Frank Stewart—who crossly informed the *Canberra Times* that it was not the responsibility of the government to pay the fares of former athletes invited overseas to receive awards[4]—that propelled Mina back into the spotlight. Pickard's fund-raising campaign not only enabled Mina to attend her induction ceremony at the International Swimming Hall of Fame (ISHOF) in Florida, it introduced her to a new generation. A generation which relished the ongoing international success of Australian swimmers and, by the mid-1970s, was increasingly preoccupied with gender equality.

The newspaper reports leading up to Pickard's public appeal highlighted Mina's participation in the 1912 Olympic Games in Stockholm over the triumphs of her later career. Her status as 'one of the first' was utilised to highlight her historical significance and to remind readers that the nation's view of itself as an egalitarian country was not without foundation. Australia, the media hinted, had been in possession of a progressive outlook towards gender long before the UK or the USA had even voiced the word equality.

The victories of Dawn Fraser and Shane Gould contributed to a popular view that it was female swimmers who were largely responsible for Australia's second position in world ranking statistics, and this too may have influenced the outpouring of support for Mina. The women's rights protests of the 1960s had brought sexual discrimination back into the public consciousness in a way, arguably, they had not been since the campaign for female political emancipation at the beginning of the century, and 1975 had been designated International Women's Year by the United Nations. The climate, therefore, was ripe for the re-emergence of a ground-breaking female athlete, particularly one who was apparently so casually dismissed by male authoritarians. Even if the staff responsible for acquisitions at the Mitchell Library had never heard of Mina Wylie prior to the Florida controversy, she now presented the perfect opportunity to fill a gap in the dearth of records of female athletes in Australia. The result was the acquisition by the library in 1976 of a group of ten photographs, including the one which had appeared in the *Sydney Morning Herald* of Pickard and Mina.

It is the timing of this donation that catches my attention. Because it had to be around this time that Mina and Harry moved from the house in Neptune Street to a nearby nursing home.[5] It also, therefore, had to coincide with the packing and storing of the boxes of memorabilia under the house, and I believe the two are related. The press interest and public support surrounding Mina's induction into the ISHOF convinced her that her past was more than personal memories.

It was an important thread within the historical tapestry of the nation. Particularly a nation obsessed with sport. The focus on her pioneering status had also made Mina aware of her achievements within the context of gender and social history and it began to dawn on her that her former swimming career held greater significance than that suggested by a drawer full of medals. A 1907 autograph album filled with girlish sentiment from swimmers at an interstate carnival was more than a selection of names and Victoriana—it was rare testament to the early days of women's competitive swimming in Australia.

This growing conviction was nurtured throughout 1975 by the ongoing interest in Mina from the media, and six months after her return from Florida she was interviewed by ex-journalist and sporting enthusiast, Neil Bennetts.[6] Bennetts had recently embarked on an ambitious oral history project focussing on outstanding Australian athletes—mainly those who had retired in the preceding ten or twenty years—and he was thrilled to discover that a 1912 Olympian had a tale to tell which was completely in tune with the mood and political preoccupations of the time.

Although the forty-minute interview with Neil Bennetts was purely for archival purposes,[7] Mina was anxious to have her facts straight. And those facts were clear as day in the newspapers and programmes and letters she had dispatched to the attic for safekeeping many decades ago. In the front room of the family home with the bay windows looking down to Henry's pool, Mina unpacked her treasures one by one until her past covered every surface of the room. When Neil Bennetts arrived at the house with his tape recorder and microphone, Harry made tea and Mina took him through her years as a champion. Bennetts admired the award from Florida and asked Mina to read the messages on the congratulatory telegrams into the microphone.

'On behalf of the government and the people of New South Wales, I congratulate you on your election to the International Swimming Hall of Fame. The response of the people of New South Wales to your election is indicative of the esteem the people of this state and nation have for you and your many swimming achievements, and for yourself. We are proud of your swimming achievements, we are proud of you and we are proud of the honour that you have brought to this country from the International Swimming Hall of Fame.'

'That's from the Premier, Tom Lewis,' Mina said. 'It was nice of him to send that, wasn't it?'

'It was indeed.'

Long after Bennetts and his tape recorder had departed, the ghosts lingered on in the front room demanding attention. Mina opened up the green cloth autograph album and heard clearly the voice of Bridgie Cloonan in her ear, 'When the distant sun is setting/ and your face I cannot see/ when you sit and think of others/ Will you sometimes think of me?' She turned the page and there was Dorothy Davies, her NSW team mate, standing in front of her, holding out her hand to take the pen and write, 'In the golden charm of friendship, consider me a link.'

Mina untied a thin red ribbon holding together a stack of postcards, and as they spilled to the floor a rush of new voices and faces floated up, infusing the air like curling cigarette smoke. 'Dear Mina, I hope by the time you have got this you will have done all in your power to bring home the ashes…'; 'Dear old sport Mina, it all helps to make things pleasant when mail arrives, especially when it comes from an old friend…'; 'Dear Miss Wylie, A line to enquire if you can pay SA a visit to assist in a couple of club carnivals from 30 Nov to 14 Dec.'

Strange, she mused, how sixty years ago was clearer to her now than last week. Often, these days, she felt as if she had swum out to wedding cake island opposite Coogee Beach and was stranded there, looking across the waves to her life here onshore. And it was blurred. Yet the voices of the long dead were clear, their faces brighter than they had ever been.

'Dear Mina, You remember I said I was going to a dance on 22 May—well I went and had a most glorious time. Had every dance but two valitas and the dance after supper. Got on splendidly and the boys would hardly believe me when I said it was my first dance…'

Vera. With her jokes and her male admirers and her peach silk evening cape. Vera, who had almost wept as she presented Mina with a bouquet of violets as she boarded R.M.S. Malwa at Circular Quay.

'Have a real good time, Mina. See as much as ever you can while you're there because you may never have the chance again. Take care of yourself. Don't lose heart go in and WIN. And accept my love and biggest hug and warmest wishes.'

What would Vera think of her old schoolmate being preserved in the vaults of the Mitchell Library? More to the point, what would her mother, Florence, think? Her only daughter a 'person of value'. That's what the Library had called her in the letter asking for photographs. Florence would have framed that letter, or at least made sure everyone in Coogee read it somehow. '… up to ten photographs of your own choosing …' Ten images to sum up a life.

A picture of the family pool, of course, and one of Henry. On the back Mina wrote his name, and added 'Founder and builder of Wylie's Baths, Coogee, NSW'. Then she hesitated. What year did the baths open? She had still been at school—she remembered that because all the girls came for a swim. Not entirely sure that she was correct, Mina wrote, 'Baths built 1912', and placed the photograph in the folder marked Mitchell. Then the picture of her with all her medals pinned to her swimsuit—she remembered they tore the light silk.

A studio portrait taken in front of a backdrop of the sea—Mum had liked that shot. And a copy of the image that had appeared on the front page of *The Daily Telegraph* in February 1920[8], showing a swimmer touching a rope ahead of another swimmer in the inside lane. To be absolutely sure there was no debate, Mina wrote on the back, 'Mina Wylie defeating Fanny Durack after the Olympics at Sydney Domain 1916'. The date mattered less than the point she was making.

'You should give them the Stockholm medal,' Harry said. 'They could put it on display.'

'That stays in the family.'

It strikes me as odd that Mina gave photographs to the Mitchell Library in 1976, but not the rest of her memorabilia. She may have believed that family members would appreciate it, or she might have been of the opinion that whilst her keepsakes were enormously significant to her, the interest in a female athlete from a bygone era did not extend far beyond a small batch of photographs. On the other hand, she may have offered the entire collection to the library and been politely turned down. Archives in the 1970s primarily recorded the lives and feats of political or artistic male figures, and whilst a handful of photographs depicting the early days of women's swimming were historically significant, a pervasive view of women's sport as irrelevant may have influenced the decision makers at the library.

The demand for the establishment of women's archives which recorded the lives of women of all race and class, in every social and professional arenas, did not gain traction until the early 1980s, driven by academics from the relatively new discipline of Women's Studies and this could explain why the library accepted the thirteen boxes offered by Meredith Clark a decade later.

The ten photographs acquired by the library in 1976 told a specific story, one that reinforced Mina's status as a champion without challenging the right of male ownership over sport. Mina's need to give credit to her father and emphasise his position within the community is obvious, but her confusion concerning dates is a poignant sign of her age and, possibly, her declining mental faculties. Nonetheless, she and Harry spent a wonderful few hours sifting through the images of people and places that had once been real as they decided on which images to give to the library.

'Look Harry, the old natatorium in the city. Remember we went and saw Dad swim there?'

'There's Cecil Healy. You were sweet on him…'

But when they had leafed through every album and read every postcard, there was nothing left to say.

'Put it away, Mina. It's done now.'

And perhaps it only meant something to them because they had been there. No one else found it as enthralling as they did. Younger family members were curious for half an hour and then bored. Who cared about a swimming race sixty years ago?

Mina cared.

*

I had a great aunt whom I used to visit in a care home in the north of England. More than once she expressed her fear to me that when she died her collection of photographs of her frilled and beribboned siblings, her handsome husband who left her a widow after only three years of marriage, her mother … would all be thrown away. A life tossed into oblivion. I believe Mina had the same fear. A growing anxiety that her existence would be tipped into rubbish bags by someone who saw it only as piles of mess cluttering up a house which had to be sold. The stark reality is this: that most lives come down to one or two boxes in the end. A broken brooch, a birthday card, a menu. And whilst it seems that nothing much is actually there, it is a life. And who is anyone to decide which lives have more meaning than others?

I believe that the train of events that led to Mina packing her swimming career into boxes and hiding them in a metal chest under the family home, began with the letter from Buck Dawson inviting her to become an ISHOF honoree. The row over fares catapulted her back into the spotlight and she realised that she had a story people wanted to hear. This was confirmed by the interest shown by Neil Bennetts and the Mitchell Library, but when it came to passing on her archive, no one seemed to want it.

Yet Mina held on to her conviction that someone would. That what she had in her possession was historical gold, or silver, and she would not, could not, throw it away. Because that implied her life had been meaningless. So, she hid it. And if that was an act which now appears irrational, well, maybe it was. Perhaps Mina was fighting the clouds of confusion which blight old age and knew only that these items must be saved. Because they were her.

*

In 2008, Meredith Clark gave the Mitchell Library an additional three boxes of Mina's possessions, which she had originally offered to the Powerhouse museum in Sydney. These boxes are not yet part of the main Mina Wylie collection in the library, and they contain items of a more personal nature than the previous boxes donated by Meredith Clark. Alongside a card from the 12th

Annual Inter-School Swimming Championship in 1915, there is a nightgown and a white shirt with the initials 'H.W' embroidered onto the collar. There are seven sets of early swimming flotation aids, family photographs, travel brochures from the cities Mina visited, school books and towels from Wylie's Baths. But the item which immediately captured my imagination was Mina's black leather writing case. The lid of the case was broken and hanging at an angle, but the front section still folded down to form a makeshift desk, complete with a pad of blotting paper. An ivory ruler with Mina's name scratched into it rested in a sleeve above a sharpened pencil ready for use. There was even a stamp in one of the pockets. I imagined I knew how grown up and important this case made Mina feel because it proved she was a someone of note. A modern woman who travelled the continents in response to a request for her presence. The postcards from Europe and the USA—the cards I had read and so carefully copied—had very likely been written on this case. I thrilled to the vision of her balancing this very case on her knees as she sat in a train compartment in 1919 penning a letter home to Henry.

'My dear Dad, We left San Francisco this morning and are now on our way to Chicago which takes three days and three nights. We have a compartment to ourselves which is very nice and well we can do with it as we are tired out...'

Just as fascinating was the discovery of a folded note tucked into a compartment designed to hold envelopes. The note was in Mina's handwriting and read: 'Won at Bath Club, 21 June, 1912. London.' The Bath Club had been established in the West End of London in 1894 as an exclusive gentleman's sporting club and housed an airy indoor pool with an impressive domed ceiling. The club was unusual for the time in that it admitted female members and entire days at the pool given over to women—that is, the right kind of women. Those whose husbands could afford the membership fee. Mina recorded swimming at this pool in her 1912 diary account of her trip to Europe.

'On Friday 21st I went to have a practice in the Bath Club with Fanny which is without doubt the finest bath in the world. The same night we raced there amongst all the Dukes and Duchesses and Lords and Earls there to witness us. At this function of course we went in evening dress—something unusual to go to a swimming carnival in evening dress.'

Unintentionally, Mina illustrates the class divide which was already beginning to permeate ladies swimming, an activity which was garnering the reputation as one suitable for respectable women. The carnival Mina refers to in her diary had been organised by the Royal Life Saving Society and was intended as friendly challenge between local swimmers and their (post) Colonial cousins prior to their departure for the Olympics in Stockholm.

The evening clearly made a huge impression on Mina as she saved four copies of the elegant pink and gold programme commemorating the event, a programme, incidentally, in which she is billed as Miss Minnie Wylie. The pink and gold leaflet embodies the early ideals of amateurism, refined ladies and gentlemen with time on their hands participating in sport for sheer enjoyment. No post-race interviews or furious tears at being denied a gold medal, simply amateur athletes doing what they loved. The darker side of the amateur ideal was, of course, a set of rules designed specifically to keep the working-class sportsman out of competition.

Apart from the evening dress and the Dukes and Duchesses, the high point of the Bath Club carnival evening in 1912 was the 110 yd Ladies Scratch Race in which Mina and Fanny Durack (billed as Annie Durack) competed against five English women. Durack took first place and Mina second and, according to the programme, they were each awarded a silver chain handbag. Due to the strict rules separating the amateur from the professional, women were often given jewellery or small silver items, such as a vase, as their prize. But the folded note in Mina's writing case claims that this was her prize from that evening at the Bath Club.

Whether she was awarded a handbag or a writing case for her second place in the 110yds race is actually neither here nor there. It is the note in the leather case which intrigues me, because the writing is in the unmistakeably shaky hand of the elderly, which means that she placed it there in old age. In other words, as she was packing the boxes. Who did she think would read it, I wonder? And why did she feel the need to elaborate on where the case had come from? Because she believed had won it at the Bath Club in London in 1912, and that thought still made her proud.

*

Mina's identity as a competitive swimmer took shape from an early age. In 1902, she competed in the inaugural NSW Ladies swimming championships, winning second place in the 27yds handicap for girls under the age of ten: the fact that she was almost eleven appears to have been overlooked. Within five years of this first appearance on the competition circuit, she was the state and national champion. By the time she retired in 1924, she had been competing, and winning, for a staggering twenty-two years. Little wonder then, that her archive in the Mitchell Library reaffirms her identity as Mina Wylie, champion swimmer: it was impossible for her to see herself as anything else.

Her reluctance to throw away signed posters and menus suggests she was aware of the significance of the particular event at the time, and her role in it. Her hoarding, for want of a better word, therefore goes beyond sentimental attachment and is intrinsically bound with her sense of self. Without the evidence of her years as a swimmer, how would she know who she was?

Mina's identity in later life was clearly influenced by the memory of the achievements of her younger self, and this was reaffirmed by the 1975 media reports which focused primarily on her participation in the 1912 Stockholm Olympics, captioning articles with phrases such as 'Australia's oldest living Olympic medallist' and, 'Ex-Olympic star racing against time'. This could explain why there is a dearth of material concerning her post-swimming life. Either she herself felt that it was not worth recording, or she believed that others would think so. It is a harsh fact that public interest in an elite athlete diminishes concurrently with the inevitable loss of ability that comes with age. The fans are there for the gold medal but turn away when the athlete fails to make the final.

When I first viewed the items in Mina's archive, I was as intrigued by what was missing, as by what was there. Olympic team mate Fanny Durack is conspicuous by her absence, yet Australian swimming sensation and later Hollywood star, Annette Kellerman, is a palpable presence. Mina apparently kept no souvenirs from the 1956 Melbourne Olympics which she attended as a VIP guest, and her forty plus years as swimming coach at Pymble Ladies College on Sydney's north shore is marked by a single card. There is almost nothing to account for either her actions or her whereabouts in the years between her retirement in 1924, and her re-emergence onto the front page of the *Sydney Morning Herald* in 1975.

It is as if, in those five decades, she simply ceased to exist. For someone whose identity was so closely entwined with her status as a competitive swimmer, perhaps disappearing is exactly what Mina felt she did. Having said that, I don't get the impression that she wallowed in self-pity at the loss of her glorious career, nor struggled with 'normal' life, unsure of how to define herself. Mina left the competition circuit behind and successfully, and from what I can surmise, happily, reinvented herself. She was a pragmatist and was under no illusion that the career of a swimmer comes with a time limit. Her father, after all, had once been a champion.

I can't possibly begin to understand the reasoning behind what Mina chose to keep and what she threw away. Her choices may have been dictated by space—a postcard from Paris instead of programmes from the 1956 Melbourne Olympics. If she was experiencing confusion due to her age, possibly even the onset of dementia, then the early years would be clearer in her mind than her more recent past.

Consequently, she saved what she remembered and threw away what she did not recognise. There may have been no cohesive rationale driving her decisions, and some of the more random items in the archive—receipts, cinema tickets, an appointment card for the dentist—hint that she saved her swimming memorabilia alongside whatever else happened to be at hand. Did she really mean to include playing cards, sewing patterns, the Port of Sydney sun, moon and tides tables for February 1940 and a series of projector slides depicting the visit of the Duke of York to Sydney in 1901, in the same collection as an autograph album from the Stockholm Olympics?

The most obvious glaring absence in the Mitchell collection is Mina's Olympic medal. None of her medals were actually recovered by Meredith Clark, due to the fact that Mina had previously bequeathed them, and the medals belonging to Henry, to her nephew. As a woman who never married, Mina did not have an engagement or wedding ring to ritualistically pass down through the family line. Her medals were her heirlooms and she endowed this inheritance with the same meaning that other women bestow upon yellowing wedding dresses or lace christening shawls.

Mina's nephew—the son of her older brother, Walter—donated the collection of medals to the Mitchell Library in 2004, but they are held separately from the rest of the archive and it is not possible to view them without first making an appointment. Perhaps if a little more attention was paid to women in Australia's sporting history, Mina and Fanny Durack's medals would be on display in the sporting museum at the Melbourne Cricket Ground, albeit in the one dark corner attributed to 'Women in Sport'. As it is, Mina's medal resides in a vault beneath the Mitchell Library, occasionally brought into the light for curious researchers to exclaim over under the watchful eye of a vigilant staff member.

I was unprepared for the sheer beauty of the Stockholm medal. And the weight of it, for something only thirty-three millimetres in diameter. I donned the protective white cotton gloves and held Mina's greatest triumph in my hand. Here it was. These few ounces of silver that I had read about, imagined and longed for myself, at one point. Here it was. This small object was what divided Mina's life into before, and after. From national swimmer, to international celebrity. This, in my gloved hand, was what remained of the event which had determined the rest of her life.

The face of the medal depicts a figure standing beside a bust of Pehr Henrik Ling, founder of the Swedish gymnastic system, proclaiming the opening of the games. Encircling the figure are the words 'Olympiska Spelen Stockholm' and the year, 1912. On the reverse side, a victorious—and for some reason, naked— male athlete is crowned with a laurel wreath by two semi-naked women. This design had previously adorned the reverse side of the 1908 London Olympic medals and may have been a deliberate reflection of the views of French aristocrat Baron Pierre de Coubertain, who had revived the Olympic games in 1896. Coubertain repeatedly expressed his belief that the purpose of the modern Olympics was to exalt and honour male athleticism and the rightful place of women was in the spectator stands where they could tender their applause as a reward to the male athletes.

Certainly, the image of the triumphant male being feted by adoring women was in tune with Coubertain's unabashed chauvinism. Mina's name and the event for which the medal was won is engraved around the edge of the medal and the silver disc nestles within velvet in a red leather box which would comfortably fit into the pocket of a sporting blazer. Unlike current Olympic games, when medal presentations take place throughout each competition, a separate medal ceremony was held on the final day of the 1912 festival. Mina assembled with some three hundred fellow medallists in the impressive newly built stadium and was handed her treasure by the Swedish Crown Prince Gustaf Adolph in front of around thirteen thousand spectators. Including her father, Henry.

I was aware that the awe inspired by actually holding Mina's Olympic medal was tied up with my knowledge of the significance of the piece of silver in terms of the sweeping changes at the time concerning how women were viewed by society. Prior to 1912, women's participation in the Olympic games had been restricted to the more ladylike disciplines of golf, tennis, croquet and figure skating i.e. sports in which the women were fully clothed.

Despite the strenuous objections of Baron de Coubertain, the International Olympic Committee announced in 1911 that the swimming and diving competitions the following year would be open to female competitors. This caused enormous consternation amongst traditionalists, both male and female, in certain countries. Sport at this time was regarded as a male prerogative and women who engaged in physical exercise were frequently derided as Amazonian or 'manly' and accused of imitating male behaviour.

Although swimming was regarded as more ladylike than, for example, hockey or cricket, the inevitable semi-nudity provoked both anxiety and outrage amongst those who held the view that the female body was not for display. Coubertain's fury at the admittance of female competitors into the swimming events was echoed by his American comrade in arms, James E. Sullivan, who was practically apoplectic at the prospect—although whether this was due to his aversion to the female body, or women in general, is unclear.[9]

Sullivan was a founding member of the Amateur Athletic Union (AAU), the governing body of sport in the USA, and had a disproportionate objection to women participating in any form of organised sport. He had once threatened to ban a boys' club from the AAU because it had allowed races for girls to take place in same the pool used earlier by the boys. No amount of reasoning could persuade Sullivan to relax his stance against women in 1912, and he expressly forbade American female divers and swimmers from competing in Stockholm. Such was his power within sport in the USA that no official dared question him.

Whilst the opposition was less virulent in Australia, although by no means absent, Mina's medal from Stockholm is symbolic of the seismic shift in attitudes towards women in the twilight years of the Victorian era. The athletic female body began to be acknowledged as a mark of the modern woman and the long-held view of the female body as innately frail was openly challenged by Australian swimmers such as Mina Wylie, Fanny Durack and Annette Kellerman. The 33mm disc of silver which I held with such reverence was the physical evidence of the changes precipitated by that day in July 1912, when Mina Wylie became 'one of the first'.

In actual fact, she was the very first woman to represent Australia in swimming at an Olympic Games as she swam in heat three, which took place at noon on Tuesday, 9 July, and Fanny Durack swam later in heat four. I'm being pedantic, but only because it occurs to me that the difference between 'one of' and 'the first' is a distinction that Mina herself would have been well aware of.

Swimming was a relatively late addition to sporting competition compared to cricket, for example, which was being played in England in the eighteenth century, or tennis, which can be traced back to the sixteenth century. The late development of competitive swimming allowed it to flourish unencumbered by centuries of tradition, and because the sport developed across the continents at the same time and at the same pace, international competition was a relatively level playing field. It is not a stretch to say that it was the success of the Australasian[10] swimmers in Stockholm that convinced authorities that this was the sport in which the newly independent Australian nation could make a name for itself on an international stage, particularly as Mina's medal was not the only Olympic glory won in the murky harbour pool. It was Fanny Durack who beat Mina into second place in the women's race, and Australian male swimmers put up a decent showing with Cecil Healy winning silver in the 100m freestyle, Harold Hardwick winning two bronze medals in the 400m and 1500m freestyle, and the men's relay team taking gold in the 4x200m freestyle. As a result, Australia finished second, behind Germany, on the overall swimming medal table, thus laying the foundation stone for the view of swimming as an Australian sport.

*

Since the mid-nineteenth century, Australians had regarded themselves within the context of Otherness i.e. they were not English, European or even American, and the formation of a unique national identity was a consuming preoccupation amongst the mainly immigrant (or the descendants of immigrants) population. Australia's difference was not yet it's strength, as exactly what that difference was had not yet been established. The cult of athleticism, however, imported from England at the end of the 19th century and pervasive in boys' schools, did offer a route by which Australians could assert their physical superiority.

As a movement, athleticism downplayed intellectual ability and focused on physical indicators of masculinity, such as the strength and aggression in evidence on the playing field. In addition, athleticism reduced the adherence to traditional Christianity, preferring instead the new incarnation of Muscular

Christianity, which reflected the sporting values of team spirit, fairness and discipline. Over time, it was sport, not religion, which came to be regarded as the path to developing these characteristics in the young Australian men who would build and lead the new nation, and early sporting triumphs encouraged the population to regard sport and sportsmanship as unique national characteristics.

The image of the healthy, bronzed Australian was a sharp contrast to the feeble Englishman and a positive signifier of the difference between the nations. Early Australian swimmers such as Barney Kieran, who, by 1905 had held no less than five world records over various distances, and Frederick Lane, who won gold in the 200m freestyle in the 1900 Paris Olympics, were a source of national pride and regarded as the epitome of the superior outdoor, recreational lifestyle on offer in Australia.

Such was the heroic status endowed on these swimmers, that the untimely death of Barney Kieran in 1905, aged nineteen, prompted nationwide scenes of grief and a monument paid for by public subscription was erected to the 'Champion Swimmer of the World' in Sydney's Gore Hill cemetery.[11] Mina's medal, therefore, stands for so much more than second place in a swimming race over a century ago. It is the beginning of a direct line which passes through Clare Dennis, Dawn Fraser, Susie O'Neill and Stephanie Rice (to name but a few) and ends today at Emma McKeon, Ariarne Titmus and the Campbell sisters.

As I placed the silver medal back amongst the red velvet of the presentation box, it became clearer to me that Mina Wylie was indeed a woman of many sides and just as many stories. Whatever story I decided to tell depended on my interpretation of the objects she had left behind. On the surface, there was the straightforward story of a determined young woman who ignored the disdain and swam anyway, making herself one of the most talked about sportswomen at the time.

If I dive deeper, I find evidence of the rise of the modern woman with her athletic body and her penchant for displaying it, and a feminist tale of young women shrugging off their corsets and running, rowing, swimming and playing cricket 'just like men'. Further still into the breaking waves of information, I find a fledgling nation looking to the beach and the outdoor environment to establish an identity, and the beginning of the ideal of the Sporting Nation. Which story is the version Mina wanted told, is the question I grapple with. And is it possible to tell one without alluding to another?

Photographs, a writing case, medals … Who can possibly understand the meanings we have invested in the things we leave behind? Relatives bicker over jewellery belonging to the recently deceased, not purely for the monetary value but because it is a tangible reminder of the person who has gone. The gold watch that signified the coming of age, the pearls that Nana always wore, the engraved cufflinks. I have a ring that I was given on my sixteenth birthday, but no one except me knows why I continue to wear it when I have other, more ostentatious pieces. The reason is simple. It reminds me of home.

We all, to an extent, desire to be remembered through the things which, we believe, have defined us. My mother had a necklace with little enamel shields bearing the coat of arms of the various countries and cities she had visited. These trinkets were tied up in her memories of a particular time or place. Somewhere she had been happy. They were also love tokens, as many of the charms had been bought for her by my father.

To the unenlightened admirer, the necklace was a status symbol or an unusual adornment worth commenting on. To my mother, they were moments in her life that she treasured. And the same could be said of all the objects in Mina's hidden boxes. I don't pretend to know what they all stood for in her life and I can only employ my imagination and invent meanings, where perhaps there are none. But to me, they tell multiple stories of a woman who enjoyed the limelight, who refused to conform, and who loved to swim. That, I do understand.

Mina in 1975 with MP Neil Pickard, during the media storm surrounding her inauguration into the International Swimming Hall of Fame in Florida.

Mina Wylie's 1912 Olympic medal

Chapter 2

My father was the champion underwater swimmer of Australasia, and also the champion plunger of Australasia. I suppose that's why I was such a swimming fanatic.

Mina Wylie, interviewed by Neil Bennetts in 1975

The story of Mina's career begins, as she herself indicates, with her father, Henry. He is a pervasive presence in her archive, transforming in photographs from a fit, muscular underwater swimming champion, to a stout and greying respected member of the community. In the space between the two images, Henry coached his daughter to swimming glory, built and managed the most popular ocean pool in the district, and travelled to Europe to attend the Olympic Games.

It was a very different life from the one his childhood in Belfast had led him to believe was in store, and Henry's upward social mobility was a result both of his tenacity, and his ability to adapt to the changing times. He and Mina were likeminded individuals who shared a passion and their relationship was strengthened by the exclusive bond between athlete and coach. While Mina's postcards to her mother describe city sights and souvenir shopping, 'I have bought some real Irish lace and my word, it is expensive', the letters between father and daughter are concerned with opponents and race times. In other words, they are letters of business. Henry relinquished his coaching duties in 1920 but continued to maintain a close eye on Mina's performance, writing to her in New Zealand in 1923, 'We were all pleased of course, to hear of your win and consider it unfortunate the verdict went against you in your first race.'*

Memories of Henry are scattered throughout Mina's possessions, and one entire box is devoted to his association with the Freemasons. To the uninitiated, the ceremonies and rituals surrounding the fraternity are bewildering, but the

---

* The 'verdict' refers to a 100yd race in Auckland in which Mina and New Zealand champion, Pauline Hoeft, dead heated, with victory, contentiously, awarded to Hoeft.

seven copies of a photograph of Henry resplendent in office bearing regalia, complete with sash, white gloves, an elaborate cummerbund and various insignia, indicate his pride in his association with the organisation. The second archival box allocated to Henry is concerned with his professional move from house painter into the swimming business as pool manager and operator.

This had begun in 1895, when he took over the lease of Bronte Baths, situated at the south end of Bronte beach, and culminated in 1907 with the opening of his 40m ocean pool in Coogee. The two accounts books from Wylie's Baths, which date from 1916 through to 1929, detail the day-to-day operation of this thriving business. Henry's handwriting meticulously records columns of figures detailing expenditure of wages, telephone calls, refreshments (and cigarettes) for the kiosk, stamps, paint and Mina's various expenses incurred by her frequent interstate travel for competitions. The remainder of the box is taken up with Henry's short lived and ill-fated association with the Elkington Park pool[12] in Balmain in 1901, including the letters regarding outstanding rent which passed between Henry and the Balmain County Clerk.

Mina's statement concerning her father's status as a champion underwater swimmer, or 'plunger', is backed up by a certificate of Honour awarded by the NSW Amateur Swimming Association to Henry in 1896, for his feat of swimming an astonishing eighty-eight yards and one foot underwater. Unlike freediving contests today where it is the deepest dive which secures the prize, the aim of plunging was to swim the greatest distance without breathing, and in 1894, Henry secured the interclub dive medal for completing seventy-five yards underwater—a length and a half of contemporary competition pools. There is no evidence that Henry competed in traditional swimming races but he must have been a good enough swimmer with a sound knowledge of stroke technique to be able to teach, which he started doing at Bronte Baths in 1895, and to coach his daughter to Olympic glory.

When Henry, a 22-year-old Ulsterman, had arrived in Melbourne in 1882, his ability to swim made him an exception amongst his fellow emigrants. Having braved the icy waves of the Irish Sea, the benign waters of the many swimming enclosures in Port Phillip Bay was a welcome revelation and he honed his skills around the beaches of St Kilda and Brighton, free from the previous threat of hypothermia.

By the late 1800s, bathing was an extremely popular activity amongst the Australian population, a response both to the warm climate and to the lack of running water in homes. Following an outbreak of typhoid in Melbourne in 1850, authorities had made strenuous efforts to discourage bathing in the polluted Yarra river by building an indoor swimming pool on Swanston Street in the heart of the rapidly expanding city. Henry was a regular visitor to the City Baths during the winter months as he slowly, but surely, carved out a new life for himself in this country promoted as the 'working man's paradise'.

A history of endemic famine and political unrest in his home country had driven Henry, like four million of his compatriots before him, to regard the far-flung colonies with a hopeful eye and gamble on the premise that the unknown was preferable to a bleak and stagnant future. A business card dated 1887, for 'Samuel Wylie, House Painter and Art Decorator' suggests that Henry had family, a brother perhaps, already living in Melbourne when he arrived.

It could not have been on one of Henry's visits to the Melbourne City Baths that he first encountered Queenslander, Florence Anne Beers, as the swimming facility denied entry to women. What she was doing in Melbourne is unknown, but the two met somewhere in the city and began a relationship. At some point in the late 1880s, Henry and Florence married and relocated to Sydney, where Henry set himself up in business as a housepainter in the inner-city suburb of Woollahra. A son, Walter, was born in 1889, and two years later the arrival of Wilhelmina, known to the family as Mina or, occasionally Bill, was duly celebrated.

By this time, Henry had moved his family to St Leonards on the north shore, a suburb more reminiscent of an unsophisticated country town, complete with a jumble of tin roofed cottages bordering dirt roads and uncultivated land. There was, however, a train line servicing the district, which gave Henry and his young family—another son, Harry, was born in 1893—easy access to the coves and beaches of Sydney Harbour. Henry joined the North Sydney Swimming Club and quickly became known for his proficiency in underwater swimming. His participation in inter club competitions introduced him to the Sydney swimming fraternity and he was soon being called upon to exhibit his plunging prowess at club carnivals. One of these events was the second annual championships of the Palace Emporium Swimming Club, held at the famed Natatorium in Pitt Street, in February 1897.

The five-year-old Mina was enormously impressed by her first visit to the city Natatorium, which consisted of two indoor pools filled with sea water pumped in from the harbour almost two miles away. Sitting on the hard, wooden seats above the water, she tried not to lean forward for a better view, but to keep her gloved hands folded in her lap and her back straight as her mother had taught her. An age had passed since the first race and Mina was impatient for the event which Florence had pointed out in the programme, encouraging Walter to recognise words and spell them out: 'An exhibition of swimming underwater by Mr H. A. Wylie (of Bronte Baths).'

At home, Mina was entranced by the colours of her father's framed certificate which hung on the wall in the front room. Blue and red, and gold highlights which glinted as the afternoon sun moved across the wall. Henry often lifted her up to get a better look and she held her hand over the gold lettering so that the sun shone instead on her.

'That'll be you one day, eh, little Bill?'

Mina liked swimming underwater. The world was different there.

'There he is!' Walter was on his feet and pointing.

'Sit down, love. He knows we're here.'

But Florence smiled as Henry's eyes searched the rows of seats above until he found what he was looking for. Now he could swim.

*

Neither Henry nor Florence had relatives living in Sydney and the country-like atmosphere of St Leonard's was a far cry from the busy Melbourne life they had both been accustomed to. Henry spent long days travelling across the harbour to paint houses in the more densely populated areas of the city, leaving Florence alone with three small children and little in the way of distractions to break the monotony. As more and more of his free time was taken up with swimming, Henry found his tribe amongst the like-minded men of the various clubs around Sydney and enjoyed the sporting camaraderie. But he was mindful that Florence was isolated on the North Shore, and, encouraged by his new swimming acquaintances, Henry began to plan a solution.

The inter-club carnivals were hosted each weekend by a different club at their own pool, and it was through these competitions that Henry had been introduced to the Eastern suburbs beaches of Bondi, Tamarama, Bronte, Clovelly and Coogee. At the south end of Bronte Beach was a thirty-metre ocean pool which was home to the prestigious Eastern Suburbs Swimming Club. Nestling under the cliffs and with dramatic views all the way back to the impressive beach at Bondi, Bronte pool was a diamond in the rough of the crudely improvised harbour pools in the many coves around the city. Opened in 1888, the pool had quickly become the focal point for men's competitive swimming in Sydney and attracted large crowds to the festive carnivals which were often augmented with displays of boxing, wrestling and exhibition swimming. The beach at Bronte was a brisk walk from the nearby tram terminus in Waverly and rivalled Bondi as a popular day trip amongst Sydneysiders. In contemporary parlance, Bronte was an up-and-coming area, offering a myriad of opportunities to a man of ambition who was prepared to take a risk.

Henry was this very man, and in 1895, he turned his back on house painting and stepped into his new future by taking over the lease of Bronte baths. He moved Florence and the three children to Coogee, a suburb little more developed than St Leonards but at least offering easier access to Bronte beach. He then transferred his allegiance from the North Shore to the Eastern Suburbs Swimming Club and daily walked the eight-kilometre round trip to Bronte from Coogee, through Gordon's Bay, Clovelly and the stunning cliff top cemetery at Waverley. Did he pause on his journey to wonder at the Aboriginal rock engravings and hidden shelters hugging the cliffs, or was he, like so many other European immigrants, unconcerned with the area's Indigenous past and population?

One of the first tasks Henry undertook at Bronte pool was to teach his three children how to swim. The four-year-old Mina proved herself to be a natural and completely without fear, throwing herself into the pool from the rocks above like the boisterous boys around her. She copied her father by holding her breath and attempting to swim the length of the pool underwater, and she was soon spending as much time in the water as Henry did. Florence does not appear to have discouraged this, even allowing Henry to recruit Mina and her siblings into a family aquatic act which performed 'fancy swimming' at carnivals throughout Sydney in the late 1890s. The young Walter, Mina and Harry swam underwater and executed expert handstands, somersaults and acrobatics to adoring crowds. The highlight of the show involved Henry tying Mina's hands and legs together with rope and the five-year old wriggling across a complete length of the pool. Clearly these were the days before Health and Safety regulations.

The one surviving photograph of the family act is undated, and disappointingly, not an action shot. It is a studio portrait in which Mina looks to be about seven or eight, and reclines on the floor wearing a striped outfit of a short jacket and leggings which cover her knees. Her two brothers wear dark swimsuits and each have one of Henry's medals pinned to their chest. Harry's swimsuit is slightly too big for him and slips off one shoulder. The boys imitate their father's sporting stance of folded arms and shoulders back, looking directly into the camera, but Mina's attention is elsewhere. Both she and Henry are looking at someone standing beside the studio photographer: the supportive Florence perhaps, radiating pride at her vigorously healthy troupe.

In the late 1890s, a studio portrait of a family group was restricted to special occasions such as weddings, and this outing to Brand studio in Sydney's Park Street would have been a thrilling event in the young lives of the Wylie siblings.

'It shows how good we are,' Walter told Mina. 'People want pictures of us.'

The rise of large-scale sporting events in the late 1800s was a new and extremely popular form of mass entertainment which drove a desire from fans for images of individual athletes. The cult of body building, first promoted by the German 'strongman', Eugen Sandow, resulted in a huge demand worldwide for images of muscular men adopting poses for the camera. Henry shows his awareness of these pictures in this portrait, hands placed strategically under his upper arms to enhance the bulge of his biceps. This picture was most likely intended for publicity purposes—newspaper items or swimming carnival programmes, for instance—or to attract potential pupils to Bronte Baths. Who knows, there may even have been a clique of devoted fans clamouring for an image of the current Australasian Plunging Champion.

Henry was not the only opportunist to respond to the wide spread fervour for swimming in Australia by enlisting his children in exhibition performances. Self-appointed 'Professor of Swimming', Frederick Cavill, leased harbour baths around Sydney at various periods in the late 1800s around Lavender Bay, Farm Cove and Woolloomooloo, and coerced all nine of his children into performing aquatic tricks to promote the new art of natation. One of Frederick's three daughters, Alice, cut her teeth in these family shows before travelling to San Francisco in 1901, where she listed her occupation as 'professional swimmer'.

For the next thirty years, Alice made her living performing in swimming exhibitions, teaching and, somewhat bizarrely, as a member of the Flying Jordans circus troupe which toured to Hawaii, Japan and Siberia. Two of Alice's' brothers, however, had less successful swimming careers. In 1896, 26-year-old Charles became the first person to swim across the Golden Gate strait in San

Francisco but drowned the following year after inhaling poisonous gas during an underwater endurance act in Stockton, California.

His younger brother, Arthur, known as Tums, also swam the Golden Gate strait but froze to death in 1914 whilst trying to swim across Seattle Harbour. The young Wylie siblings showed no inclination to tackle similar feats of endurance in freezing temperatures. They remained content to handstand and fancy dive their way across the many pools of Sydney, lapping up applause as they linked hands in the water to form a serene floating star.

*

In 1895, when Henry joined the Eastern Suburbs Swimming Club, there was no ladies branch to accommodate the growing number of women who were engaging with the new past time of bathing. Women were permitted to swim at Bronte pool only during designated hours and not at all on Sundays or public holidays which were reserved for men. This was common practice throughout public pools where there was not a separate facility for women, and the disproportionate amount of time set aside for male swimming reflected the view of sporting activity as more suitable for men. This attitude was challenged by the bicycling craze of the mid-1800s, which had been taken up primarily by women.

When the 'safety bicycle', with pneumatic tyres, a steerable front wheel, chain drive and wheels of equal size, was introduced in the 1870s, it became so popular amongst women that American feminist Susan B. Anthony labelled it the 'freedom machine'. Australia was not immune from the bicycling craze and one Sydney woman, Sarah Maddock, was feted throughout the country for her long-distance cycle rides, covering the 1600 miles from Sydney to Brisbane and back in five weeks in 1895, accompanied by her likeminded husband. Whilst these 'lady cyclists' delighted in their new-found liberty, not everyone was so enthusiastic about this modern incarnation of womanhood.

Newspapers and periodicals frequently ridiculed the 'red-faced' cyclists, and women who wore bloomers or divided skirts to ride were treated to displays of outright hostility and often had their safety threatened. One of the arguments regularly employed against women participating in sport was the assertion that only men possessed a competitive spirit, and such a thing was unseemly in women who were, it was claimed, morally superior. The clergy went one step further and avowed that the fostering of this masculine competitive streak in women would lead to unnatural, or uncontrollable sexual urges. Despite the condemnation and accusations of un-ladylike behaviour, determined women set up cycling clubs across Australia and staged road races, relishing the thrill of competition. They then began to row in crews, play tennis, cricket, hockey and golf. And, when the restrictive hours at public pools allowed them to, they swam.

The patriarchal notion of femininity at this time defined women as Other, that is, their feminine qualities were the antithesis of the strength and muscularity which defined masculinity. Women were frail and passive, it was believed, and their function was primarily to reproduce or to be decorative. Society was fixated on the correct body shape and demure behaviour for young women and girls, and these notions were grounded in an ideal of femininity that was balletic and graceful. Because the female swimmer was seen neither to sweat, nor display outward signs of exertion, swimming was regarded as a sport in which a woman could engage without compromising her all-important femininity. Over protective (or controlling) husbands and fathers were more favourably disposed to their women engaging in swimming than playing lacrosse or cricket, because swimming did not develop unsightly muscles, and, in the water, the lady swimmer remained elegant and graceful.

In addition, swimming took place behind closed doors, away from prying eyes. But it was exactly this separation which drew women in droves to the swimming pool. Free from the peeping tom who lurked around the hockey field hoping for a glimpse of ankle, and liberated from the suffocating restrictions of ladylike behaviour, women could swim in peace, uninhibited and unabashed. Here, they could perfect their technique away from male frowns and disapproval. Here, they could learn to swim just as well as the men did.

In the early swimming competitions of the late 1890s, the fastest stroke was the trudgen, a combination of an overarm move and a scissor kick, named after English swimmer John Trudgen, who reputedly learned it from South American natives during a trip to Argentina in 1873. This may well be a myth, but Trudgen's superior form of side stroke undoubtedly laid down the roots of what was to eventually become front crawl. Breast stroke was the more common stroke in the early days of swimming and the stroke which was taught to beginners, but trudgen was utilised in freestyle races due to its superior speed.

In 1901, during Henry's management reign at Bronte Baths, a now legendary incident in the history of stroke development is said to have taken place. A fifteen-year-old Solomon Islander named Alick Wickham, competed in a race and amazed onlookers with his unique over arm style accompanied by a four-beat continuous kick. Local coach, George Farmer, is reputed to have exclaimed, 'Look at that kid crawling!' thereby giving credence to the claim that it was the early Sydney swimming community which invented the Australian crawl, today known as freestyle.

The story does have a sense of the apocryphal clinging to it, given that at the Olympics in Stockholm over a decade later, only two of the seven-member Australasian team were able to swim the stroke, and six of the team were Sydney based. 'Professor of Swimming' Frederick Cavill, maintained for years that it was his son Tums who first developed the crawl stroke, and US gold medallist from Stockholm in 1912, Duke Kahanamoku, insisted that it had been practised for years in his native Hawaii.

The origins of the stroke continue to be contested, but the Wickham myth persists in Australia due to an ongoing desire to position the early nation at the forefront of the development of the sport. If the story is true, then Henry was not sufficiently impressed to take the time to learn the stroke from Wickham, sticking instead with the more reliable trudgen stroke.

Henry thrived in his new role as pool manager and introduced swimming lessons and the latest health cure of hot sea baths, said to provide relief from arthritis, to the pool. Close inspection of the one photograph of Bronte Baths in the archive, reveals that all the male swimmers are naked: little wonder then, that swimming was segregated. But this image must have been taken before the pool was officially opened as one of the rules of entry stipulates that 'each person using the Baths shall wear an appropriate bathing dress'. Both of Henry's sons competed in junior inter club races, with Harry proving more successful than Walter, but Henry was frustrated by the lack of organised competitions for girls. Mina continually pestered him to allow her to race in the boys' competitions and he was tired of having to think up new excuses.

'It's not fair. I'm a better swimmer than Harry and he gets to race.'

'He's a boy. It's different.'

The ten-year-old Mina was not alone in her frustration. As the numbers of women enjoying swimming continued to rise, so did their demand for organised competitions. Although there is no evidence in Mina's collection of any official ladies' carnivals occurring during the 1890s, the number of competitors at the inaugural NSW ladies' championships in 1902, does suggest that women had joined together to form their own clubs and were unofficially competing between themselves. As Henry registered Mina's name on the list of competitors participating in the first official ladies' championships in Woolloomooloo Bay pool in 1902, he was almost as excited as she was.

'You're in the 27 yards for the under tens. You need to keep a steady pace, don't rush the start …'

'But Henry,' Florence protested, 'she's almost eleven.'

'Well, they don't know that. Do they?'

Mina came second in her race, but her real thrill of the day was watching the fourteen-year-old Annette Kellerman[13] easily win the 100yds freestyle.

'One minute twenty-two seconds,' exclaimed Harry. 'That's a new state record.'

'I could do that,' said Mina.

'No, you couldn't.'

'I could if I practise more.'

Kellerman was slender and tall for her age, and already displaying the overt femininity for which she later became known. As she stepped up to receive her prize as the first female state champion, Mina had only one thought.

I want that.

Prior to the 1902 ladies' championships, Henry may have been aware that his daughter swam well, but it was only when he saw how favourably she compared to the other competitors that he understood she had real potential, certainly more than either of her brothers had. His daughter, Henry realised, could be a champion. Just as he had been. And he could now be the coach of a champion. Sporting relationships between father and daughter are not unusual: witness the tennis partnerships between Steffi and Peter Graf, sisters Serena and Venus Williams and their father Richard, and, more troublingly, Jelena Dokic and her controlling father, Damir.

When the American swimmer, Trudy Ederle, attempted to become the first woman to swim the English Channel in 1926, it was her father, 'Pop' who boarded the support boat in France to guide her, whilst her mother sat beside a wireless with her other children in Connecticut waiting for news. Pop Ederle spurred his daughter on by holding up a drawing of the red Roadster he had promised to buy her if she was successful, and as the history making swim progressed, Pop added wheels and doors to the drawing of the car until the English coast was within reach and the car was complete.[14]

*

Following the success of the ladies' championships of 1902, women's clubs were officially formed and female swimming carnivals became a regular feature during the long summer months. The favourable reception shown towards women's competition by both the public and the press was partly due to the increasing debate concerning what it meant to be Australian. The climate and the beach were beginning to be central to a sense of a separate 'Australian-ness', and it therefore followed that swimming was integral to a unique Australian way of life which revolved around the beach. In addition, the late emergence of the sport internationally resulted in both women and men being involved from the very outset, unlike disciplines such as cricket where women were regarded as infiltrating male territory.

Contrary to expectations, given the virulently patriarchal society that Australia had become by the end of the nineteenth century, competitive swimming in Mina's era appears to have been more gender neutral than elite swimming today. Men and women competed over the same distances and the early endurance swimmers were more likely to be female than male. The success of Frederick Lane at the 1900 Paris Olympics, where he took first place in the 200m freestyle and the 200m obstacle race (sadly, no photographs survive of the latter) confirmed the conviction that Australia had the potential to dominate this new discipline.

Lane was awarded a statue of a bronze horse as his prize for the freestyle event and he single-handedly raised the profile of swimming as a competitive sport in Australia, elevating it to a national preoccupation, one in which women appeared to have a status bordering on equality. Certainly, the positive position adopted by the press towards women's swimming in the early 1900s gave it a legitimacy other women's sports were denied, thereby contributing to its wider acceptance.

With the establishment of club, state and even interstate championships for women, Mina's love for swimming became an obsession. The winter months were an agonising interlude between racing seasons and the hurried July dips in the chilly Bronte baths were no compensation for the hours of training she put in during the summer. Henry shared, and guided, his daughter's passion, and under his watchful eye Mina's form quickly improved. She was renowned as a breast stroke swimmer but swam the faster trudgen in freestyle races and by 1905, the only swimmer who regularly beat her into second place was fellow Sydneysider, Fanny Durack.

Durack was two years older than Mina but despite their rivalry and distinctly different backgrounds—Durack's father was a publican in a less than salubrious inner-city suburb—they became friends. Mina belonged to the newly formed Sydney Ladies Swimming Club, and Durack to East Sydney, meaning they were regularly drawn against each other at interclub competitions. Mina would beat Durack in breast stroke, and Durack invariably took the freestyle honours.

'Well swum, Miss Wylie.'

'Why thank you, Miss Durack.'

In some accounts of Mina's career, Henry is credited as coaching both his daughter and Fanny Durack, but nothing in the archives confirms that this was the case. Durack is credited as having swum the Australian crawl in Stockholm whilst Mina swam trudgen, which strongly implies they had different coaches. I also suspect that religion would have coloured any relationship between members of the Durack and Wylie families: Henry was a Protestant from Ulster and Durack's family were practising Catholics. The issue of Home Rule had provoked bitter divisions and civil unrest within Ireland, and even if Henry was only half hearted about the cause, the traditional deep-seated antipathy between members of the two religions may have ensured he conducted relations with his daughter's friend—and her family—at a distance. Sydney in the late nineteenth and early twentieth centuries was a city awash in sectarianism, so much so that the Catholic Foy family, who owned the enormous Mark Foy's department store in the city, were said to only employ members of their own religion and refused to stock school uniforms for schools which were not Catholic.

Henry and Mina's first foray into ladies competitive swimming came at a time of immense change for Henry. At the end of 1901, after six years at Bronte Baths, he took over the management of the Elkington Park pool in Balmain, a lively harbour suburb populated mainly by workers from the nearby shipyards and factories. What prompted this move is unclear, but it was a larger pool under council authority and Henry may have considered it a step up the professional ladder. The foreshore area in Elkington Park had been an unofficial swimming spot for some years before the wooden surrounds of the pool were put in place by Sydney Municipal Council in the early 1880s in an effort to regulate informal (and nude) bathing.

When Henry took over the lease, the baths were home to the oldest swimming club in Australia, and in 1888 had been the site for the first game of water polo to be played in the country. The position of manager required him to live in a cottage onsite and to be sworn in as a special constable in order to have the authority—as outlined in the lease agreement—to 'prohibit, stop and suppress all improper conduct or bad language within the reserve called Elkington Park as well as in the baths.' Foiling potential muggings in an area with the dubious reputation Balmain had, appeared to be above and beyond the call of duty of a pool manager. Nevertheless, Henry signed the three-year lease on 31 December 1901.

From the letters and postcards in Mina's archive, it is impossible to deduce if Florence and the children moved to Balmain with Henry, or if they remained in Coogee. All personal written communication in the Mitchell Library collection is addressed to one of two Coogee addresses, suggesting that Florence objected to a move to the overcrowded and dirty Balmain. Large loads of coal from Sydney Harbour Collieries were transported through the steep, often barely accessible streets, and the suburb increasingly attracted unemployed men who were unable to afford accommodation in more attractive area. It was not a healthy place for children, especially not those who were used to fresh air, open spaces and the more refined Eastern suburbs. A couple of signatures in Mina's earliest autograph album are from girls in Balmain, so she certainly spent time at the Elkington Park pool, but where exactly the Wylie family was living throughout 1902, remains confusing. Not that it really matters.

If the family did move away from Coogee, their Balmain sojourn was not a long one. Within six months of signing the lease, Henry breached the terms of the contract by failing to pay two instalments of the quarterly rent in advance. When he failed to pay the third instalment in October, the Clerk of Balmain Council, J. M. Hetherington, contacted Henry's guarantors informing them that, 'The Mayor now instructs me to give you and your co-surety seven days' notice for which to pay the amount (£160) otherwise he will put the bond in suit.' The matter did proceed to court and on 23 December, less than a year after signing, Henry surrendered the lease. His time at Bronte Baths had proved that Henry was a good manager and trustworthy in business, so it is strange that he fell into debt so soon after signing the Balmain lease.

The outdoor swimming pool business, however, is a fickle one, relying on favourable weather for healthy gate receipts. Perhaps the summer of 1902 was not as sunny as Henry had hoped, resulting in his actual income falling short of his predictions. In addition, upon signing the lease, Henry had been required to outlay a significant sum of money from his own pocket to purchase items such as towels and bathing suits for the customers, and cleaning and safety equipment for the pool. He was also expected to hire and pay for two members of staff: 'a man who shall be strong and an accomplished swimmer and adept in saving life of persons in danger of drowning', and 'a lady who shall be a thoroughly qualified swimmer and who shall be in charge and in attendance in the Baths during and for a reasonable time after the hours of prescribed attendance of ladies...' Reading between the lines, the lease does give the impression that Balmain Council wanted a public pool under its jurisdiction but was not enthusiastic about paying for it.

Leaving Bronte Baths for Elkington Park had been huge miscalculation on Henry's part. His honour as a businessman had been called into question and he now had the reputation as someone who was not reliable where finances were concerned. Licking his wounds and nursing injured pride, Henry returned to Coogee and went back to his former occupation as a housepainter to support the family.

'Is Dad not going to have a pool anymore?' asked Mina.

'Ssh, love.'

Henry was, however, astute enough to keep the items he had purchased for the Balmain pool rather than sell them back to the Council as part of his separation agreement.

*

If the disaster of Elkington Park taught Henry one thing, it was that being beholden to an authority such as a town council was not the best fit with his personality. At Bronte, he had implemented changes which were forward thinking, thus revealing a character which embraced modern ideas. But when he had requested permission from Balmain Council to open Elkington Park pool on Sundays he received a stern rebuke from the Council Clerk stating: 'your request cannot be complied with, furthermore I am instructed to point out to you most decisively, that, you must adhere to the terms of your agreement in respect to closing the Baths on the Sabbath.' Better that the whole sorry affair was consigned to the past. At least now he was back in the eastern suburbs, and with the electrification of the tram to Coogee in 1902, the suburb was booming.

*

By the end of the 1800s, an attitude which associated beach-going with a sense of a unique (white) Australian way of life was taking hold amongst the population of Sydney. The beach as a place for recreation was a familiar concept to the tens of thousands of British immigrants now living in the city, and the early development of the beachside suburbs of Manly, Bondi and Coogee attempted to ease the homesickness of the new immigrants by recreating the atmosphere of popular English resorts such as Brighton or Southend.

An English day at the seaside involved amusement arcades, a show at the end of the pier and bandstand concerts, and this was exactly the experience that the new Sydney beachside suburbs sought to replicate. In the idyllic cove of Tamarama, between Bronte and Bondi, a popular amusement park modelled on New York's Coney Island opened in 1901. Named Wonderland City, the park boasted fun fair rides, a miniature railway, waxworks, a circus ring and movie theatre, a Japanese tearoom and a music hall which could seat an audience of over one thousand. From 1887, Coogee had the Palace Aquarium complex which housed an aquarium, a great hall which could be utilised as a roller-skating rink, a bandstand and a variety of swings, toy boats, aviaries and a herd of donkeys.

Although the eight-hour working day was not achieved nationally in Australia until the 1920s, different states and various industries had been gradually adopting the practice since the mid-1800s, resulting in an increase in leisure time amongst the working classes. In the first decade of the twentieth century, amusement parks such as Wonderland City and Coogee Palace Aquarium were instrumental in attracting tram loads of workers with free time on their hands to the eastern suburbs beaches.

Visitors came to have fun and to escape the industrial grime of the inner city and, given Australia's hot and sunny climate, they came to swim. Photographs of Bondi in the early 1900s, however, attest to the fact that few day trippers could swim well enough to cope with the strong surf and spent the day paddling at the water's edge or enjoying the ocean view from the safety of a deck chair. In addition to the treacherous rip tides, shark attacks were common, and women

51

faced the additional hazard of voluminous bathing outfits which became dangerously heavy when wet.

Under these circumstances, it was hardly surprising that prior to the inauguration of the Surf Bathing Association of NSW in 1907, drownings at Sydney beaches were a frequent occurrence. As the popularity of swimming continued to grow, so too did demand for safe places to swim and the early 1900s saw an explosion—literally—in the construction of harbour and ocean pools around the city.

On his frequent walks along Coogee beach with Florence, Henry noted the swelling number of visitors disembarking from the extra weekend trams and the overcrowding of the pools at either end of the beach. The natural rock pool on the northern rocks, known as the Bogey Hole, was so popular that long queues of men awaiting entry stretched all the way down to the sand.

On the southern cliffs, the twenty-metre secluded rock pool for women that had once been a sacred space for Aboriginal women was just as busy. Mina frequently reported to Henry that the pool was so crowded it was impossible for her to train seriously. There was an indoor twenty-five metre pool within the Aquarium complex, but this had been taken over by the serious (male) swimmers of the Randwick and Coogee Amateur Swimming Club who firmly discouraged the recreational swimmer. Henry became convinced that the booming suburb could support another, larger and better equipped, public pool.

'Look at the crowds, Florence. They need somewhere else to go.'

'They could go to Bronte, or Bondi.'

'But they're coming here. And I already have everything we need.'

In 1906, Henry took his biggest gamble yet and obtained a lease from Randwick council for land below the cliffs at South Coogee with the intention of building a forty-yard pool. Where he had found the money is anyone's guess. Perhaps there was already a high demand for interior decorators amongst the well-heeled residents of the eastern suburbs, or perhaps Florence had acquired a legacy from her family in Queensland.

In Henry's account legers for Wylie's Baths present in Mina's archive, there are a number of references regarding borrowing, or paying back money to Florence, suggesting she had access in later years to money that did not belong to Henry. With his borrowed or saved money, and a signed lease for land only a five-minute walk from the popular Coogee Beach, Henry began consultations with architects and builders. Plans for the largest pool in the suburb quickly took shape and an air of restrained excitement infused the Wylie household throughout 1906.

The site Henry had acquired below the southern cliffs was ideally suited to a tidal pool due to a natural plateau surrounded by overhanging cliffs. The pool would be blasted out of the rocky level area with steps leading down from the changing rooms on the clifftop above. The northern and eastern walls of the pool bordered the ocean with walls high enough to keep out the ever-present threat of sharks, yet low enough to allow waves to break the edge at high tide. This close proximity to the ocean gave swimmers in the pool the impression they were actually swimming in the sea, as well as ensuring that the water in the pool was constantly refreshed by the breaking waves and high tides. The fact that fish and shells were washed into the pool furthered the impression that the enclosed space was, in fact, an extension of the wild ocean beyond. Here, visitors would be able to engage with nature and the unique Australian environment free from the dangers of rip tides and the occasional freak wave.

Henry unlocked a metal trunk and pulled the five hundred white towels he had bought for the Elkington park pool out of storage. He added a red stripe with the words, 'Wylie's Property Coogee Baths' down the centre to foil any light-fingered customers and took a similar precaution with the children's swimsuits, the hire of which was included in the price of entry. His team of workers constructed a wide wooden boardwalk on the clifftop to house the male and female changing rooms and a small kiosk selling sweets and cigarettes.

A set of stairs at the south end of the boardwalk led down to the pool itself, which graduated in depth from the near side to the eastern sea wall allowing children and non-swimmers to enjoy the roped off shallow area. Ten yards short of official competition length and with no provision for spectators, Henry clearly intended this as a leisure pool and by 1907, he was ready to unveil his most ambitious plan to date.

When Henry's pool opened to the public, it was one of only a few pools operating in Sydney as a private enterprise, and from the first day of operation it was clear that this was a family business. Walter, then eighteen, resigned from his position as clerk with shipping merchants, W & A McArthur, to join his father in the new enterprise, and Mina and Harry were also drafted in to help. Like Professor Cavill and his brood of nine, the Wylie family was now, more than ever, a swimming family. They even had their own pool to prove it. Henry clearly regarded the business as a bond which united his family and his cards to Walter and Harry from Europe invariably ask about 'the work'.

In a letter to 'My dear Flo' sent from London in August 1912, Henry writes: 'I am glad to hear Walter is getting on so well with the work, you can tell him I have not seen any better system for locked rooms or lockers than we have ourselves.' There are numerous entries in the swimming pool accounts book reading, 'Wages, Ada', indicating that an outside female employee was brought in to supervise the women's changing room. But even with Ada, Henry kept his cards close to his chest: Ada was the daughter of a neighbour with whom Florence had struck up a close friendship. Strangers would not be involved in any way with the running of Henry's new enterprise.

Mina taught swimming at the baths and when she visited San Francisco in 1918, she sent a postcard of the Lurline Baths with its impressive colonnade to Harry, writing, 'It would be a good idea if you could bring Wylie's Baths over here. We are enjoying ourselves very much, the people are fine, Love Mina. PS there are 47 employees at this bath!'

It is possible that part of Henry's motivation in building Wylie's Baths was tied up with Mina's flourishing swimming career. As her coach, Henry wanted her to succeed, and as a former champion himself, he understood her desire to be the best. Her success reflected well on him and may even have contributed to Henry re-establishing himself within swimming circuit following the disastrous Balmain interlude. The lack of swimming hours available to women in public pools was an obstacle for the father/daughter team and the two ocean pools in Coogee, the Bogey Hole and McIvers Baths, were strictly segregated. Mina could swim in the latter, but Henry could not watch and instruct her. The nearest pool which could accommodate them both, and then only in the few hours allocated to women, was Bronte Baths. But the eight-kilometre round trip could only be undertaken by Mina outside of school hours, placing still more restrictions on the time she could devote to perfecting her stroke technique and building up stamina. Because whatever it was that Henry was doing as Mina's coach, his methods were paying off.

By 1906, four years after her first competition, Mina had established herself as one of the fastest female swimmers in the state, and Henry was becoming increasingly frustrated at the out-dated segregation rules. He was her father, after all. If Henry was in charge of his own pool, and that facility was on the family doorstep, the issue of scrabbling to find Mina training hours would be a thing of the past. It would also reinstate Henry into the pool management business, a job he thrived on.

Wylie's Baths was an instant success. At forty yards, it was the biggest facility in the district and the rocky surroundings offered a natural playground for over-excited children. There was the thrill of the diving platform to contend with, and the fact that the hire of a swimsuit was included in the nominal admission fee made it accessible to all. The lack of affordable recreational facilities throughout the city resulted, as Henry had predicted, in long lines forming at the locked gate a full hour before he and his keys arrived. But the main bonus of ownership had to be the fact that now Henry and Mina had somewhere to pursue, unhindered, their plan for her domination of Australian ladies swimming.

In 1908, the then 17-year-old Mina finally beat Fanny Durack to win the 100 yards freestyle in the NSW Ladies' championship. Surely this was the pinnacle of Henry's dreams. In only six years, his daughter had gone from being a child who lied about her age in order to secure a place in a race she was too old to be in, to being the fastest female swimmer in Australia. Balmain had been a distressing glitch, but the Wylie family was back on track. Henry had trusted his instincts and here he was, back doing the thing that gave him enormous pleasure, in the place he had come to love, in a pool he had built and owned. Here in Coogee, Henry did not have to answer to anyone. Except perhaps his wife.

*

In the 2008, boxes of memorabilia donated to the Mitchell by Meredith Clark, there is evidence of those early successful days of Wylie's Baths. A number of the thin white towels with the red stripe and proprietorial message are there, but disappointingly, not the swimsuits that were included in the admission fee. It is possible, however, to view one of the suits online on the Australian Dress Register.[15] It is a child's swimsuit, most likely for a boy or a very young girl given the lack of shoulder coverage. Prior to the onset of puberty, girls and boys shared the same swimsuit design—a simple one-piece garment with a singlet top half, a row of buttons down the front and shorts ending above the knee.

As the bodies of the young girls matured, they graduated to a two-piece swimsuit, shorts and an early long t shirt which covered the shoulders and had a higher neckline. The child's swimsuit on the Australian Dress Register looks to be made from a rough, hessian type material which has been dyed a vibrant blue. The suit is trimmed with two white buttons and vertical white stripes running the length of the suit proclaim 'Wylie's Baths'. Did it fall to Florence, I wonder, to maintain the running repairs on these well used suits? Replacing buttons and ties and patching what had been torn on the rocks. I doubt that the suits were ever washed, or at least, not until they were so stiff and stained with the repeated immersion in the ocean pool that they were virtually unwearable. I doubt too, that the boisterous 10-year-olds running around the boardwalk cared.

Amongst Mina's photographs is a delightful one of three girls posing in front of the rocky cliff face at the pool, wearing Wylie's swimsuits. The confidence of the girl on the left, who has her hands on her hips and an attractive self-assurance, makes me smile. As does the impish child in the middle who cares not a bit that her swimsuit is too big and has slipped off her shoulder. In the background, another child can be glimpsed attempting to climb up onto the rocks. To me, the image encapsulates the freedom and fun this pool offered to girls who would soon enough be constrained by corsets, high buttoned boots and ladylike rules.

I can hear them calling to each other, giggling and shrieking at the jellyfish which have sneaked in over the far edge. I know that on windy days they stand on the eastern wall facing the breaking waves, screaming with delight as the force almost pushes them back into the pool. I know too that they splash each other in the shallow end and exaggerate the pain of a sea urchin spike sticking in their heel. I know for certain they are reluctant to leave, and make plans to meet the next day before going their separate, tired out ways at the top of Neptune Street. The image reminds me of how it was possible to spend hours with friends at a swimming pool and be completely unaware of how much time had passed. How did we spend it—my friends and those grinning girls in Mina's photo? Where did those hours go?

They went in pushing each other in, dive bombing the boys, jumping from the board, racing each other, picking up coins or black bricks, trying to swim butterfly, showing off by doing handstands, somersaults, bellyflops, fighting over goggles and guzzling bottles of fizzy drinks.

Above the three girls enjoying their afternoon at Wylie's Baths, I imagine Henry and Florence up on the boardwalk surveying the crowded mayhem beneath them. At the entrance hut, Walter is feverishly taking entrance money and distributing swimsuits. Harry is somewhere near the pool trying to maintain order. And their daughter is the Australian champion. Henry takes his wife's hand and surreptitiously presses it to his lips.

'We're alright, Flo. We're alright.'

*

In the 1920s, Henry strung lights across his pool to enable visitors to swim after sunset on stifling city nights. It must have been magical – a scene out of a fairy tale. What would it be like, I wonder, to swim through a full, silver moon reflected on the surface of the pool as it must have been on at least one of those summer nights? Does moonlight penetrate the water like the sun does, throwing shimmering shapes on to the body of the swimmer? I picture myself diving down through a shining ball of light, pulled on like the tide to the beckoning silver moon. Searching for Mina.

The Wylie Family Aquatic Act, circa 1897.

Henry Wylie, Freemason.

Wylie's Baths 1907, with Coogee Pavilion in the background

Wylie's Baths, date unknown but the presence of women indicates post 1912.

Girls at Wylie's Baths wearing rented swimsuits.

Chapter 3

I met Annette Kellerman of course, as everybody knows...
Mina Wylie, interviewed by Neil Bennetts, 1975

A number of women who influenced Mina and aspects of her career appear throughout her archive. There is Rose Scott, the influential feminist and social reformer, who became President of the NSW Ladies Amateur Swimming Association upon its inauguration in 1906. And Marion McIntosh, the younger woman who succeeded Scott as President after the 1912 controversy concerning mixed competition. Mina's mother, Florence, is more of an image on the receiving end of Mina's postcards than an actual presence, and Fanny Durack, Mina's greatest rival and supposed best friend, is notable for her absence. On the evidence of the archive boxes, however, the woman who wielded the greatest influence over Mina and her career was Annette Kellerman.

The life of Annette Kellerman and her transformation from a lower middle-class daughter of genteel musicians to a Hollywood film star famed for her physical attributes, is one of the defining stories of the age of glamour. Born in 1886 in the Sydney suburb of Darlinghurst, she began to swim at the age of six following a childhood blighted by rickets and leg irons. Within a matter of years of learning to swim, she had mastered all the strokes and left her childhood affliction far behind her.

Following her record-breaking 100yd swim at the 1902 NSW championships, her family moved to Melbourne where her mother had accepted a position as music teacher at the private Mentone Girls Grammar School. Kellerman's father, Frederick, however, struggled to find work as a violinist and as the economic downturn deepened, his private pupils gradually disappeared. While she was still at school Annette started giving displays of her aquatic prowess in a tank filled with tropical fish at the Melbourne Exhibition Aquarium. If this was an attempt to boost the family coffers, it worked, and she was soon drawing large crowds. Sometime around 1904, she moved the act to the Princes

Court amusement park on the Yarra River and began giving exhibitions of the balletic diving which she later became known for.

By 1905, the Kellerman family finances were in a precarious situation and, after a benefit concert to raise the fares, Frederick took his daughter to London in the hope of capitalising on her earning potential as a professional swimmer.

This was not as fanciful as it seems as a fellow Australian and contemporary of Annette, named Beatrice Kerr, had already built a considerable name for herself as a swimmer and was giving exhibitions up and down the coast of England. Annette and Frederick set themselves up in London where Annette became the new darling of the front pages following a twenty-six-mile swim in the Thames river from Putney to Blackwall. In August of 1905, she made the first of her three attempts on the English Channel, and in September she was the only female competitor amongst seventeen men in the twenty-four-mile Seven Bridges race in the Seine in Paris.

Astonishingly, she took third place. Her real talent, however, was not for long distance swimming, but exhibitionism, both personal and professional. She had a driving need to be the centre of attention and by 1906, she was performing her diving and 'fancy swimming' routine at the enormous Hippodrome theatre in London, earning herself the nickname of the Australian Mermaid.

Her reputation soon spread across the Atlantic and when she received an offer in 1906 to appear at the White City Amusement Park in Chicago, Annette and Frederick boarded a White Star liner and headed for the Windy City. Within a year, Frederick's health began to fail, and in the summer of 1907, he returned to his wife in Australia leaving Annette to take up a new contract at Wonderland amusement park on Revere beach in Boston. It was on this beach that the famous incident which has endowed Kellerman with the reputation as the woman who freed other women from the tyranny of corsets took place. In the summer of 1907, Annette was allegedly arrested on Revere Beach and charged with indecency for wearing a one-piece bathing suit with black stockings. I say, allegedly, because despite the incident now having legendary status, there is no proof, either in newspapers or in court records, that it actually happened.

It is probable that she was cautioned or told to cover up by a patrolling police officer, but the court case may be no more than a myth. Regardless, Kellerman had long been critical of the cumbersome regulation bathing suits for women, arguing that they restricted movement in the water and were lethal when wet. When she appeared on Revere beach in her one-piece suit, arrest or no arrest, she became an overnight sensation. Her growing fame was boosted the following year when Dr Dudley Sargent, of Harvard University, compared the measurements of her figure with those taken from the statue of the Venus de Milo and concluded that Kellerman was The Perfect Woman.

When the announcement was made in 1911 that women would be admitted to the Olympic Games swimming events the following year, Kellerman was one of the highest earning vaudeville stars in the USA. As a professional, she was ineligible to compete, but the competition circuit had ceased to be of interest a long time ago, cast aside in favour of the larger crowds and bigger financial rewards of exhibition swimming. Billed as the Diving Venus, Kellerman's act involved a series of acrobatic dives into a glass tank, followed by a sequence of underwater ballet.[16]

Newspapers of the time were quick to admit that it was Kellerman's figure, displayed in her now signature black stockings and figure-hugging black swimsuit, that was the main attraction, and Kellerman seemed perfectly happy to be objectified. American theatrical promoter A. F. Albee even went as far as to hang mirrors above Kellerman's onstage tank to enable audience members a clearer view of her buttocks as she swam. 'What we are selling is backsides,' he is quoted as saying, 'and a hundred backsides are better than one!' Kellerman raised no objection.

Vaudeville was all very well, but any ambitious performer at this time had their eye on Hollywood, and Kellerman was no exception. Her first underwater adventure, or 'fairy tale films' as she herself referred to them, appeared in 1911. Kellerman played a mermaid in the film which was somewhat unimaginatively titled, 'The Mermaid', designing and making her own costumes. Her underwater frolics proved enormously popular and, three years later, press reports of the premiere of her second underwater epic, 'Neptune's Daughter', described patrons waiting in line for up to four hours in Chicago to be admitted to the cinema.

Objections were raised (mainly by women) to the indecency of the film, but these were lost in the general enthusiasm for the opportunity to view The Perfect Body onscreen. The fact that the perfect body was semi-naked throughout almost the entire film only added to the appeal. With the release of 'Daughter of the Gods' in 1916, Kellerman earned the dubious honour of being the first woman to appear onscreen completely naked. The film was also the first with a production budget of one million dollars, an indication of how highly the studio regarded her appeal to the public. The massive marketing campaign around the film shamelessly focussed on Kellerman's figure. Her cardboard cut-out was positioned in cinema foyers and women were handed tape measures and encouraged to compare their measurements with those of Kellerman—proof, if any was needed, that body anxiety amongst women was in place long before waif life teenagers strutted the international catwalks half a century later. Pre-publicity for 'Daughter of the Gods' drew attention to the artistry and ethereal beauty of Kellerman onscreen, a diversionary tactic designed to reassure the audience that what they were witnessing was legitimate art, not erotica, thereby endowing it with a respectability at odds with the content. Not everyone was fooled however: in Toledo, Ohio, a woman appeared in court charged with assaulting her husband after he viewed the film three times in as many days and unfavourably compared his wife's figure to that of Kellerman's.

In addition to her film career, Kellerman set herself up as a self-styled expert of women's health, writing columns for magazines and undertaking lecture tours throughout the USA. She returned to Australia during the Second World War and outlaid her considerable fortune producing lavish aquacades featuring hundreds of female swimmers to raise money for the Red Cross. Given that the money raised did not equate to the money spent on producing them, the aquatic spectacles were more of a vehicle for Kellerman to maintain her public profile and, possibly, resurrect a lost career.

As she aged, Kellerman clung stubbornly to her former image as The Perfect Body, as if, in letting it go, she would destroy the identity she had manufactured for herself. She was devastated in 1952, when the star of Billy Rose's famous Aquacades, Esther Williams, was signed to play Kellerman in the musical bio-pic, 'Million Dollar Mermaid'.[17] Kellerman was then 65 years old to Williams' 31, but she refused to concede that she was too old for the role. Ageing was not something Kellerman ever countenanced, and publicity shots of the time show her touching her toes or defiantly stretching one leg high in the air to demonstrate, in her eyes, her still perfect body.

*

I have searched for evidence to substantiate Mina's claim that she met Kellerman, 'as everyone knows', but I have drawn a blank. There is no signature in any of Mina's three autograph albums nor a photographic record of their meeting, but that is not to say it did not take place. Mina could have been referring to the 1902 NSW championships where the teenage Kellerman and the 10-year-old Mina may have exchanged a few words. But her 1975 assurance to Neil Bennetts that she had met Kellerman could have been another instance of Mina's tendency to exaggerate, often to elevate her own standing. Certainly, Mina and Kellerman never raced against each other as Kellerman turned professional before arriving in London in 1905.

The fact that Mina saved more items relating to Kellerman than anyone else—with the exception of Henry—is a good indication of the effect she had on Mina's choices, and possibly, her aspirations. Kellerman was the first female sporting celebrity of the age and although her fame resulted more from her Hollywood success and not competitive triumphs, it was her swimming prowess which had enabled her to attain star status. It is hard now, in our overtly sexualised culture, to fully comprehend the enormous impact of Kellerman on a relatively sheltered public.

The Victorian era was defined by a brand of puritanism which designated the female body an object which should be hidden from view. Female sexuality was regarded as a dangerous and corrupting influence and in some households, it is said, the legs of the grand piano were covered up to ensure that forbidden lust was not inadvertently stirred amongst gentleman callers.

Into this stuffy and strictly regulated atmosphere dived Annette Kellerman, with her brazen one-piece swimsuit and near naked aquatic displays in a glass tank. She made the female body visible in a way it had never been before, and her feats of endurance swimming challenged the accepted view of women as frail and physically passive. Little wonder, then, that Mina idolised Kellerman and looked up to her as a role model. While she may not have had the proverbial posters adorning her bedroom wall, she did have a set of six postcards depicting Kellerman in full flight displaying perfect dives from a high board.

Interestingly, the cards each carry the caption, 'Miss Annette Kellerman Champion lady swimmer and diver of the world'. Kellerman never competed in an Olympic Games, so to bill herself as a 'champion of the world' was more than a slight exaggeration. But Kellerman, even more than Mina, had a tendency to embellish her achievements to increase her personal standing.

Although there are no traces of cinema stubs or film programmes amongst Mina's possessions, I cannot believe that she had did not see Kellerman's filmed aquatic 'fairy tales', probably more than once. I believe Mina both admired

Kellerman and fantasised about a similar career for herself. She had, after all, been performing in swimming exhibitions and executing 'fancy tricks' since she was five years old. Mina had professional calling cards made and on the back of one she wrote, 'Australian crawl, American crawl, breaststroke, backstroke, sculling, fancy swimming, revolving backwards, somersaults, submarine, torpedo, porpoise.'

These cards do suggest that she was looking to present herself as an exhibition swimmer and although it is undated, the inclusion of both the American and the Australian crawl puts it beyond the 1912 Olympics where an early version of the stroke we now recognise as freestyle made its debut.[18]

Mina clearly modelled herself on Kellerman and possibly regarded herself as her natural successor, but I am not persuaded that Mina was as convinced as Kellerman was, that the worth of a woman lay in her femininity and her subsequent appeal to men. Although she was a fierce advocate for women's involvement in physical exercise, Kellerman nursed a powerful dislike towards women who displayed physical strength and stamina: the irony, of course, was that she herself had built her early reputation in long distance swimming. When she abandoned her third attempt on the English Channel in 1905, her comment, 'I had the endurance, but not the brute strength', typified her conviction that women were physically weaker than men. Yet she had been in the water for ten and a half hours, a feat unmatched by any other woman for the next twenty-one years. Kellerman frequently declared her belief that women should be 'balletic and graceful', and supported gender division of all sport, writing in her 1918 book, 'How to Swim': 'If women were to go in for the sports that men do, it would indeed result in physical development that would be anything but pleasing or beautiful.'[19]

In the same book, she disparaged women who attempted to move beyond conventional patriarchal constraints, stating, 'The present leaders of athletic sports for women fully recognise that a woman is a differently organised creature, and only makes herself ridiculous when she attempts to compete man-fashion in man's sports.' And yet she herself had been an enthusiastic competitive swimmer and had swum against men in endurance races. Perhaps there was a touch of sour grapes about her 1918 pronouncements, coming as they did, in the midst of Mina and Fanny Durack's well-publicised tour of the USA. Her loathing of female athletes did not, obviously, extend to swimmers as she appeared to regard swimming as exercise, but not strictly a sport, and therefore beyond the masculine associations of the playing field.

A woman should confine herself to swimming or skating, Kellerman pronounced, and 'appear in all her gracefulness.' Being feminine and attractive to men characterised her view of what a woman should be, and she urged women to take up swimming not just for health reasons, but because it was 'a great beautifier'.

Kellerman has been lionised as liberating women from that symbol of patriarchal control, the corset, but in actual fact, the ideal of femininity that she espoused trapped women in an even tighter set of restrictions. Women should be thin, she argued, to please their husbands, and should exercise to retain youthful appeal. In her 1919 book, 'Physical Beauty: How To Keep It', she maintained that 'not only does the girl who fails to possess beauty of body fail in finding love, but the woman who loses her body fails to keep that love which she has found.'[20]

It is a stretch, I admit, to accuse Kellerman of inciting the beginnings of an ongoing culture of body anxiety amongst women, but her aggressive promotion of the body beautiful certainly contributed to the growing view that it was a woman's duty to be attractive and physically desirable to men. It is worth bearing in mind that she was a film star and therefore expected to offer an image of perfection to an audience seeking escape through fantasy. The brand of perfection that Kellerman was selling was, however, unobtainable for the majority of women.

What Mina thought of this side of Kellerman, is unrecorded, and if she owned a copy of 'Physical Beauty: How To Keep It', she did not consider it important enough to store in the boxes under the house. Kellerman's influence on Mina is apparent in a 1918 studio portrait in which Mina adopts a pose identical to that of an image of Kellerman from 1905. Lying on her stomach, head resting against one arm and her hair cascading over her shoulders, Mina appears slightly self-conscious and faintly uncomfortable at her own objectification.

In photographs taken around various swimming pools, however, she is relaxed and unashamed of her body. Images of Kellerman confidently posing for the camera whilst wearing very little, suggest that the two women expressed their identity in very different terms. Mina was a competitive swimmer and her athletic body and racing swimsuit corroborated this definition. Kellerman was a film star and her slender figure and revealing swimsuit represented her financial security in a society moving towards the commodification of the female body. Each in their own way, both women were redefining the puritanical Victorian ideal of femininity.

Kellerman may have been elegant and graceful, but she was far from the invisible feminine ideal and more than happy to exploit the demand for images of her body. Mina's feminine ideal, if indeed she ever gave it much thought, had a foundation firmly planted in athleticism and a female body that was strong and capable. Ironically, for a woman whose appeal was primarily her physique, Kellerman has a strange, asexual quality in photographs. Her femininity is exaggerated by heavy make-up and flowing silks, but she, in no way, exudes sexuality. Images of her in her later years hint at cosmetic surgery, an inability to accept a natural loss of the beauty she deemed so vital in a woman's life.

In one of the boxes from Meredith Clark's later donation to the Mitchell Library, is an artefact which suggests that Mina was intent on emulating Kellerman in more ways than one. Three pieces of lightweight onion paper reveal that Mina attempted to write an essay or an article for publication entitled, 'The importance and advantages of the art of swimming and its effects as an exercise upon the growth and development of the body.' Since her (alleged) arrest on Revere Beach in 1907, Kellerman had established a reputation for herself as an expert on women's health and on lecture tours throughout the USA, she dispensed advice on issues such as how to combat menstrual pain, weight loss and exercises to achieve firmer breasts.

Australian women had the benefit of her wisdom through her regular column in Snowy Baker's sport and health magazine[21], which carried articles such as, 'Corsets—Of Course I Wear Them' (although not when swimming, which she decried as 'foolish') in September 1912, and 'A Waist Like Mine' in April 1913. Mina's article attempt, with many rewritten sentences and crossed out words, is undated, but undoubtedly imitative of Kellerman's style and subject matter. She reassures the reader that swimming will not develop unsightly muscles—a tell-tale sign of manliness—and a later paragraph reveals Mina's adherence to theories of the era which sanctioned the belief that there was a natural superiority in swimming amongst certain races:

'Nature intended us to swim and we find the south sea islanders and nations in other parts of the world are splendid natural swimmers, but among civilised people it seems to have grown into an art or science which can only be acquired by most of us after long practice.'

Mina was a product of late Colonialism, which explains her use of the word 'civilised' when she clearly means 'white'. This view of South Sea Islanders as 'natural' swimmers was popular at the time, and influenced by the success of US 1912 Olympic champion, Duke Kahanamoku, who hailed from Hawaii. When Kahanamoku visited Australia in 1915/16, the local press showed remarkable deference towards him, utilising terms such as 'bronzed islander' or 'brown marvel' to describe him in reports.

This was a searing contrast to the overtly discriminatory attitudes towards the Aboriginal population in Australia, and virulent institutionalised racism designed to deny Aborigines any inclusion in the societal structures of power. The uncharacteristic respect shown towards Kahanamoku by the Sydney press pack reproduced attitudes common amongst the white population, that South Sea Islanders, such as Alick 'look at that kid crawling' Wickham, or Hawaiians, held a higher racial status than their Aboriginal or African/American counterparts. They were thus consequently framed in terms of the exotic, and Mina's view of an innate racial superiority in swimming amongst South Sea Islanders was influenced by this portrayal.

*

The enthusiastic lady cyclists of the 1870s were mainly responsible for igniting the desire amongst women to breech the male exclusion zone that surrounded organised sport. One of the most frequently utilised arguments against this desire came from (male) medical experts who pronounced that women who engaged in vigorous exercise would jeopardise their ability to bear children, not least by dislodging their uterus. Religious leaders were quick to concur and condemned women who played sport as immoral, due to their apparent disregard to preserving their bodies for childbirth. So deeply ingrained was the belief that to be female involved being a mother, that a woman who had not given birth was regarded as deviant, or not a real woman.

By the time Mina and Kellerman came to public attention, it was generally acknowledged that exercise was, in fact, beneficial to childbearing, but the practices associated with being female continued to centre around motherhood. Kellerman married in 1912, but she never had children, and her overstated femininity may have been a response to a society which equated sport with men, and female-ness with motherhood. As a woman without children who was in the public eye, she had to establish her feminine credentials in other ways.

In reassuring men that her slim body and balletic grace were cultivated for their benefit, she ensured that the combination of her childlessness and athletic prowess did not prevent her acceptance as a woman in the public sphere. Coincidentally, Mina never married, a fact (infuriatingly) noted in all of her obituaries, but neither did she display the same need as Kellerman to construct herself as graceful and girlish to compensate. Admittedly, she did not have the 'pin-up' status of Kellerman, but Mina's identity as a successful sportswoman was, going on the evidence of photographs in her archive, more important to her than presenting herself as an attractive, unthreatening ornament, designed to appease the male eye.

Although I failed to find any evidence that Mina actually met Kellerman beyond 1902, there is proof that she saw one of her performances in London. In a small Letts diary, Mina noted the places and sights she and Henry visited in Europe in 1912, and her entry from London on Friday 9 August reads, 'Went to Hippodrome to see Ching Ling Soo 2.30. Also to Palace—Annette Kellerman'. Kellerman was playing the title role in a show billed as 'Undine. An Idyll of Forest and Stream'[22] and Mina saved the theatre programme. The synopsis outlines a rather bizarre storyline:

'Jacqueminot, the daughter of Lord and Lady Rosehill, has lost all interest and pleasure in her little world. The shepherds, wood nymphs and court clowns fail to arouse her from the lethargy into which she has fallen. She cares not for books or gifts, and in despair, her father offers a purse of gold to the one who will awaken her from this mood. It is then that Naola, one of the wood nymphs, brings Undine, who with her dancing and diving in the stream that flows through the woodland, so exhilarates Jacqueminot that she entirely recovers her fallen spirits. At her invitation, Undine leaves her glade and retires with Jacqueminot to Rosehill Castle where they live happily ever after.'

London audiences, with their well-established pantomime tradition, were presumably so inured to witnessing cross dressing onstage that they saw no reason to question the subtext behind two young women setting up home together following the emotional awakening of one by the other. As Mina sat in the Palace theatre watching Kellerman's onstage cavorting, I wonder how seriously she fantasised about a similar career for herself. How did the applause of a theatre crowd compare to the standing ovation she and Durack had received in Stockholm? Did Mina present herself at the stage door and request a meeting with her idol, I wonder?

It's possible, although surprising, that she would come away from such a meeting without some souvenir—a signature on her programme, for example, or a publicity shot from the show. What I really can't bear to imagine is the scenario where Mina gives her name to the stage door keeper and waits whilst a runner takes a note up to the number one dressing room. After a few moments, the boy returns, breathless and bearing the message.

'Miss Kellerman says thank you for coming around, but she's too tired for visitors.'

Because Annette Kellerman would not be upstaged by anyone. Especially not an Olympic swimming medallist from her own country.

Mina continued to cut out articles about her idol from magazines for another ten years. And perhaps, in the space between 1912 and 1975, Mina imagined meeting Kellerman so many times that it became real for her. She had met her. Everyone knew that.

*

Mina's mother, Florence, is an elusive presence in Mina's archive. The number of cheerful postcards beginnings, 'My dear Mum …' indicate a close and loving relationship between the two women, yet the lack of any additional information relating to Florence makes it almost impossible to recreate her character without resorting to imagination. There is one photograph amongst Mina's possessions of a woman I assume is Florence, purely due to the likeness to Mina. Florence is seated and a group of four young women, one of whom is Mina, is standing around her. The photograph is undated and the women in it, unidentified, but the presence of Fanny Durack suggests to me it is swimming related. The woman who I am assuming is Florence, is wearing what appears to be a chiffon tea gown and has her hair elegantly swept up. I was surprised at the image, as the impression I had formed of early swimming as a sport was solidly working class.

One of the attractions of swimming in Mina's era was that it did not require expensive equipment or membership to an exclusive club, and the financial incentives on offer in long distance swimming and aquatic exhibitions attracted a disproportionate number of young working-class women to the sport. It may have been my knowledge of Henry's immigrant and tradesman background that led me to blithely assume that his wife would be of a similar social class, but the quiet refinement displayed by Florence in the photograph, suggests otherwise. She has the stillness and posture equated with good breeding. A hint of a smile plays on her lips, yet I get the impression that this is a woman who would never be so uncouth as to laugh out loud in public. A woman, I believe, of a higher social class than Henry, and how she came to marry a house painter from Ulster living in Melbourne remains a mystery.

Once I realised that Florence was not the archetypal 'Aussie battler Mum' that I had pictured, a number of things which had puzzled me about Mina began to make more sense. From Marseilles, for example, Mina sent Florence a postcard which opens:

'My dear Mum, We went ashore here and had a good time. We can speak French fairly well now but it is so funny, but it is so wonderful how you can find your way about with a little French...'

How on earth, I had wondered, had this young woman from Coogee learned to speak French? When I unearthed a 1911 programme for 'Mrs Stuart Doyle's Annual Student Recital' featuring a piano solo—'Pass de Cymbales (Chaminade) by Miss MINA WYLIE'—I began to question the version of the Wylie family that I had formed in my mind. I discovered that Mina had, in fact, attended a private school, Carleon College in Randwick, where she had not only learned French as part of the curriculum, but also Latin, elocution, arithmetic and the classics. And mixed with the right kind of girl.

Henry's accounts book for Wylie's Baths hold another clue to his wife's higher social background. One entry reads, 'borrowed from Flo £20' and another, 'repaid Flo £100'. The latter was a considerable amount of money in 1919, and I wonder if Florence came into a legacy at some point after the debt crisis which brought about the disaster that the Elkington Park pool became. It could explain where money was found to pay for school fees and private piano lessons.

There is also evidence in the account books that Mina's constant interstate and overseas travel for competitions was paid for by her family and not a swimming authority:- February 1917, 'Mina Brisbane £2/10', February 1918, 'Mina Melbourne £2', May 1918, 'Mina fare USA £20' and June 1919, 'Mina America £15'. Sustaining a career as a champion swimmer was not cheap, and

Henry's letters betray a constant preoccupation with money. I do believe that it was Florence who, later in life, provided the financial safety net that enabled both her husband and her daughter to pursue their dreams.

In short, contrary to my working-class imaginings, the Wylie family was lower middle class with money to pay for piano lessons, education, overseas travel and, in time, a large family home. In teenage and earlier photographs of Mina, she is well turned out, wearing white lace dresses and her hair held back with a white ribbon. She invariably wears jewellery, in particular a bangle on one, or both wrists[23], and the impression she presents is of a girl from a 'good' family. The fact that Mina first took up paid employment at the age of 37 suggests that Florence and Henry never intended she would have to earn her own living.

In the hour-long interview Mina gave to Neil Bennetts in 1975, she refers to Florence only once, saying, 'Mother always made sure I got a fillet steak on the day I had to race.' Apart from proof that the Wylie household was a long way from starving, the comment indicates that Florence was fully supportive of Mina's swimming and ensured she had what she needed to perform at her best. This scenario might have been different had Mina chosen cycling or cricket as her favoured past time, but the presence of highly respectable women such as Rose Scott and Lady Poore at the Ladies Amateur Swimming Association, and Lady Chelmsford at the Sydney Ladies Swimming Club, bestowed a sense of decorum and decency onto ladies swimming.

The prevailing view of swimming as a more refined way of exercising for women made the disciplines attractive to mothers, such as Florence, who had no desire to see their daughters engaging in behaviour they regarded as rough or uncouth. The graceful swimmer or diver was the antithesis of the boisterous, loud women charging around a field wielding hockey sticks and attacking a ball.

There was, however, an unspoken division between the young women who participated in competitions, and the female swimmers who performed in exhibitions or, in Annette Kellerman's case, the vaudeville circuit. Whilst Kellerman succeeded in convincing her audience that what they were viewing was artistic and therefore socially acceptable, a fine line existed between aquatic artistry and exhibitionism. This line became more rigid as swimming, or at least, a version of it, began to make an appearance on the disreputable burlesque circuit.

An enormously popular act in the first decade of the 20th century involved a female performer singing a song about swimming while executing a series of stylised stroke movements and simultaneously disrobing. Whether the singer had ever actually swum a stroke in her life was neither here nor there. In fact, the closest many of these performers ever came to full immersion was under a cascading stream of water onstage designed to heighten the singer's sexual allure as, once wet, the silk underwear left little to the imagination. In this context, it is easy to understand the obsession with sex segregation and the outfits women wore in the water which dominated women's swimming at this time. It was a bid to distance competition swimming from any seedy associations with vaudeville, or, heaven forbid, the even more downmarket burlesque.

The Victorian era was one in which respectable women were not readily visible in public, and when they were, they were rarely unaccompanied. The high-profile campaign for political emancipation, however, enticed women out of their homes and into public halls as they rallied in support of the cause.

An invigorating sense of confidence began to emerge, fuelled by a burgeoning feminist movement demanding marriage reform, access to higher education and the right to stand for parliament. I like to imagine Florence Wylie as one of these revolutionary women: someone who insisted on an education for her daughter as well as her sons, and refused to listen to nonsense about the supposed dangers of sport for women. For all I know, she may have been one of the thousands of women liberated by the invention of the safety bicycle and was adamant that her daughter would not spend her life as a frail wallflower, reclining on a chaise in a darkened room complaining of breathlessness and fatigue. Henry, as Mina's swimming coach, took full responsibility for her swimming regime, but the fillet steak-bearing Florence was undoubtedly the support team.

*

A second woman who is not a pervasive presence in Mina's archive but who had an enormous influence on her swimming career is celebrated feminist and social reformer, Rose Scott. Born in 1847 in Singleton, NSW, to a police magistrate and his wife, Scott moved to Sydney after the death of her father in 1880. She was a founding member of the Women's Literary Society, established in 1889, and it was from the ranks of these members that the Women's Suffrage League of NSW emerged in 1891.

Scott quickly established a formidable reputation as an educated and intellectual woman who was not afraid to take on the authorities in her quest to reduce men's institutionalised power over women. She was a leading campaigner for the political emancipation of women and held weekly salons at her Woollahra home which were patronised by judges, politicians, academics and writers. Following the success in 1902 of the campaign to extend voting rights to women in NSW[24], Rose Scott became the first President of the Women's Political Education League, founded to educate women on the use of the vote.

Beyond her political and social reform activities, she was an enthusiastic supporter of ladies swimming, and in 1905 she was a driving force behind the instigation of Mina's club, the Eastern Suburbs Ladies Swimming Club. By this time, women's competitive swimming in Australia had become so popular that the formation of a separate association was deemed necessary, and in 1906, the NSW Ladies Amateur Swimming Association (LASA) was officially established with Rose Scott elected to the Presidency.

A photograph of a group of women including Rose Scott and Mina confirms the middle-class aura surrounding ladies competitive swimming in the early 1900s. The image, like so many of Mina's souvenirs, is undated, and Mina looks to be about twelve or thirteen. The group is a mixture of ages and the younger women at the front, including a young Fanny Durack, have medals around their necks. The older women behind the girls are a magnificent confection of lace, gloves and elaborate hats trimmed with flowers and yards of material. The gauze of one woman's hat cascades gloriously down her back like a water feature in an ornamental garden.

Scott has assumed her natural position centre stage and she sits majestically in the middle row, the focal point of the picture. She holds a large bouquet of flowers and has a stylish posy pinned to her hat. An extravagant feather boa— surely more suitable for a night at the theatre—is draped around her neck, and she regards the camera lens with faint disdain. There is no mistaking her status in either this group, or this image. She commands respect merely by sitting there. Interestingly, it is Mina who has been awarded the honour of sitting immediately to Scott's left. Fanny Durack is in the front row, the only girl wearing a dark dress amongst the froth of white lace. She, and the girl sitting next to her, are also the only two figures in the picture not wearing the white gloves that were considered mandatory for women of this period. Should I discern something from this about Durack's lower social status?

The dress she is wearing is too big for her, suggesting a hand-me-down, and crude stitching is visible on the inside of both arms. In contrast, Mina is the epitome of middle-class gentility. Her gloved hands are folded demurely in her lap, her back is straight and she too has an elaborate beribboned hat which appears to hover above her head. The formality of the photograph indicates this was a special occasion and Florence had made sure that Mina was dressed appropriately. I do notice that none of the women, not even the young girls, are smiling. Was Rose Scott really so intimidating?

Because there is no evidence to contradict this image, it is easy for me to conjure up a portrait of Florence as fully engaged with Scott's feminist causes, which would account for Mina's favoured position in the photograph. I picture Florence at Scott's weekly salon in Woollahra, attempting to exude a self-confidence she did not quite possess, but fired up for any campaign led by Miss Scott which would improve the lot of working-class girls.

'They turn to prostitution because they have no other option. And why? Because the father has abandoned them and is free to take no responsibility at all for his actions.'

'These girls require protection, not judgement, Miss Scott.'

'And especially not judgement from men, who are the cause of the problem in the first place. An imbalance of economic power, Mrs Wylie. That's the real issue. Oh, will you excuse me, there's the Prime Minister ...'

And off she sweeps, leaving Florence to be polite to the Vice President of the LASA, Marion McIntosh. A woman Florence disapproved of, due to her raucous laugh and disreputable sporting promoter husband.

If this was the Hollywood version of Mina's story, there would be an inspiring scene with rousing underscoring as Florence cycles after the tram carrying Henry and Mina to the boat which will take them to Europe, and Olympic glory. Her bicycle has a large sign affixed to the handlebars—'Good Luck Mina'—and Mina leans out of the tram window waving to her mother as bystanders smile and applaud. But this is not Hollywood, and much as I enjoy the fantasy, it is a result of my over stimulated imagination. And too much exposure to period dramas.

The only letter I located in the archives from Florence to Mina makes a fleeting reference to the 1914 small pox epidemic in Sydney: 'My word the small pox is still spreading one is almost afraid to go out into town. I do wish it was all gone but we must trust in God to protect us from it'. Other than that, the card is concerned with family matters and whether or not Florence will be able to get a rabbit and a cauliflower for dinner. I suspect the reality was that Florence was never invited to Rose Scott's home to mingle with the intelligentsia of Sydney. They may have exchanged a few words at swimming carnivals, but Florence, a wife and mother, had little in common with the resolutely single and independent Scott, who had once remarked that life was too short to waste in the service of one man.

Florence's life was, I believe, like so many women's lives, consumed with the needs of her family. Supporting her husband's professional endeavours, guiding her daughter, feeding her sons ... If Florence was involved with any women's organisations, she would almost certainly have taken Mina along with her to meetings. Yet Mina, despite her contemporary reputation as a feminist advocate, showed no signs of political activism and nothing in her archive suggests she was a member of a women's organisation or a feminist group. That, of course, does not mean that she was not, only that she chose not to save the evidence.

Mina's diary from London reveals that her association with Rose Scott did not ignite any blazing feminist fire. She writes of a walk in Hyde Park where, 'we went down along the banks of the Serpentine and also heard the Suffragettes spouting.' Not the most supportive terminology that she could have used.

Much as I would love it to be true, I find it hard to believe that the mother and daughter duo I found in the archives donned identical 'Women for Peace' sashes and joined Rose Scott in the campaign against conscription in 1916. Florence and Henry were members of the lower middle class, the aspirational class. The class, arguably, least likely to speak out or rock the boat for fear of losing their newly acquired and hard-won social position. Rose Scott had the confidence to lead campaigns and argue against male authoritarian control because, as a member of educated and ruling class, her social position was never under threat. While Florence may have admired Scott, she certainly would have found her an intimidating figure, and any vision of the two women crossing the entrenched class divide and socialising together is pure fantasy.

Florence's support of Mina's swimming does, however, indicate that she was a woman who was quite prepared to embrace the societal changes concerning the role and place of women. This reflected a wider view amongst white Australians of their country as both modern and egalitarian, (these attitudes, it goes without saying, did not extend to the Aboriginal population). Many

Australians saw themselves as belonging to a forward-looking nation, one willing to embrace changing ideologies and apparently free from the class constraints pervasive in British society, and although Rose Scott and her ilk would have been quick to disavow them of the latter notion, it was a pervasive view throughout the Lucky Country.

In Florence's mind, any development which rebounded positively on the life of her daughter was a good thing, but that did not necessarily mean she felt the need to go out and actively campaign for it. The impression I have formed is that Florence was content with the life she had in Coogee. She was a good wife and mother, her children were well educated and secure, and her husband a successful businessman. What more could she want? The fact that her only daughter was a swimming champion was a bonus she delighted in.

*

Two later photographs of young women wearing labels marked LASA, further confirm the 'respectability' of ladies swimming. Mina and Durack, dressed in long silk dresses, are now older and wear their hair up, a sign that they had progressed from childhood to womanhood. An older woman, possibly a chaperone if this was an interstate event, is seated in the middle of the group and all four women stare unsmiling into the camera lens. Dignity, is the key word here. Refinement. 'You may be swimmers', I hear Rose Scott caution, 'but there is no need for boisterousness'. The absence of men from photographs associated with women's swimming confirms one of the most notable facts about early women's competition in Australia: it was governed entirely by women.

The issues faced by female swimmers at the same time in the USA, most noticeably from James E. Sullivan, frequently related to chauvinism and a belief that sport was the privilege of men. But in Australia, male sporting authorities seemed perfectly happy to hand over the organisation and governance of women's competition to other women, with no inference at all that they were incapable of managing it. There is always the possibility that they did so in the belief that women's swimming was so trivial compared to the real issue of men's competition, that it scarcely mattered if it was well organised or not. But just as the sex segregation of pools contributed to women's eagerness to swim, the absence of male authoritarians dictating the operation of women's clubs and competitions appealed to women living within a resolutely patriarchal society.

Swimming, and the organisation of ladies' competitions, offered a rare opportunity to spend time with other women beyond the confines of the home.

Upon her election to the LASA, Rose Scott's first priority was to protect the semi-naked young swimmers from prying male eyes, and her proposal to close ladies' competitions to male spectators was quickly approved by her committee. This action firmly drew the line once and for all between women who swam in amateur races, and women who performed in burlesque wearing a swimsuit. It also, however, excluded Henry from competitions in which Mina was racing, and Florence consequently assumed new responsibilities as the person who scrutinised Mina's performance and reported back to her coach. She was now more than the support team. She was essential. And Henry's eyes at the interstate championships in Brisbane in 1909.

'Will you sign my autograph book, Mum?'

'I'll be the oldest person in it.'

'That doesn't matter ...'

After a moment of careful thought, Florence took the pen and wrote on the final page of Mina's album: 'All's well that ends well.'

Mina's team mate, Lily de Beaurepaire, however, had the last word, writing underneath Florence's signature:

'By hook or by crook/ I'll be last in this book'.

*

When I found a letter to Mina, dated July 1922, from a neighbour expressing her condolences at the death of Florence, I felt I was intruding. That this letter had never been meant for my eyes and I was betraying a trust by reading it. Florence was 56 when she died and the letter from Mrs Watson refers to a long illness: 'Deeply as you regret the loss of a loving mother, you have the consolation to know she is now at rest and free from all the pain and suffering she must have gone through for a long time.'

Mina had not married and was still living at home, which make it safe to assume that, as the only daughter, much of the caring responsibilities for the ailing Florence rested on her shoulders. How did she cope, I wonder, seeing the life slowly ebb from her beloved mother? Was swimming her welcome escape from a house filled with the messy business of terminal illness and impending death? The condolence letter is heartfelt, an older woman recognising the isolation and distress of an only daughter:

'The sweetest word in the English language is mother. We never miss a mother till she is gone and no one in this world, Mina, no matter how good they be, can ever replace her. You have still your father left you Mina, and my earnest hope is that you may be long spared to be a comfort and solace to him in his declining years as we all know you were to your dear mother in the past.'

I was sad reading it. Sad for Mina, and sad that I had not succeeded in knowing Florence better. This gentle woman who lent her husband money and supervised her daughter's piano practice. Who had watched her daughter grow from a child wriggling across the pool as a novelty act, to a woman feted by the Australian public for her ability to swim fast. Even when Mina only had a few hours somewhere, Atlantic City in 1919, for example, she sent a card to 'My dear Mum'.

From Belfast in 1912, Mina she enclosed some shamrock seeds within a card saying, 'thought you would like to try to get it to grow. If you did, it would be a real Irish shamrock'. I like to think that the gold bangle Mina wore on her wrist, even when competing, had been a gift from Florence. She wore it, not just for luck, but because it made her feel safe. It reminded her of her mother.

Annette Kellerman, undated

THE PALACE THEATRE

Managing Director - - Mr. ALFRED BUTT

FIRST APPEARANCE HERE

ANNETTE KELLERMANN

AND HER COMPANY IN

"UNDINE"

An Idyll of Forest and Stream

By MANUEL KLEIN

An entirely new production, revised by JAMES R. SULLIVAN

Characters

The Lord of Rosehill - - - Mr. DOUGLAS PAYNE

Programme for Kellerman's stage spectacular, Undine, Palace Theatre, London 1912.
Florence Wylie, undated.

Rose Scott, centre with flowers. Mina on Scott's immediate left. Fanny Durack front row in dark dress. Circa 1906.

Mina at left, Fanny Durack far right with an unidentified swimmer and chaperone. Undated.

Chapter 4

When we went to the games in 1912, the men hadn't anything to do with ladies' swimming and they didn't think it was right that women should be sent from Australia to Stockholm.

Mina Wylie interviewed by Neil Bennetts, 1975.

The assertion that Mina and Fanny Durack were initially denied places on the 1912 Olympic team by authoritative men who favoured male competitors, is one which has gained traction within contemporary recording of the events. This framing of Mina within the context of sexual prejudice has become part of her myth, but it is completely without foundation. It is a myth, however, first introduced by Mina herself in the 1975 Bennetts interview, when she assured him that she and Durack had 'a long fight' with male authorities before they were 'allowed' to go. Three months after Mina met with Bennetts, a feature article appeared in *The Canberra Times*, and opened with this paragraph:[25]

'Mina Wylie, 77, had to overcome male chauvinism before she could become one of Australia's first women Olympians. When she was 13, Miss Wylie, of Coogee, won a silver medal in the 1912 Stockholm Games when she came second to her compatriot Fanny Durack. But before the two women could represent Australia they had to overcome strong objections by the Men's Swimming Association. 'They didn't want women in their team,' was Miss Wylie's simple explanation.'

Considering the storm which came to surround the selection of the 1912 swimming team, it is bizarre that Mina misremembers the events so completely. She may have been aware of the political preoccupation with women's rights in the 1970s, and was responding, however unintentionally, to the current climate. There is also the possibility that, at 84 years old, she remembered very little concerning the controversy which led up to her and Durack's inclusion on the team and was merely saying what she thought was the right answer.

What is certain is that once the story of Mina battling men intent on keeping women out of the Olympics appeared in print, it became accepted as truth and attached itself to the reconstructed image of 'feminist heroine, Mina Wylie'. Perhaps the very notion that it had been other women who had almost prevented the participation of the female swimmers seemed to be so absurd that no one ever considered it. But that was indeed the correct version of events.

*

In 1911, the NSW Amateur Swimming Association (ASA) made it known that funding would allow for five swimmers to represent Australia at the forthcoming Stockholm games. A supportive press speculated that Fanny Durack, a serious gold medal contender, would certainly be included in the five and the subsequent announcement of an all-male team infuriated her supporters, particularly as only one member of the team, Cecil Healy, was a medal contender.[26] The Australian Olympic selection committee justified the exclusion of Durack as a financial consideration, citing the six individual male events over the one female event. Male swimmers could be utilised for more than one race, the committee reasoned, including team events, thereby offering additional medal opportunities. But alluding to financial concerns was an odd defence to employ against Durack when a perfectly valid reason already existed. The 1906 rule instigated by the NSW LASA which forbade their members from competing in front of men, was still in place in 1911. This meant that the men of the Australasian Olympic selection committee were forbidden to attend a competition in which Durack was swimming and without seeing her race, they could not offer her a place on the team. More significantly, the rule rendered Durack ineligible for selection in the first place, as the Olympic competition would be held in front of a mixed crowd.

Initially, the outraged attention was focused on Durack, but Mina was also entertaining a vision of swimming in Stockholm. Her club, now known as the Sydney Ladies Swimming Club (SLSC), produced a pocket sized blue and cream card every competition season which listed the office bearers and rules of organisation. In the card for the 1911/12 season (which lists Mina as Captain of the club and Rose Scott as President), Rule 13 made Mina's position with regard to the Olympics, perfectly clear:

'Any member competing in any race outside the club, to which the general public is admitted, shall be struck off the Roll.'

'General public', of course, meant men. Rule 18 then outlines the consequences:

'Any member violating the rules or by-laws, or who shall misconduct herself or act contrary to the general wishes or policy of the Club, may be expelled by the votes of two thirds of the members present.'

On the off chance that Mina harboured a vague notion of switching clubs, rule 21 reminded her:

'All races shall be governed by the Rules of the NSW LASA to which this club is affiliated.'

As indeed were all the ladies swimming clubs at this time. And the segregation of competitions had been introduced by the LASA under the stewardship of Rose Scott.

'It's not fair,' said Fanny. 'I'd get gold before any of them, and they get to go.'

'They're men,' said Mina. 'It's different.'

The grumblings concerning the apparent snubbing of the female swimmers by the Olympic committee faded quickly. That is, until February 1912, when Fanny Durack broke the world record for the 100yds freestyle at the NSW championships. The refusal by James Sullivan in the USA to sanction the participation of the American women in Stockholm now elevated Durack to the position of favourite for the gold medal. Dissention swelled amongst the general public, fanned by the press which questioned the judgement in maintaining a rule which could deny the country Olympic glory.

As a woman who valued education above all else, Rose Scott did not place the same significance on sporting achievement that her fellow Australians appeared to do, and she remained steadfast in her refusal to even discuss the possibility of Durack going to Stockholm. Because in order for that to happen, the segregation rule would have to be abolished. Vice president of the LASA, Marion McIntosh, was equally determined that Durack would compete in the Olympics and claim glory, not just for Australia, but for women.

Marion McIntosh may have lacked Scott's education and social connections, but she had one major advantage over Rose Scott—her larger-than-life husband, Hugh D. McIntosh, also known amongst the sporting fraternity as 'Huge Deal'. Hugh McIntosh wielded enormous influence within the press and it was largely due to his insistence that support for Durack was stimulated by the media.[27] Rose Scott was someone who was accustomed to getting her own way, but so too, was Hugh McIntosh, and what his wife wanted, he wanted. Marion McIntosh and Rose Scott eyed each other across the ring and warmed up for the fight.

The ensuing bitter divide within the NSW LASA, with Scott on one side and McIntosh on the other, was not simply a difference of opinion or a class conflict i.e. brash new money confronting the establishment. Nor was it primarily an age issue, despite McIntosh being thirty years younger than Scott. It was a more profound clash between the traditional feminism favoured by Scott, which maintained that women should seek equality in some areas but retain their feminine difference in others, and the ideal, advocated by McIntosh, of equality in all areas.

Rose Scott was a product of the Victorian era and she resolutely believed that women were the moral guardians of the sexes, and that that maintaining distance between the sexes, retained dignity. McIntosh refused to accept the negative connotations associated with the word difference and she wholeheartedly rejected the traditional Victorian restrictions on women's behaviour. Instead, she embraced modern ideas which promoted visibility and display as female agency, and exhorted women both to be seen, and to show themselves.

As a social reformer dedicated to improving the lives of working-class women, Rose Scott was acutely aware that the imbalance of power in relations between the sexes resulted in the easy exploitation of women. Her work with female prisoners meant that she was well attuned to the predatory nature of some men ('most', she would have said), and where this could lead. Scott agreed that exercise was beneficial for the mental and physical health of women but she was against anything which challenged the innate decorum of women, because she saw it as reducing their moral superiority.

Scott insisted that many of the men who came to watch women's swimming were there not to admire the skill of the swimmers, but to leer at the female body. Men, she insisted, could not be trusted to control themselves, and it was therefore up to women—the natural guardians of morality—not to place temptation in their path. The fact that men might take responsibility for their own behaviour was not something Scott ever countenanced. Experience had taught her that this was a pipe dream.

Women in the Victorian era were denied a voice in the societal structures of power due to beliefs which asserted that women required protection and could not be trusted to think for themselves. The ideal Victorian woman was one who was invisible, physically passive and who accepted male rules regarding codes of behaviour. Little wonder, then, that the lady cyclists who donned bloomers and careered through city parks were often attacked by furious men:- the women were flagrantly rejecting a set of rules designed to contain and confine them.

Fears concerning the erosion of female modesty which had begun with the bicycling craze, had reached fever pitch by the early 1900s, as the 'modern girl'—with her bobbed hair and unselfconscious flaunting of her body—first began to make herself known. Up until then, the female form could only be found on public display in two places. The art gallery, where the study of the female nude by middle class men was considered educational and therefore entirely respectable, or in burlesque, regarded as entirely unrespectable and patronised by lower class, uneducated men. The female swimmer was positioned somewhere in between the high-brow culture of the art gallery and the bawdiness of the lower forms of vaudeville, and Scott's conviction that it was the near nudity on display which attracted male spectators to ladies' competitions was not without foundation.

Between the years 1880 and 1930, there existed a subculture amongst men in Sydney which came to be defined as a 'bachelor' or 'sporting' culture. Men congregated to drink, to gamble and to experience sexualised entertainment. This group equated masculinity with sport, and women with sex, and so it was inevitable that these men would view semi-naked women in a swimming pool only in terms of sex. When Scott closed the doors of women's competition to male spectators in 1906, she did so in the firm conviction that the young female swimmers were in danger from the men who presumed a connection between the female body on display and his right to possess it.

Banning men from competitions was the obvious way to protect female swimmers from voyeuristic men, but the additional fixation with the style and cut of swimsuits is puzzling given that the women were racing in front of an all-female crowd. Mina's copy of the NSW LASA rule book for the 1912/13 season lays out an extraordinarily detailed set of stipulations outlining what competitors must wear. Swimsuits had to be black or navy with shoulders straps no less than two inches wide. The front of the costume could not be lower than two inches below the base of the neck, it had to be buttoned on the shoulder and 'the armhole shall be cut to fit closely round the shoulder'.

Rule f in the book is even more explicit, stating, 'the costumes shall extend not less than eight (8) inches from the inside measurement of the leg downwards and shall be cut in a straight line round the circumference of the leg'. Women with tape measures stood by to ensure that competitors complied with regulations, and only after their swimsuits had been meticulously assessed were the young women permitted to compete.

Even then, another rule decreed that, 'At all public carnivals, the competitors must go cloaked to the starting post, and must resume their cloaks on the conclusion of the heat in which they are engaged.' To avoid any undignified scrambling amongst swimmers attempting to locate their discarded cloak, each competitor was assigned a cloak maid. The cloak maid was required to remove the full-length garment from the swimmer as she stepped up to the starting post, then hover on the side-lines, ready to swiftly envelop her at the end of the race. From a twenty-first century perspective, the swimsuit and cloaking regulations strike me as a less of a protective measure and more about controlling young women's behaviour. Who, after all, were the swimmers being protected from in an all-female environment?

The antipathy towards women in sport was an ongoing issue in the first decade of the 1900s, and however unreasonable the swimsuit rules now seem, they did pacify detractors who condemned sportswomen as lacking in moral fibre in their desire to emulate male behaviour. Ensuring that the female body was covered maintained the all-important impression of swimming as a respectable activity, but it also sent a clear message to the swimmers. One which told them they could swim, even engage in races, but they were still required to conform to the societal rules dictating feminine behaviour.

A contemporary interpretation of the regulations would conclude that the more pervasive message the young swimmers were absorbing was that the female body was something to be ashamed of and to be kept hidden. Interestingly, the stringent regulations did not dictate a specific material for the swimsuits, which was a glaring oversight considering that the light silk favoured by many competitors, including Mina, became transparent when wet. With all these rules and measurements and constant scrutiny, the women who swam competitively in this judgemental climate were engaging in an act either of daring, or outright defiance.

'A little more modesty would do you no harm, Miss Wylie. Bare shoulders won't win you the race.'

Mina caught Fanny's eye and giggled. Mrs Chambers was not amused. 'Cloaks on, girls. You know the rules.'

*

After Durack's record-breaking swim in February 1912, the Sydney newspapers began agitating for the LASA segregation rule to be removed and for Durack to join the Olympic team. The ensuing campaign provoked divisive debate and came up against fierce opposition from various sections of the community including, it goes without saying, the clergy. But Michael Kelly, the Catholic Archbishop of Sydney, was far from being a lone voice in his belief that mixed bathing would 'undermine the fabric of society.' Rose Scott stayed true to her conviction that young, female swimmers racing in front of a mixed crowd would be open to exploitation by opportunistic men, and swimming correspondent of the sporting newspaper *The Referee*, a reporter who wrote under the pseudonym, 'natator', echoed her sentiments, writing:

'I believe in the mingling of the sexes on our beaches and under proper supervision; but the cad is much more in evidence at a swimming meeting where women figure, than he is in the surf.'

The real issue at the heart of the debate was again related to control, in this case, controlling access to the female body. Scott wanted women to maintain this control, but she failed to appreciate the appeal of appearing in public to a younger generation who rejected the Victorian notion of a woman as someone who was neither seen, nor heard. What Scott classified as immodest or unladylike, Marion McIntosh, Fanny Durack and Mina Wylie regarded as progressive.

Surprisingly, in all the newspapers cuttings filling three boxes of Mina's archive, there is almost no mention of the heated controversy which dominated NSW newspapers for almost two whole months. Durack was the subject of the initial campaign which could explain why Mina chose not to save the newspaper reports concerning the mixed bathing debate: her motive behind her choice of articles which she selected to cut out and save, appeared to be whether or not her name appeared in it.

Because there is nothing in the archive to guide me, it is impossible to say for certain who it was who first raised the prospect of Mina accompanying Durack to Stockholm, but my instinct leads me to Henry. The race times posted by the British women, who were medal favourites after Durack, were not as fast as Mina's personal best, positioning her as favourite for the silver medal. If the two women could somehow be manoeuvred onto the team, Australia could easily dominate the women's competition. And Henry Wylie would become the coach of an Olympic medallist.

The public support for Durack was growing daily into a movement for change, and in an attempt to quell the rising rebellion, the LASA instructed all their affiliated clubs to hold an emergency meeting to discuss the crisis. Mina's club, the SLSC must have met prior to the 3rd of March, as that is when a report appeared in the *Sunday Times* headlined, 'Miss Mina Wylie: For Olympic Games', and opened with: 'The SLSC proposes making a strong move in the direction of endeavouring to have Miss Mina Wylie sent to Stockholm as one of the Australasian representatives at the Olympic Games'.

The statement is perplexing as Rose Scott was also President of the SLSC, and was extremely unlikely to support a motion which would allow a member of the club to swim in a competition at which men were present. Unless, of course, she was required, as President of the LASA, to declare an interest and exclude herself from the vote.

The sole surviving newspaper report which Mina kept of these tumultuous events is from the *Evening News* on March 7th, and is headlined, 'Lady Swimmers: Should Men Look On? Sydney Club's Decision'. The report opens with the claim that, 'Discontentment has reigned among members of the NSW LASA for a long time …'—not the best commendation of Scott's leadership skills—and then outlines the two questions that all affiliated clubs were being asked to vote on. 'The advisability of sending Miss Durack to Sweden, and the matter of allowing men to witness the ladies' carnivals.'

I picture a stuffy hall retaining the summer heat of the bright day. Irate women with large hats and diametrically opposed views. Fanny Durack, a fixed centre point around whom the maelstrom of furious debate swirled. And Mina, becoming increasingly impatient with arguments which seemed to go round and round without reaching any conclusion.

'Why should women be hidden away as if we are something to be ashamed of?' Mrs McIntosh demanded. 'We have voted alongside our husbands for over a decade, but they are forbidden to watch us swim. Are we in the Middle Ages, Miss Scott?'

Fanny laughed, a little too loudly. Florence frowned.

'Australia is in danger of being regarded as a backward nation,' Mrs McIntosh continued. 'This is our opportunity to show the rest of the world that this country is progressive and modern, and favours equality for women.'

Miss Scott drew her impressive self up, a galleon in full sail.

'Parading around in front of men will result in a loss of respect for our girls. How do you propose, Mrs McIntosh, to control the crowd when it becomes unruly?'

Mrs McIntosh waved a dismissive hand and laughed.

'Have policemen present. That'll sort them out.'

The laughter which erupted around the room convinced Rose Scott that enough was enough. It was time, she declared, for a show of hands amongst the committee members. Mina and Fanny sat up, straining to see.

'All those in favour of men being allowed to witness ladies' carnivals, raise your right hand.'

Mina counted feverishly. Ten for, twelve against. There was a smattering of applause, mumblings, a cry of 'ridiculous' from the back of the hall. It was over. But Mrs McIntosh was back on her feet.

'A show of hands does not comply with the regulations of the LASA,' she announced. 'We have to cast a ballot.'

This was true, and as the ballot papers were distributed among the twenty-two committee members, Marion McIntosh surveyed the crowd.

'Are there any points we have not yet taken under consideration?'

Mina's heart thudded in her chest. Her mouth was dry, and her hand shook as she removed it from her mother's and rose to her feet.

'Miss Wylie?'

All eyes in the room turned to stare. Mina took in the journalists, Marion McIntosh, the ladies of the SLSC. And she knew that what she was doing would hurt the one person who had kind and supportive and specifically requested that she sit next to her in official photographs.

'My father and brothers have never seen me compete,' she said, in a voice that had a strength she did not feel. 'And I would like them to see me.'

And she sat down with a bump, avoiding her mother's eyes.

The result of the ballot was a surprise that was greeted with cheers. Two women had changed their minds since the show of hands and there were now fourteen votes in favour of allowing men to watch ladies' competitions, and eight against. Excited women crowded around Mina and Durack, and Henry grinned broadly as Cecil Healy shook his hand. Only Florence noticed how Miss Scott's voice wavered as she announced her resignation as President of the SLSC.

Scott would not, however, resign from the more influential LASA, holding onto the glimmer of hope that the men's association would not accept the committee's recommendation that the two women should compete in Stockholm. Without the approval of the men's ASA, the ballot which had just taken place was meaningless and nothing, with regard to women's competition in NSW, would change. The question of money gave Scott a good reason to remain positive. The fares of the men were covered, but who would pay for another two swimmers? As her ally, secretary of the LASA, Mrs Chambers, pointed out, the Olympic committee was hardly likely to remove two men to accommodate two women, favourites or not.

*

Mina was quoted the following day in the report of the meeting carried by the *Evening News*, but a clipping in her archives contradicts her claim that her father and brothers had never seen her compete. On April 2nd, 1904, *The Australasian* carried a picture of an unnamed ladies swimming carnival at which Henry is officiating and Mina is competing. Admittedly, the carnival took place before the LASA segregation rule was implemented, but her use of the word 'never' was a deliberate move to gain sympathy and support for her cause. And another example of her tendency to exaggerate.

Mina and Durack now faced an agonising wait until the men of the ASA met to decide whether or not they would accept the LASA recommendation that the women join the Olympic team. Almost two weeks after the rowdy SLSC/LASA meeting on 6 March, an article appeared in *The Sun* asking the question, 'Lady Swimmers: Will They Go?'[28] The paper quoted Ernest Samuel Marks, an Alderman of Sydney Municipal Council and an Olympic sporting official[29], as confident that the answer would be yes:

'Personally I am in favour of the girls going, and though there is an old argument that girls should not swim in competition in the presence of men, I believe the majority of the remainder of the council will take the same view as I do and adopt the recommendation of the Ladies Association ...'

The same report, however, quoted Honorary Secretary of the SLSC and LASA, Mrs Chambers, as saying: 'under no circumstances should men be allowed to witness ladies' competition.' Rose Scott had clearly schooled Mrs Chambers well.

Sixty years after these events, in 1975, Mina's retelling of the controversy painted a vivid picture of men refusing to countenance women on the team, yet the evidence in her archive clearly shows that the greatest opposition against the inclusion of the female swimmers came from other women. The further irony is that these were the very same women who were involved in the governance of ladies swimming which was regarded as a liberating experience for young women. The eight committee members who voted against Durack going to Stockholm and opening up competitions to the male spectators did not record their reasons for doing so, but undoubtedly there were women, Mrs Chambers being one of them, who agreed with Scott that it was undignified for young women to appear semi-clothed in front of men and it would result in a loss of respect. It is safe to assume that there were other women who simply did not feel comfortable at the prospect of appearing in front of strange men wearing only a swimsuit.

There were competitors on the ladies' circuit at this time who swam under a false name to hide their participation from an overbearing husband or father, and there were also women who were allowed to compete by male relatives purely because the carnivals were closed to men. These issues related to ownership, of course, but on a more basic level they held potentially disastrous consequences for participation rates at ladies' carnivals.

Whatever the reasons behind the voting choices of the committee members, an issue that should have united the female officials of the sport and celebrated the fact that two Australian women were going to compete in Olympic swimming for the first time, caused instead bitter divisions amongst and the snubbing of Rose Scott who had been a driving force in women's competitive swimming for over a decade.

*

Wylie's Baths became the unofficial meeting place for a group of men who had a vested interest in Mina and Durack being granted places on the swimming team. 'Huge Deal' McIntosh, because it would make his wife happy, and because there was potential money to be made out of public appearances by the women on their return from Stockholm. Henry Wylie, for obvious reasons. Ernest

Samuel Marks, who would be going to Stockholm as team manager and fervently wanted to see Australian competitors bring home medals, and the only male medal favourite, Cecil Healy, whose wholehearted endorsement of the two women had appeared in print in the *Referee*. It is possible he had more personal reasons, but I am merely speculating.

The men's association and the Olympic committee duly accepted the proposal that Mina and Durack join the team for Stockholm, causing Rose Scott to immediately resign from the NSW LASA, famously stating: 'It would be alright, perhaps, if the men would behave themselves properly, but a lot of bad men would be attracted who would make all sorts of nasty remarks and who would go rather for the spectacle than for the skill.' Mrs Chambers, however, stayed put, and Marion McIntosh, unsurprisingly, assumed the Presidency of the organisation. Scott's reign, and the segregation rule, was now a thing of the past.

Modern ideas had trumped Victorian values and Scott was left angry, hurt and bewildered at this changing of the guard. She had campaigned tirelessly for decades for women's rights, but this, in her eyes, was not female liberation. This was playing into the hands of men by giving them exactly what they wanted: easy access to semi-naked young women displaying their bodies. Albeit dressed up with some vague notion of respectability. That was not the feminism that Scott espoused, and she was impatient with those who regarded the outcome of the Durack/Wylie controversy as a victory for women. Why, she wondered, would any woman want to engage in an arena designed specifically to pay homage to masculinity? That was not equality, Scott mused. That was lowering one's standards.

It is impossible to know what decision the Olympic committee would originally have arrived at if the segregation rule not provided them with the perfect excuse to ignore the female swimmers. It is highly possible that Durack would still have been snubbed by the all-male committee who retained an obvious bias towards male athletes. There were many, however, who regarded the initial omission of the female swimmers as out of synch with the egalitarian ethos which supposedly defined this modern nation, a country which had already demonstrated progressive political values with regard to women and voting rights. Nationalists were well aware that the former Colonial power, Great Britain—a nation lagging behind Australia in the political enfranchisement of women—was sending a female team to Stockholm. Australia's failure to do so would therefore depict the new nation as backward and clinging to traditional principles, instead of projecting an image of a modern and democratic society built on egalitarian ideals.

While the support whipped up by the press for the female competitors does suggest a population committed to gender equality, this was not entirely true of the virulently masculine society that Australia had become by 1912. Young women frequently left Australia for Europe at this time, citing the lack of opportunities available to women in education, professions and the arts in their home country. And there was no doubt that the concept of the Sporting Nation placed men in the foreground and relegated women to the spectator stands.

It could be argued that Mina and Durack were among the first examples of the politics of inclusion in sport (in the USA, Hawaiian swimmer, Duke Kahanamoku was another). That is, they were useful when they were likely to win, but expected to remain in their subordinate position dictated by societal rules when they were not. The fact that Australian sportswomen continued to experience discrimination for decades following 1912, indicates there was no real commitment to gender equality in Australian sport at this time, and that the outcome of the Durack/Wylie selection controversy was a triumph of nationalism, not feminism.

The demand to include the women in the team had, in actual fact, very little to do with their sex and was a reflection of an insatiable national lust for sporting glory and international relevance. An impressive medal tally in Stockholm would not only corroborate Australia's sporting superiority over other nations, it had the additional benefit of ridding the country, once and for all, of the most pervasive by-product of colonisation, a national inferiority complex. The healthy and victorious Australian athlete dispelled the humiliation of the 'convict stain' and allayed fears of a degenerate gene being passed down through subsequent generations. In addition, with two women on the swimming team, Australia could utilise Stockholm to demonstrate to the world that here was a country which valued gender equality, unlike the oh-so-modern American nation.

The nationwide support for Mina and Durack was a sharp contrast to the USA, where only a handful of voices were raised in protest against James Sullivan's edict forbidding the American women to compete in Sweden. The Amateur Athletic Union (AAU) had been formed in 1888 to regulate and govern amateur sport in the USA, and Sullivan, unsurprisingly, had been a founding member. The AAU barred women from participating in any event sponsored by the Union—the majority of all sport in the country at the time—and repeated calls from women to incorporate women's events went unheeded. Ida Schnall, the country's leading female high diver, sent a furious letter to the *New York Times* in which she accused Sullivan of:

'… always objecting, and never doing anything to help the cause along for a girls AAU. He objects to so many things that it gives me cause to think he must be very narrow minded and that we are in the last century. It's the athletic girl that takes the front seat today and nobody can deny it.'

But Schnall received little support for her campaign to compete, neither from the public nor from sympathetic athletes and officials.[30] The latter were probably intimidated by the overbearing Sullivan, and unwilling to cross him, but the lack of wider support for her campaign could suggest two things. It could intimate that the USA did not consider equality and women's rights an issue of any importance, and that female athletes were a not a particularly welcome addition to society.

It could also suggest that the country did not, at this time, regard sport as a means of gaining international status in the way that the Australian officials did. The USA had been independent for well over a century and was possibly further down the road than Australia was in developing confidence in its own ability as a separate nation.

*

The Olympic officials imposed two conditions on Mina and Durack joining the swimming team: they would have to pay their own fares and they would have to travel with a chaperone. Out of context, these conditions could be misinterpreted as grudging acceptance, but in 1912, there was no official sporting organisation in place to raise money to enable Australian athletes to compete internationally, and previous Olympians had paid their own fares, often by raising money through their local communities. (This reliance on public generosity remained a feature of Australian participation in international competitions into the 1930s, often to the detriment of women as male athletes were given priority.)

The insistence by the committee that Mina and Durack travel with chaperones was standard practice within the moral codes of the era. Despite press reports giving her age as 14[31], Mina was 21 and Durack, 23, and Victorian respectability deemed it unthinkable that two young women would travel to

Europe unaccompanied. Durack elected to take her sister Mary and there was no question as to who would accompany Mina. The father who had introduced his daughter to swimming and who had spent as many hours on her career as he had on his own. Henry Wylie would go to Stockholm as Mina's coach and chaperone. This made perfect sense, but I wonder if Florence perhaps hoped for one minute that she might be the one to go? Perhaps she too longed to see European cities, to buy Irish lace and speak French in Marseilles.

Marion McIntosh immediately took advantage of her husband's contacts within the press and established a public fund to raise money for the four additional fares to Stockholm. In Mina's archive is a sheet of paper headed, 'Olympic Funds Towards Sending Miss Mina Wylie to Stockholm'. The page is divided into two columns labelled 'name' and 'amount' which suggests that McIntosh and/or Henry were soliciting individual donations to augment the public fund. As gold medal favourite, Fanny was first in line when the requisite total was achieved, and on 10 April, she and her sister Mary Durack set sail from Sydney bound for Europe. Fundraising efforts on Mina's behalf continued in earnest and one of her newspaper cuttings gives a good indication of the community support she received:

'To Ald. T R Gilderthorp, Mayor of Randwick. Sir, we the undersigned Ratepayers of Randwick, hereby petition you to hold a Public Meeting in the Randwick Town Hall, for the purpose of Raising Funds to enable MISS MINA WYLIE to visit England to take part in the Olympic Games, as one of the NSW Lady Representatives. Yours faithfully, E G Hamilton Browne, J. Le Carpentier, S N Cornan, H Poole, T R Alldritt, Thomas Murphy and others.'

Time, however, conspired against her, and Henry finally made up the £100 shortfall in the public fund from his own purse (or possibly Florence's) in order to enable his daughter to compete.

*

Why Mina has gone down in history as a woman who battled a male conspiracy to keep her out of the Olympics, says more about Australia's need for female sporting role models, than the unreliability of memory. Beyond 1975, Mina's image was reconstructed to give the public a more triumphant figure, one who had overcome the odds to emerge as the victorious 'hero' so beloved of Australian mythology. And Mina herself continued to repeat the version of sexual prejudice instead of retelling the saga of Rose Scott and the segregation rule.

Twenty years after the 1976 *Canberra Times* article, an ABC National radio documentary entitled *Anzac Mermaids*[32], incorporated excerpts from an (unidentified) interview Mina had given in 1980, in which she again claimed sexual prejudice, saying: 'Nobody wanted us to go. The ladies swimming association were with the men, and the men were against the women going to the games.' While this may not be technically correct, there is no denying that sexual discrimination was enormously relevant Mina's era, particularly in sport. And the fact remains that Mina and Durack were not initially offered places on the team due to issues concerning their sex.

If I analyse Mina's reasons for reframing the events of 1912, I have to consider that, in later life, Mina was actually revealing her personal experience of the Olympics as she now remembered it, and that this version had emerged with hindsight. So, although it is possible to argue that there was no overt discrimination in the selection procedure, what Mina might be alluding to is the pervasive undercurrent of hostility towards women which permeated sport in her era. An attitude which she only felt empowered enough to name in 1975. The prejudice story gained traction in the 1970s because it resonated with the current political climate and illustrated the ongoing inequalities and discriminatory practices rife throughout wider societal institutions. Nothing had changed in sixty years, argued the furious activists. Just look at Mina Wylie.

The figure who emerges badly both from the mixed bathing debate in 1912, and the retelling of it in contemporary accounts, is Rose Scott. And yet this is unfair. At the time, she was portrayed by the press as out of touch with a society reinventing itself as modern, and this is the definition which makes an appearance in any current account of Mina, Durack and the 1912 Olympics. True, she does come across as a woman who was incapable, possibly due to her class, of regarding a situation from anything other than her point of view. She was completely unable to comprehend why two young women would want to compete in an international sporting competition, and she refused to accept that the values of the Victorian era were rapidly being displaced by modernity.

The fact that the issue of the sexualisation of female athletes continues to pervade the contemporary sporting arena, actually makes Scott's observation regarding voyeuristic male spectators ahead of its time. One only has to glance at a women's beach volleyball contest to be left in no doubt as to what the real attraction is. With hindsight, Scott now appears as more aware than most of where 'equality' in sport could lead in terms of the exploitation and commodification of women.

Perhaps she was also conscious that whilst the female swimmer was regarded as a novelty in 1912, she was unlikely to be granted the same recognition and respect for her achievements as her male counterpart.

*

Mina and Henry boarded the RMS Malwa at Circular Quay on the 4th of May, 1912, and Mina's diary confirms the momentousness of the occasion: 'On my arrival at the Quay I was surprised to see many of my friends waiting for me with floral tributes and tokens of remembrance...' Marion McIntosh was amongst the heaving crowd, flanked by members of the LASA and the SLSC. So too, was 'Huge Deal' McIntosh.

'Bring back a medal, Miss Wylie, and I'll turn you into the next Annette Kellerman.'

How many of the hundreds of women who thronged Circular Quay that day were there because they viewed her as an inspiration, the embodiment of the fearless New Woman? Here was proof that women were just as good as men. Mina stood on deck entangled in coloured streamers and looked at the crowd. There was Vera, and Bridgie and Dorothy and Esme, all as excited as Mina was. Lily, who would certainly be aboard this ship in four years' time[33]. And there was Florence, as beautiful as ever, holding up a delicate lace handkerchief. Before they had left Coogee, Florence had taken Mina aside.

'It doesn't matter what happens over there, Mina. You've already changed things.'

'But I want a medal.'

'If you're nothing without a medal, you'll still be nothing with one.' Florence kissed her daughter. 'You're not nothing, Mina.'

Then, as Mina wrote later in her diary, 'The Customs Clock struck 12, the Malwa commenced to move and we waved and waved until we could no longer see the Wharf.'

As the ship passed Double Bay, I wonder if there was a lone figure standing on the beach watching. And as the RMS Malwa disappeared beyond the harbour heads, did Rose Scott turn and walk slowly back to her home in nearby

Woollahra, pondering the transformation of a society into something she no longer understood? She remembered the polite girl who had sat next to her in club photographs. Who had curtseyed the first time she was introduced and never spoke unless she was spoken to. She missed that girl in white lace.

She missed everything.

Chapter 5

Everybody spoke of the great send-off you got. The worst of it was Walter or myself could not get a word in edgeways.

Letter to Mina from Harry, 7 May 1912

Mina's brothers, Harry and Walter, were so infuriated at being muscled to the back of Mina's Olympic farewell celebrations by women in large hats brandishing bouquets, that they requisitioned a rowing boat and attempted to follow the RMS Malwa out into Sydney Harbour. 'Dear Mina, it was hard luck we could not get out close enough to you on Saturday, but you were too far out,' wrote Harry, three days later.

The image of the two young men in a tiny boat battling the wake of the ship, driven on by the desire to wave to their sister, is beautiful. It encapsulates the feverish excitement among the crowd at Circular Quay, and the closeness of the Wylie siblings. As children, they had joined hands and created patterns in the water. As adults, they were reluctant to let go. When the news of Mina's medal came through to Sydney, Walter, interim pool manager in his father's absence, made a large sign stating, 'Home of Olympic Medallist Mina Wylie' and displayed it at the entrance of Wylie's Baths.

The first port of call for the Malwa was Melbourne, three days after leaving Sydney. Mina writes in her diary of taking the tram to St Kilda and having a swim, 'the water was nearly down to freezing point. I was so cold that I was numb, and the manager, Mr Kenny kindly prepared a hot salt bath for me and I was soon warm again.' She also found the time to buy a new autograph album: a more sophisticated affair than the previous book, this had a black leather cover and her initials embossed in gold. She was now an Olympian and required trappings which reflected this status.

As a young woman from a modest background, Mina would have had no reason to imagine she would ever make the pilgrimage 'home' that was the seminal event in the lives of middle-class Australian women in this era. This rite of passage trip was such a feature in the late 19th and early 20th centuries that newspapers frequently carried reports of who had left Australian shores, when they did so and on what ship. The voyage to Europe was regarded as culturally and educationally liberating for young women and, in addition, offered a more palpable way of engaging with the Empire.

Mina was fascinated by her introduction to new countries and cultures and, in tune with the times, she later recorded the details in a diary which she titled 'My Trip Abroad'.

After stopovers in Adelaide and Fremantle, it was a ten-day voyage to Ceylon, during which Mina became better acquainted with her fellow travellers and immersed herself wholeheartedly in the life of the ship. In Ceylon, she and Henry travelled by train from Colombo to Kandy, the last capital city of the ancient Kings located in the central hills: 'The scenery going up in the train is just magnificent to see, the lovely way in which the rice fields are laid out is quite a sight.'

In Suez, Mina and Henry visited a Mosque and she noted in detail the feet washing rituals of the men, and the headwear of the women. In the diary, she displays a keen interest in a religion she is probably encountering for the first time, and in 'some very ancient script supposed to be hundreds of years old'. After Suez, Mina reports to Florence that she and Henry are, 'both having a good time, now the heat is over. Dad got prickly heat very bad now he has got boils on his arm but he will soon get rid of those. Love Mina'.

From Marseilles, she assures Florence she has been speaking French (the private school education had not gone to waste) and notes, with spectacular understatement, that, 'there are some beautiful buildings here'. While the diary and letters home are descriptive and fascinating to me, one hundred years on, a sense of emotional detachment pervades Mina's writing. As if she is engaging only up to a point. She does admit to Walter that, 'since we left Sydney, it seems all like a dream to me, I can't seem to realise it', but her remaining cards are unusually straightforward. I say, unusually, because this was a young woman who had never been out of Australia and yet her reaction to her new experiences often feels muted. Perhaps she was being deliberately casual, restraining her enthusiasm in a dignified Victorian manner.

It is evident throughout the diary that Mina clearly identified with the English colonisers and assumed an automatic position of authority. This was a common attitude amongst the white inhabitants of Empire territories, a deliberate positioning of themselves as superior within a cultural and racial hierarchy. Mina noted in the diary in Ceylon, 'how peculiar it is to be served by black waiters', and later, on leaving Suez, 'it is a seven-day run up to Marseilles and it seemed quite natural to be associated with white people once again after all the blacks but still they were not English-speaking people'.

Once Mina and Henry arrived in London, however, any sense of cultural superiority was quickly dispelled and her awareness of her lower position in the British social hierarchy is apparent in her awe at swimming before the 'Dukes and Duchesses and Lords and Earls' at the Bath Club on 21 June. This dichotomy of superiority in the colonial territories and inferiority in England was a common contradiction experienced by Australian travellers in the early 20th century. It was, however, a shock to Mina when she realised that here in London, it was she who was regarded as the unsophisticated colonial.

In London, Mina 'went to Highgate Ponds where I met Fanny Durack and some of the English lady swimmers and we all had a swim and the water was very cold.' Highgate Ponds were three ponds located on Hampstead Heath: one was for men, one for women and one for mixed bathing. Presumably the English ladies, mindful of the well-publicised Australian horror of mixed bathing, took Mina and Fanny to the women's pond. In which case, when the Australian women swam on the 22 June in the King's Cup lifesaving competition and carnival at the mixed pond in Highgate, it was the first time in six years that they had raced in front of male spectators. Which also means it was the first time in six years that Mina's father and coach had watched her race.

The next day, the four Australians, Mina, Henry, Fanny and Mary Durack, left London bound for Sweden. Mina's diary records in meticulous detail the arduous journey which involved two ferry crossings and four separate train journeys, finally arriving in Stockholm twenty-four hours after they had left from Victoria Station. After settling into their accommodation in the city, an Australian team official arrived and 'took Dad, Fanny and I down to Djurgardsbrunnsviken where the swim stadium was specially erected for the Olympic competitors.'

And here, at the pool in the Djurgarden, Mina's diary infuriatingly ends, and blank pages occupy the rest of the unassuming hard backed notebook. Mina wrote her account of the journey to Europe retrospectively, starting the journal three days before she arrived back in Sydney in October. This could indicate she wrote it at someone else's suggestion, possibly with a view to having it serialised in a newspaper or sporting magazine, which would account for the slightly formal language she uses throughout the entries, often giving Fanny Durack her full name or referring to 'my father' instead of 'Dad'.

It also explains the emotional detachment I sensed: she was recording what she had remembered, and not of how she felt as she experienced it. If she did hold out hopes for publication, it may have been a lack of interest from the press that caused her to stop the account so abruptly.

More likely, she simply became too caught up in the social swirl of congratulatory lunches and dinners laid on for her benefit back in Sydney.

Faced with the half empty notebook, I felt as if I had been served the appetiser and was now being denied the main course. I desperately wanted to read how Mina felt at being a competitor in the Olympics. Who she met, who she socialised with and where she went in her free time. More than anything, I longed to read her account of the 100m freestyle final and the reaction of the spectators. And to gain an insight as to what it was like to stand with all the other medal winners in the newly built stadium and be presented with one of the first women's Olympic swimming medals. Perhaps it was something so personal and so profound that she found it impossible to commit the depth of her own feelings to a page in a diary.

*

The pool for the Olympic aquatic events had been constructed on the north shore of the small island of Djurgarden, located in Stockholm Harbour. There was a bridge connecting the island with central Stockholm and the bay was a popular spot for picnickers and swimmers. The pool was an enormous 100m long with high diving boards at one end, spectator stands running the length of the southern side and the opposite side left open to the Bay. A wooden boardwalk ran all around the pool and a two-storey office to house the officials had been built at one end. The changing rooms were in a large canvas marquee which had been erected in the park beside the pool. It was an impressive facility to look at, but not necessarily the best place to swim as the water was cold and murky, making it difficult to see.

For Mina, however, her first vision of the pool was thrilling and proof that she was really here. She was at the Olympic Games. The nerves in her chest began to flutter in time with the international flags waving from the poles around the pool. She was aware of shouts, a babble of different languages, the sun in her eyes, splashes, women's laughter and a whistle being blown. There was Billy Longworth treading water and grinning, a young woman soaring from the high diving board and there was Cecil Healy, waving from the next stand.

'Oh my …' breathed Fanny, as she and Mina surveyed the scene around the pool. 'Miss Scott would have a heart attack.'

For the pool was a mass of semi-naked men and women mingling on the boardwalk and lounging in the spectator stands chatting and laughing. A number of men had rolled the top half of their swimsuit down to their waist and they strolled casually, their bare torsos soaking up the Scandinavian sun.

Few women had bothered to don their mandatory full-length cloaks and no official appeared to be concerned. Mina and Fanny were physically on the other side of the world from Sydney, but this was light years away from the swimming carnivals they were used to.

'Better get in there and swim,' said Henry, as if this scene was something he encountered every day. 'That's what's you're here for, isn't it?'

There were two whole weeks in between Mina's arrival in Stockholm and her first heat on 9 July, and those fourteen days were spent thoroughly immersing herself in the Olympic experience. As a competitor, she was issued with a brown booklet containing the programme of events and the regulations of the games, many of which were concerned with the all-important amateur status of the athletes. There was no doubt about Mina's amateur status and so the regulations were irrelevant, but rule 8 in the booklet states that, 'the minimum age for competitors in the Games is 17 years, subject to exceptions in special cases where the entry is accompanied by a doctor's certificate testifying to his fitness.'

I'll ignore the casual assumption that all competitors are male and focus instead on the fact that the rule lays to rest the claims that Mina was fourteen in 1912. Admittedly it was a better news story—'schoolgirl swims in Olympics competition'—and Mina's age had been a moveable feast since the NSW championships of 1902. But if she had been 14 as the press insisted, instead of 21, she would not have been permitted to compete.

Mina and Fanny joined their team mates to train at the pool twice a day and the rest of the time appears to have been taken up with shopping, sightseeing, boat trips, postcard writing and socialising at occasions organised for the visiting teams. Like a squirrel storing up nuts for the long winter, Mina hoarded every little thing that would remind her of this glorious time in years to come. She saved three of the brightly coloured commemorative stamps which, like the medal, depicted a naked man, this one waving streamers, surrounded by the flags of competing nations and yes, even more, naked men.

A daily programme was produced for the swimming and diving events, each day distinguished from the last by a different colour, and Mina saved ten of these, some duplicated, although, surprisingly, not one from Friday July 12th, the day of the ladies' final. She bought numerous postcards of the city, cards being a cheap souvenir, and those she didn't send were easy to carry home.

She did send a card to Walter of the newly built athletics Stadium, the Stadion, and on a card of a Stockholm street, Mina carefully marked a cross on a building, then wrote: 'Dear Harold, This is one of the prettiest parts of Stockholm. Where the cross is, is the street we live in'. She saved the programme from a memorable evening at the Olympic Festival, held on Tuesday 9th July at Skansen, an open air museum and zoo located on the same island as the Olympic pool. The evening's festivities ran from 8-11pm and included 'songs and military music', the traditional 'illumination by burning tar barrels' and a torchlit procession.

Mina had had her first taste of competition that afternoon, winning the heat which had officially made her the first Australian woman to compete in Olympic swimming, and she was still buzzing as she rode the funicular up Skansen Hill with Henry to take in the festival. Men from other sports recognised her and tipped their hats, fellow swimmers waved, and Cecil and his new American friend, Duke Kahanamoku, stood next to her for the procession, their faces illuminated by the fire of burning torches.

In short, she was—as she relayed in a postcard home—'having a ripping time'.

*

Mina may have, frustratingly, ended her diary with her arrival at the pool, but I discovered an extraordinary collection of photographs which pick up from the very point where she left off. Also housed in the Mitchell Library, the images in the collection are arranged in two albums entitled 'On the Wallaby' (Volume I and II), and were taken by the Australasian team manager, Ernest Samuel Marks.[34] The first album documents the journey to Europe and many of the images depict the male athletes finding ingenious ways to keep in shape during the long voyage.

To me, many of the pictures are unnervingly beautiful. The sepia tint bestows a romantic element upon the gentlemen athletes and provokes a wistfulness for a less complicated time. The men in straw hats and white flannels relax on deck in the sun, casually smoking. They don shorts and long socks and box or skip. They sit on the floor of the deck in a row, their knees against the back of the man in front and practise their rowing technique. One man has rigged up a complicated series of ropes and weights and is working out in such a dignified manner that he defies even sweat.

At the resolutely upper-class Henley rowing regatta[35], the Australian men are imprisoned in time standing in the dressing tent in their blazers and caps and cricket sweaters, amidst drying socks and abandoned school ties. The image they present is the antithesis of the classless, egalitarian Sporting Nation and more reminiscent of an English public school. But the appeal is not solely in the 'Chariots of Fire' echoes, nor the knowledge that many of these young men are doomed to die in the mud of a foreign field. It is the quality of gentleness. An absence of the macho swagger and posturing we are accustomed to in elite sport today.

In the second album are the wrestlers, the runners, high jumpers, discus throwers, gymnasts, footballers and equestrians going through their paces in the Stadion. And here too, are the swimmers and divers. Image after image of Mina and Fanny and the men of the Australasian team during the practice sessions at the harbour pool. Here is everything Mina failed to record, and more, because the atmosphere captured in Marks' poolside photographs tell a story which would have horrified Rose Scott. One which depicts the swimming pool as an erotically charged space where men and women display their bodies, socialise and even flirt.

The casual observers sitting in the stands confirms the growing view of the athlete as a performer, someone who deliberately placed themselves in a position where they would be watched. For the young female competitors, this notion of being looked at was new, and something they had to learn how to accept and accommodate. Marks' photographs reveal that, for some women, showing themselves in a swimsuit in public was a demand that did not always sit comfortably.

Given the restrictions on men at women's competitions in Australia, this was very possibly the first time the unmarried E. S. Marks had been in such close proximity to a semi-naked female body and, judging by the sheer volume of images of female swimmers and divers, it was an experience he did not find unpleasant.

For someone more used to competing in an all-female environment, Mina appears surprisingly relaxed in Marks' photographs, revealing herself as a young woman with few reservations when it came to exhibiting herself semi-naked in front of a camera and male onlookers. This may have been the influence of Annette Kellerman who, for all her talk of dignity and passive femininity, clearly rejected any notion of women as modest and invisible. In Marks' photographs, Mina is only ever pictured alone or with Fanny Durack, unlike the female Swedish competitors who happily pose with their male team mates.

I suspect this was due to Henry's hovering presence keeping a close watch on his daughter in what he recognised as a potentially exploitative situation. Mina posing as a competitor wearing a swimsuit was one thing, but Mina wearing a swimsuit surrounded by grinning, bare chested men was a different thing altogether. Would Florence approve, Henry often asked himself. And if the answer was no, then that is what he relayed to E.S. Marks.

In all the photographs taken by Marks of Fanny Durack, she deliberately covers her breasts, but Mina, notably, does not always do the same. This conscious act of covering up may have been an edict issued to the female competitors from male team officials, as the British swimmers adopt exactly the same pose, their arms crossed in an unnaturally high position over the chest. It is, however, not a stance that either the Swedish or German women take on board, indicating a lack of communication between officials of the competing nations as to what was, and what was not, considered acceptable where women in swimsuits and male photographers were concerned.

Durack's body language is fascinating because, although she pointedly covers herself, she does not appear self-conscious. It is an odd juxtaposition but one which suggests to me that Fanny was confident enough in her own body to set boundaries and to resist pressure to appear in a way she did not want to be seen. Mina, on the other hand, saw no reason to hide her body and was perfectly willing to be photographed without her cloak and with her arms by her side.

What I love most of all about Marks' poolside photographs, is the insight they give into Mina's character. For these are the only images I have found where she is not formally posing for photographs. Improvements to cameras at this time had resulted in a smaller and more portable model which allowed the photographer to step outside the confines of a studio and snap informal and spontaneous images. In Marks' pictures, Mina is relaxed and unguarded, clearly enjoying the attention from her male team mates. I see flashes of a bright personality in this young woman who oozes the confidence that accompanies the knowledge of being good at something. She is lively and, I imagine, fun to be around.

In one image, Marks has surprised Mina at the edge of the pool, but she smiles broadly into the camera, unfazed by his intrusion. In another, she adopts a racing dive pose and turns her attention to the camera with a grin, seemingly oblivious to the men only yards away, fixated on her derriere. Or perhaps this is why she grins.

*

As the daily practice sessions became routine, Mina gradually became accustomed to being looked at by the men on the pool deck. She noticed that the Swedish girls only wore their cloaks when they were cold and never folded their arms across their bodies when they were being photographed. She noticed too, their ease in the interactions with their male team mates and the absence of the stifling formality which dictated such relations at home.

The British girls were friendly but watched over by a stern and tightly corseted chaperone whose dark, pinstriped dress and lace collar seemed out of place in the cloud of nonchalance hovering over the pool. Most of the Australian men in the team had abandoned the one-piece swimsuit for high waisted trunks cut up to the thigh, and Mina smiled as she imagined the reaction to this back in Sydney. Her eyes lingered on team mate, Harold Hardwick, lying on his stomach at the edge of pool soaking up the sun. He had hitched up the legs of his trunks and rolled the waist band even further down his bare back, and Mina gazed, curious. She had never seen such an expanse of male flesh, not even on Coogee Beach. Hearing a burst of laughter from the stands, she turned to see one of the German men wearing the cloak of a female team member. Daringly, a young woman tied the cord around his waist and stepped back into the laughing group to admire her handiwork. Miss Scott would indeed have a heart attack.

In the beginning, the Australian men were shy, almost embarrassed at being confronted by Mina in a swimsuit standing next to them. Once they swam together, things changed. She and Les Boardman paced each other over two laps then hung onto the side watching Duke Kahanamoku swim the new crawl stroke.

'Reckon we'll have to learn how to do that,' said Les.

And Mina agreed. It was exactly what she had told Dad back in Sydney. Fanny could swim the stroke, but not as well as Cecil Healy who endlessly discussed arm recovery and a rotating kick with his new American friend 'the Duke'. In this easy-going atmosphere, even Henry began to relax, leaving his charge to her own devices as he networked the great and the good of Australia's sporting society. He wasn't entirely happy when he saw his daughter being introduced to Kahanamoku—even shaking his hand. But Ernest Marks was with her, that kept it decent.

After a week of sessions in the pool, Mina felt confident enough to slip her new autograph album into her bag as she and Henry left the apartment they shared with Fanny and Mary Durack.

'Don't bother people, Mina,' Henry said, when he saw her take out the album at the pool.

'I have to have something to remember it all by,' Mina said.

'Well, put your cloak on,' Henry flustered. 'Your mother wouldn't like it.' As he held it up for her to put her arms through the sleeves, he added, 'And don't go near that Yank.'

*

There are three autograph albums amongst Mina's possessions, dating from 1908-1919. These are, essentially, memory books. Records of the fleeting encounters that were commonplace in the era of ships that passed in the night. Personal cameras were not common in the early 1900s, and a signature accompanied by a thoughtful comment was a touching reminder of a brief encounter on long overseas visits. Some signatures in Mina's albums are accompanied by drawings or, in the case of Dorothy Davis from Balmain, a dainty watercolour depicting a bunch of forget-me-nots. Mina's earliest album is filled mainly with signatures from the young women she met on interstate swimming carnivals. Victorian sentiment pervades the comments in stanzas such as, 'Tis not the things that you do, dear/ but the things that you leave undone/

That gives us a bit of heart ache/ At the setting of the sun', from Esme Carlos in 1908. And there is the typical teenage preoccupation with romance: 'Fall from the ocean from a deck/ fall from a horse and break your neck/ fall to earth from Heaven above/ But Mina, never fall in love, from Ella Robinson of Toowoomba. I hear the young women giggling as they sign the book at the side of the pool in Brisbane. I hear their promises to write as they depart for the train and the boats which will carry them away from their new friends. And as I turn the pages of the green cloth album, I see Mina holding out the book to Florence—'will you sign my autograph book, Mum?'—and pondering what it means to have a life that 'ends well'.

The black, embossed album from Stockholm is, to me, an object of wonder. More so than the photographs, and I am unable to comprehend why this should be so, the signatures bring the names and faces to life. Perhaps it is because the writing of a note is such a personal undertaking that it subsequently reveals the personality of the writer in a way that a photograph of the same person does not.

I studied at length the handwriting on the pages of Fanny and Kahanamoku and Cecil Healy, without really knowing what it was I was hoping to find. What would I write, I wondered, if I had only one line in an album to convey my outlook on life, or how I felt about the owner of the book? Why did Australian freestyler, Harold Hardwick, quote Dante's 'He who knows most, grieves most for wasted time' above his signature? And what, if anything, can I read into boxing trainer, Alec Goodman's lines of, 'It is a far, far better thing that I do, than I have done/ It is a far, far better rest that I go to, than I have ever known'?

The jokes and poems and gentle teasing throughout the 1912 album confirm the relaxed atmosphere of the pool surroundings and the camaraderie between competitors. Mina was clearly well liked, as this note from Malcolm Eadie Champion attests: 'If scribbling in albums/ friendship ensures/ With the greatest of pleasure/ I'll scribble in yours'. And Fanny had an irreverent sense of humour: 'May you be in heaven before the devil knows your (sic) dead'. Hawaiian swimmer Duke Kahanamoku uses Mina's album as an opportunity to make a point about his birthplace, writing in his native language, 'Ua mau ka ea aka aina I ka pono no', translated as, 'The land is still in possession', possibly a reference to his familial ties to the Hawaiian royal family.

From a historical point of view, the 1912 album is a unique and fascinating record of the 1912 swimming competition. The international aspect of the games is evident in the signatures of team members from the USA, Canada, Germany,

114

Sweden, South Africa, Greece and Great Britain. The names of all the female swimmers on the British and Swedish teams, however, highlights the absence of the American women and the lingering objection to women competing.

I wonder if Baron de Coubertain ever made his presence felt at the practice sessions at the pool or if the thought of all that female flesh repulsed him. I like to think that at some point, the firelit festival at Skensen, perhaps, the figure of Coubertain was pointed out to Mina, and she laughed. The signature of the virulently misogynistic James E. Sullivan is also notably absent from the American names in her album.

The one thing that is strikingly obvious from this autograph book, is that Mina was having fun. She was mingling with the best swimmers in the world and they treated her as an equal. She was gregarious and confident, and not at all intimidated by the male swimmers. This album may, in fact, have provided her with the perfect excuse to make initial contact with fit, muscular young men under the guise of collecting autographs. Men such as team mates Les Boardman and Cecil Healy.

'Think before you speak, then keep thinking.' Mina read the words Les had written and feigned outrage.

'What does that mean?' she asked.

'It means you talk a lot, Miss Wylie.' Cecil laughed loudly and took the album.

'And so say all of us', he spoke as he wrote.

Mina received a letter from her friend Vera in Sydney in which there is a veiled reference to a relationship between Mina and an unnamed team mate: 'I suppose "he" is having a blistering time in Stockholm'. Knowing what I do of her background, it seems to me that if Mina was going to gravitate towards any team member, it would be Cecil Healy. Healy was the son of a respected Sydney barrister and had been prominent in Australian swimming for the previous decade, winning state and national titles.

He had been a vocal campaigner in favour of the inclusion of Mina and Durack on the Olympic swimming team, making it likely he knew Mina, or had at least met her, before the games in Stockholm. He was well-educated and charming, and photographs reveal him to be an attractive, if somewhat stocky, man with a ready smile. Exactly the kind of husband Florence had in mind for her only daughter. Given the circumstances, it would be more noteworthy if Mina did not have a romantic interest in Healy, than if she did, and it is tempting to imagine a relationship blossoming around the pool deck. How did it feel in 1912, I wonder, to stand in front of the man you had a crush on, wearing a wet silk swimsuit?

There were plenty of opportunities for the competitors to socialise outside of the competition and Mina's pocket diary notes a 'Trip on the "Brevik" 11.30pm to 3am' on Saturday, June 29th, and a further 'trip up the archipelago' a week later. Was Healy present on these boat trips, I wonder, and did Henry's watchful eye turn the other way for a while? In the official Australasian Olympic team photograph, Mina is sitting in the front row and Healy is standing directly behind her wearing a dapper straw boater and leaning nonchalantly against a post. I like to think he had deliberately positioned himself there to be closer to Mina, but that could be a product of my imagination fuelled by the memory of what occurs on swimming trips away from home.

Healy is credited with a display of good sportsmanship in Stockholm deemed typical of the Australian characteristic of the 'fair go'. Due to a misunderstanding (or a lack of communication) the USA swimmers missed their semi-final heat for the 100m freestyle, resulting in their disqualification. Healy apparently intervened, and the three Americans swam in a specially arranged heat, enabling two of them, Duke Kahanamoku and Ken Huszagh, to proceed to the final.

Healy's action effectively cost him the gold medal, which was won decisively by Kahanamoku, relegating Healy to silver, but Healy graciously maintained that winning the 100m freestyle title would have been meaningless to him if his greatest rival had not also swum in the race. Like Mina, however, the memorialising of Cecil Healy has been shaped over the century by myth and rewritten to tell the story Australians want to hear. It was, in fact, Ernest Marks who pleaded the case of the American swimmers to the Olympic officials, but depicting Healy as the unselfish hero who sacrificed his chance at victory in the name of integrity corroborates the national ideals of mateship and fair play which Australians are quick to claim as being at the core of national identity.

Like the autograph album, the photographs of Mina at practice sessions taken by E. S. Marks confirm that she was having her time of life. Stockholm was a world away from the tightly managed, single sex competitions in Sydney, and Mina soon discovered she enjoyed being looked at and admired and developed a new sense of confidence in her own body. There are only two images of Mina where she is not smiling, and both of these are official occasions. One is the team photograph and the other is the opening ceremony where she is marching with the Australasian delegation. On both occasions she is wearing the full-length cloak issued to herself and Durack, and it could be this, rather than a sense of being overwhelmed by officialdom, that accounts for her stony expression.

Fanny held up the long green cloak and pulled a face. 'Cloaks on, girls. You know the rules.'

'It's silly. None of the girls from other teams have to wear these,' said Mina. 'Why can't we wear our blazers like the men?' [36]

'If you don't put that on,' said Henry. 'You won't march.'

And Henry desperately wanted to be in the parade.

*

Although Mina was having a wonderful time, she was constantly reminded of the pressure on herself and Durack to bring home medals. A postcard from Walter tells her, 'Don't forget to keep up your practice for you know the eyes of—I might say—Australia—are upon you. I've had a lot of enquires and well wishes at the bath so for goodness' sake don't disappoint and keep up your end of the stick.'

Vera too, informed Mina that, 'We are all terribly interested "down under" but almost everyone is confident of Australia winning almost everything.'

Mina and Fanny both made it through the semi-final on 11 July and would take their places in the final with three of the British women who had taken them to Highgate Ponds in London. World record holder, Daisy Curwen was the biggest threat to Australian glory, but on the evening before the final she was struck down with appendicitis and had to withdraw. Her place was taken by the German swimmer, Greta Rosenberg, who had posted a time one second faster in the heats than Mina's qualifying time. The remaining British women, Jennie Fletcher and Annie Speirs, had also swum faster than Mina in their heats. The race therefore, was by no means a foregone conclusion.

On Friday, 12 July, at 7.30 pm, the pool was electric with anticipation. This race would go down in history as the first women's swimming final in any Olympic games. These 100 metres were what had bitterly divided opinion in Australia and resulted in the humiliation of the country's leading feminist. This race was everything James E. Sullivan in the US and Baron de Coubertain in France stood against, but in many eyes, the next couple of minutes would mark the end of puritanical Victorian values regarding women and usher in the more liberal modern movement. Little wonder the spectator stands were full and dozens of small boats floated in the bay with passengers craning to see.

The crowd hushed as the five finalists discarded the full-length cloaks swathing their bodies and stepped up to the edge of the pool. At the command, they crouched in a low dive and 'faced the water'. Muscles twitching, every sense on high alert. Silence. A shout from the stands. The cry of a gull. A breeze. Then a loud crack from the starter's pistol, an explosion of cheers and five young women dived into the history books.

Swimming the new Australian crawl, Fanny Durack led from the start and was never in danger of losing first place. In an outside lane, Mina collided with the wall within the first twenty metres and trailed behind the other four women until beyond the halfway point. Was it the thought of Florence and her brothers that gave her the burst of speed she needed, or the chance to show Rose Scott how wrong she had been? Perhaps she simply could not bear to miss out on a medal. In the last fifteen metres, Mina pulled ahead of Spiers and Rosenberg, finally eclipsing Jennie Fletcher to take second place. She looked for Henry in the stands, but he was lost amongst the raised hats and waving flags. The noise around the pool was deafening. She and Fanny found each other, and grinned.

For such a significant event, it is strange that the only evidence in Mina's archive of the inaugural 100m ladies' final in Stockholm is an undated postcard from Harry in Sydney. And even then, the race seems to hold less significance than the work at Wylie's Baths.

'Dear Mina, It must have been a great race at the Games according to the papers. Dad must have been a little down hearted when he saw you laying last but how exciting it must have been to see you pull up and get second place. We have been getting on alright with the work and expect to be finished by the time you arrive. We had some rock washed into the bath during the recent storm, so Walter and I had to get to work on it as it was as much trouble getting men as it was to do it ourselves. The bath looks a big place with the two new platforms and the concreting done. Tell Dad although I have only been out fishing twice that they are still biting one after the other. From Harold.'

Given the circumstances, it's an odd card. No congratulations, no mention of pride. As if what Mina had just achieved was all very well, but less important than the reality of the day-to-day existence. Harry's card is a curious contrast to the fervent excitement which had built up around Mina's departure and possibly the Wylie family was exercising Victorian modesty in the face of the jingoistic boasting prevailing in press reports. *The Referee*, for example, carried a rather self-congratulatory article on 28 August, stating:

'The hoisting of the Australian flag on the first and second flagpoles was received with loud cheers, which could certainly not have been given by the small contingent of Australasians present, and as the girls walked along the platform in front of the stand to their dressing room, accompanied by Miss Mary Durack, their chaperone, and Captain Vicary Horniman, the president of the Australasian team, round after round of applause followed their progress ultimately breaking into an ovation.'

This report was designed to appeal to the Sydney readership on number of levels. It endorsed an Australian view of themselves as world class athletes and assured the reader of the popularity of Australians amongst an international audience. But it could be interpreted as suggesting that the poolside lap of honour by Durack and Mina established their status as symbols of a progressive, modern nation which embraced gender equality.

The report implies that the spectators standing to salute Durack and Mina were not simply applauding the winners of a swimming race, they were congratulating the Australian nation on demonstrating an enlightened viewpoint towards gender equality. This image of Australia as a nation committed to gender equality was a useful one to promote at global events such as the Stockholm Olympics, but in subsequent years the preference for male athletes and male disciplines defined Australia's relationship with sport. In 1912, however, Mina and Durack were national heroines and held up as the embodiment of what it meant to be an Australian woman.

On 15 July, Mina sent a postcard of Stockholm to Harry which read, 'Dear Harold, How are you all getting on? I suppose you are used to us being away now. Well, the Crown Prince presents us with our Olympic medals today and we say goodbye to the Olympic Games. Best love to all, Mina'. Again, the sentiment is understated, as if being presented with an Olympic medal by the heir to the Swedish throne is a regular occurrence. But I detect a sadness, a wistfulness at the passing of these glorious few weeks. Coogee, even Sydney, would seem tame after this.

*

A couple of years ago, I travelled to Stockholm nursing a faint hope of encountering Mina Wylie lingering somewhere in the shadows. I walked around the island of Djurgarden trying to locate the exact spot where the Olympic harbour pool had stood. I took a boat trip on the archipelago, just as Mina had done, and I wondered if she too was waved at by swimmers and fisherman enjoying the water. As the boat passed the magnificent Royal palace at Drottningholm, I imagined Mina staring at the scene in front of her in awe. Committing every window, every fountain, every statue to memory, to be recounted to Florence back home. She would tell her how green the city surroundings were and what a complete contrast it was to the sunburnt landscape of Coogee. She would casually announce that the city was just like Sydney really, apart from the Royal buildings and ancient churches. There was a harbour just like ours, with ferries criss-crossing the waters to suburbs on another shore.

On my trip, I whiled away a rainy morning at the National Sports Museum of Sweden watching silent black and white footage of the 1912 Games. I saw the special trams that had been laid on to take competitors and spectators to the venues, and the streets lined with children waving flags. I saw cyclists on country roads being urged on by excited locals, and a ladies tennis match with players wearing long white dresses. I sat entranced by high jump and pole vault competitions with no landing mat, a tug of war and a display by female gymnasts in the opening ceremony at the Stadion. The harbour pool flickered into view with a water polo match and then shot after shot of the victorious female Swedish divers, the same young women whose signatures are inscribed in Mina's autograph album. Footage of alternately shy and smiling women gave way to images of the medal presentation ceremony and athletes first being crowned with a laurel wreath then handed their medal by Crown Prince Gustaf Adolf. [37] Mina was somewhere in that crowd, standing with Fanny and Cecil and Harold, nervously awaiting their turn.

My romantic (or slightly absurd) notion that I would find Mina in Stockholm turned out to be not as ridiculous as it seemed. I did find her, or at least the ghost of the young woman I had studied endlessly in the photographs of E.S. Marks. Because although the harbour pool had long since been dismantled, the 22 000 seat Stadion still stands. I stood at the impressive arched entrance and imposed Marks' image of the sporting officials and members of the Swedish military silhouetted in this same arch, with the packed stadium beyond. And the colours of my bright summer afternoon transfigured into Marks' black and grey and whites.

As there was no one to stop me, I passed through the unlocked turnstiles which, in a nod to the novelty historical factor, had not been upgraded since the stadium was built. I sat on the decorated wooden bleachers which are visible in Marks' images, and I was, quite simply, stunned. If I removed the bright green Astro turf and the banks of floodlights, I was in Marks' photographs. Perhaps even sitting where he sat. Or Mina, when she came to watch the athletics competition.

I knew so well the story this stadium still held within it, because I had been here before with the photographs Ernest Samuel Marks left behind. I had seen the triumphant steeple chase runner being carried by his team mates after collapsing beyond the finish line. I had seen the military officers urging powerful and impeccably groomed horses over the water jump. I had felt the awe at the arrival of the Royal party into the stadium in a procession of horse drawn carriages. And there it was: the canopied Royal Box with gilt decorations. The clock with the three gold crowns beneath. Exactly as it all should be. Yet no one amongst the thousands of people captured in Marks' photographs, would be alive today. No one.

I sat in the stand for a long time, until I could hear the bands play to the packed stadium and hear the cheers as the team of each nation entered the arena. My eyes scanned every corner: I had come all this way, I was not leaving until I found her.

And there. There she is. Marching behind Henry and wearing a long green cloak. Unsmiling and unusually self-conscious. And is that Cecil Healy directly behind her, his eyes on Mina and not the crowd? When Mina returned here two weeks later to receive a medal, where exactly did she stand as she waited for her big moment? Did Duke Kahanamoku cheer when her name was called and did Cecil catch her eye as she returned to her place clutching the little red box? I think they did. I know they did, because I see them do it. Here, in this stadium unlike anything Mina had seen before, here she is. Still. Lingering in the shadows in all her youthful glory. An elite performer on the world stage. And here I am, watching her.

Mina's diary from Stockholm

The harbour pool in Djurgarden, Stockholm

Mina and Fanny poolside, Stockholm. Ernest Samuel Marks collection.

Members of the Australasian Swimming team, Stockholm. Cecil Healy is second from right wearing a swimming hat. Ernest Samuel Marks collection.

The Australasian Olympic rowing team training on board ship during the voyage to Europe. Ernest Samuel Marks collection.

Australian rowers in the changing tent at Henley regatta. Ernest Samuel Marks collection.

Mina, poolside, Stockholm. Ernest Samuel Marks collection.

Fanny Durack at a changing tent in Stockholm. Ernest Samuel Marks collection.

Duke Kahanamoku poolside in Stockholm. Ernest Samuel Marks collection.

Mina posing for the camera, poolside in Stockholm. Ernest Samuel Marks collection.

Mina's autograph albums

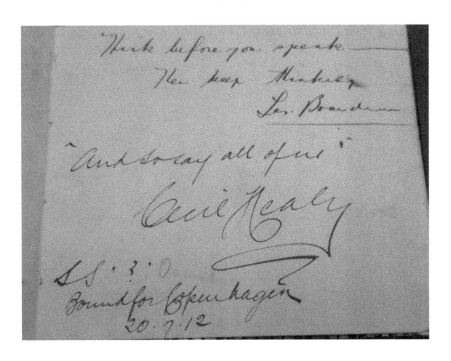

Cecil Healy's entry in Mina's Stockholm autograph album

Official Australasian Olympic team photograph. Mina is second from left front row. Henry is front row, holding hat. Cecil Healy is behind Mina wearing a straw boater.

Australasian team marching in opening ceremony. Mina is between Mary Durack (in white) and Henry, in straw hat.

Chapter 6

When the Australian flag went up for one two in Stockholm, of course Australia
sort of took the credit, for which they really weren't due, I don't think.

Mina Wylie to Neil Bennetts, 1975

At the conclusion of the inaugural 100m ladies freestyle in Stockholm, photographers, including Ernest Marks, clamoured around the medallists on the pool deck requesting that they pose for the cameras. Jennie Fletcher was hesitant, but Mina was more than happy to oblige.

'It's history,' Mina told Jennie, quickly removing the unflattering bathing cap and arranging her wet hair. 'And I'm not wearing this.'

She slipped off the long green cloak and placed it far enough away that it would not feature in the resulting photograph. Fanny had already done the same and Jennie, unable to ignore the entreaties from the photographers, reluctantly handed her cloak to team mate Annie Speirs, watching on the side-line. Mina took up her position next to Fanny and basked in the noise of the crowd. Beyond the group of photographers, she could see Captain Horniman, president of the Australasian team, accepting the congratulations from officials of other countries. Patting himself on the back. 'Of course, we knew they'd do it …' The cat with the cream, Mina thought. But wasn't he the same person who had said it was a waste of money to send women to the Olympic games?

'Over here, Miss Durack. Miss Wylie …'

The cameras were ready. The three women folded their arms across their chests as they had been told and straightened their backs. Knowing how many people would see this photograph, Mina pulled in her stomach and pushed her shoulders back. She was an Olympic medallist, she wanted to look good. And then, without even really thinking about it, she uncrossed her arms and held them at her side. Fanny and Jennie can hide themselves, she thought, but I won't. And she stared steadily at the cameras in front of her. Let them look.

*

In the Marks photograph of the Durack/Wylie/Fletcher trio, it is obvious that Mina is utilising her body to make a statement, one which clearly indicates her refusal to be ashamed of her female form. Next to the self-conscious Fletcher, Mina exudes confidence in her own body and appears to relish the experience both of displaying herself, and of being the subject of the gaze. That she seems to take this new way of being and of presenting herself in her stride suggests she was a young woman with an ability to adapt to changing circumstances. She clearly understood the trade-offs involved in marketing herself as a successful female athlete and was quite prepared to commodify herself and promote her own image. Annette Kellerman, after all, had done very well out of turning her body into a spectacle.

Back in Sydney, the news of the Durack/Wylie triumph was hailed by activists as a victory for feminism. The assertion that the female body was unsuited to physical exertion had been exposed as a myth designed to keep women out of the male sporting arena and, by implication, the wider societal structures of power. Mina and Durack were celebrated as the embodiment of the 'Australian Girl', a constructed national type which avowed that freshness, a natural look, a lack of affectation and a passion for sport were characteristics of the archetypal Australian woman. The obvious bias towards male athletes and male sport in Australia had left women with few role models of their own and Mina and Durack now stepped into that gap, enabling women to include themselves in the emerging ideal of national identity. Above all else, the Durack/Wylie victory confirmed the growing belief amongst Australians of their country as the Sporting Nation.

At the conclusion of the medal presentation ceremony, the Games were officially over. But Mina's European adventure was not. On leaving Stockholm, Mina and Henry travelled to Germany with other members of the Australasian swimming team to compete in the national championships in Hamburg on 20 and 21 July. She purchased, or was perhaps given, a mounted photograph of herself which had been snapped as she was climbing the steps out of the pool in Hamburg.

Like Ernest Marks, the photographer who caught this moment was intent on pushing the boundaries of sporting photography by capturing the athlete unawares or in mid-action, thereby conveying a more visceral sense of the thrill of the sporting event. The photograph of Mina exiting the Hamburg pool gives the viewer a ring side seat at the swimming competition, but it also clearly illustrates the main issue concerning the use of silk in ladies racing swimsuits, and why there were such strict rules regarding the wearing of cloaks.

The photographer is positioned on Mina's right-hand side, but her attention is on someone directly in front of her. Her hands are occupied with pulling down the right leg of her swimsuit which has risen high up her thigh during the race. The top of the swimsuit does not cover the shoulders—a direct contravention of the NSW LASA rules—and the wet silk offers no defence against prying male eyes. Her breasts and the contours of her body are clearly visible. Mina may have been unaware that she was being photographed but nothing about her body language suggests she is uncomfortable at being so exposed in close proximity to the fully dressed men and women who crowd the edge of the pool.

Cameras in 1912 were not sophisticated enough to capture the thrill of a swimming race as the absence of a zoom lens resulted in pictures of heads and arms amidst a lot of splashing, but not much else. In contrast, Marks' photographs from the Stadion of men running, wrestling, jumping and throwing convey both the skill of the athletes and the physical effort involved. Swimming had been accepted as a suitable sport for women precisely because this exertion, which was considered masculine, was not visible, and this could account for the fact that Marks took a number of images of the women divers in graceful and feminine action, but did not photograph the swimmers actually swimming.

His portraits of Mina and Durack may have been his way of reassuring the disapproving viewer that no comparison needed be drawn between the unthreatening and passive women at the pool, and the aggressive, muscular men wrestling or throwing a discus in the Stadion. I believe that Marks simply enjoyed the novelty of being able to photograph female swimmers, and the fact that he photographed the start of a women's heat suggests it was indeed the technical shortcomings of cameras of the era which contributed to the lack of action shots from early swimming competitions.

A result of this was that Mina had never seen a photograph of herself swimming in a race, and the Hamburg image where she is exiting the pool was the only proof she had that she was a woman who actually competed at the highest level of competition, rather than watched and applauded the efforts of others. While I look at the image and see a woman being stared at because her swimsuit does not disguise her naked body, Mina looked at it and saw an elite swimmer exiting the pool during an international competition.

To the contemporary eye, the German photograph and many of Marks' pictures veer perilously towards exploitation, not simply because the swimsuits are so revealing but because women of Mina's era had scant understanding of how the camera would represent them.

What did Florence think, I wonder, when she saw the Hamburg photograph? In later years, Jennie Fletcher claimed to hate a photograph of herself and her three team mates who made up the victorious British 4x100m freestyle relay team, and although she gave no reason for this stance, I imagine it is due to the fact that through her wet swimsuit, her nipples and underwear are clearly visible. In a number of the Marks' pictures there are men in the background blatantly staring at the women being photographed, and although Mina appears perfectly relaxed with this, the body language of a number of women, including Fletcher, projects anxiety. Perhaps Fanny Durack, who always blocked her breasts with her folded arms, had a better understanding than Mina did in those early days of how easily women could be transformed from athlete into object.

After the German championships, Henry and Mina took leave of the Australasian team and headed to Belfast for Henry's first visit to his home town since he left some thirty years ago. In 1975, Mina told Neil Bennetts that, 'there wasn't a man in Ireland at that time who could beat me', suggesting that she took part in races in Ireland, but there is no evidence of this amongst her possessions. She sent a postcard to Florence to tell her she has bought Irish lace ('and, my word, it is expensive') but she makes no mention of triumphing over male swimmers.

Henry's only comment to Florence concerns Mina's exhibitions: 'I enjoyed the trip to Belfast and the people treated Mina in a splendid way, they wanted us to stay longer so that they could arrange for a public exhibition, but those who saw Mina at the private exhibition she gave said they had never seen anything like it.' That is not to say the Irish competition did not happen and, if it did, it would have been the first, and only, time that Mina swam in the same race as male competitors.

From Ireland, father and daughter returned to London where Mina took to heart the advice given to her in Vera's letter: 'Have a real good time, Mina. See as much as ever you can while you're there because you may never have the chance again.' She met up with her British swimming friends and they took her to that new palace of modernity, Selfridges department store. She went to the cinema, strolled through Hyde Park, peered through the gates of Buckingham

Palace, rode London buses and went back to the theatre more than once. She saved a brochure from Restaurant Frascati in Gerrard Street, a grand looking affair with private dining rooms and the dark furniture and heavy drapes so particular to the period. What she and Henry were doing dining in such sumptuous surroundings when money was a constant worry, is anyone's guess.

They were more regular diners at Flemings on Oxford St, from where Mina saved a handful of menus, or at the Bedford Hotel where the uninspiring fare did not deter Mina's menu hoarding.

I find the fact that Mina saved such unimpressive menus—Flemings offered a pot of tea and two slices of bread and butter for 3d, and the Bedford Hotel had stewed tripe and onions every evening from 6pm—strangely touching. It reminds me of how young and sheltered she was at this time. Eating in a restaurant, even one as ordinary as Flemings, was a thrill she had rarely encountered in Sydney and it made her feel grown up and sophisticated. She often mentions food in letters home—eating too much on board ship, the fruit on sale in Ceylon, what she ate in the USA—and it strikes me that what she ate, where and when, was inexorably tied up in her memory of that particular time and place.

The food itself was not the reason she kept the menus, it was the context surrounding the meal which transformed the menu into an item of emotional value. She often asked the other diners present to sign it—at a farewell dinner on the occasion of Durack's retirement, for example, or onboard ship. She then had in her possession a document which bore witness both to the occasion and to the people present.

Mina took in so many sights in London that she airily informed Harry on a postcard, 'We have seen all the places and in fact everything worth seeing in London. Love Mina.' On 8 August, Henry wrote to Florence from the Bedford Hotel in London, displaying his familiar concern regarding money, 'I think we will just about have enough money to get us home. I hope you are getting on alright with money matters at home.' But he does go on to inform his wife that, 'Next week we are going for a three-day trip to Paris', an impossible excursion if the money was indeed about to run out.

A later sentence reveals that the business was never far from his mind, 'I am glad to hear Walter is getting on well with the work you can tell him I have not seen any better system for locked rooms or lockers than we have ourselves'. Interestingly, he also sounds a note of caution about their, now famous, daughter, 'I was afraid Bill might get tired or get a big head.'

Harry's words on a postcard to Mina reading, 'we were very pleased to hear you have had a good time but thought you would be glad to be coming back home', could not have been further from the truth. She loved everything about London—the buses, the buildings, the theatres, the shops.

Often, as she walked the graceful wide streets of Bloomsbury with Henry, or the closely packed lanes around Covent Garden with Jennie Fletcher, she would look up at a window and picture herself living in the room behind it. She mentally mapped out her route to the nearest swimming baths and imagined herself walking there, unchaperoned, for her daily practice sessions. The vision of herself living alone in London was so vivid she knew which museums would become her favourites, where she would meet friends for tea and which theatres would acknowledge her as a regular attendee. She knew she would send letters to her mother once a week and together they would plan and save for the day when Florence would come and visit. And Mina would show her the same sights she had just seen.

On 23 August, Mina and Henry boarded the RMS 'Morea' in Plymouth for the return voyage to Sydney. They had been away from home for almost four months—a considerable period of time given that Henry ran a business. On September 3rd, afloat in the Indian Ocean, Mina asked fellow passengers to sign her dinner menu and she placed this last souvenir into a suitcase already overflowing with theatre programmes, postcards, the Olympic booklets and handbook, tram tickets, a London bus timetable, the Irish lace, her black leather autograph album, her Olympic blazer and her silver medal in the red box lined with velvet.

*

When Mina arrived back in Sydney on 3 October, a large crowd was waiting at Circular Quay to greet her. Amongst those present were Marion McIntosh and NSW LASA officials, keen to bask in the glory Mina's medal bestowed upon the organisation. Mina was inundated with bouquets of flowers and congratulations, and reunited with Florence and her loyal brothers. She had her first taste of her new celebrity status as she gave an impromptu press conference to the waiting posse of reporters, declaring that, 'Sweden was just lovely, and the Swedish people are surely the kindest people in the world.'[38]

Buoyant from all the attention, she then claimed to have shared her skills with the female Swedish swimmers, stating, 'Whilst in Stockholm, Fanny and I showed them the crawl stroke and left them busily practicing it'. This is highly questionable given that Mina swam the trudgen stroke in Stockholm and only Durack, Cecil Healy and Kahanamoku have been recorded as swimming a version of the crawl in the 1912 Olympics. But her exaggeration demonstrates her eagerness to be part of a popular narrative that had Australia positioning itself as the nation at the forefront of the development of swimming techniques and teaching the world how to swim. The success of the Australasian swimmers in Stockholm, combined with the claim to ownership of the new crawl stroke, enabled the populace to regard swimming as a sport with national identity connotations: Australia was now 'home' of the crawl as Lords was the home of cricket.

The following day, 4 October, Mina and Durack were honoured at a reception hosted by Marion McIntosh at her large Darling Point home, 'Benoni'. The gilt-edged invitation was a thing of beauty and Mina added hers, and the one addressed to Florence and Henry, to the growing store of mementoes now taking up a whole box. In hosting the reception for the victorious swimmers, McIntosh was consolidating her new position of authority within the NSW LASA, as well as making a point to Rose Scott concerning the success of the swimmers she had refused to sanction.

Her husband, the irrepressible Huge Deal, had not yet fully established himself as the newspaper magnate and theatrical impresario he was to become[39] but he was a well-known figure in Sydney society, albeit a branch of society built on new money and therefore not what Rose Scott would term as 'society'. To have a reception held in her honour was an enormous thrill for Mina, especially one in such a grand house as 'Benoni', and I imagine she adored being the flame around which the admiring moths fluttered for one afternoon.

The McIntosh reception was a clear indication of how far Mina's life had changed in just a matter of months. The evening after the reception at Benoni, an official NSW LASA dinner was held in the spirit of 'we went, we swam, we conquered', and again, Mina asked all the guests to sign a menu. Three weeks later, there was luncheon at the Town Hall with the Lord Mayor and Lady Mayoress, where, for once, Mina was too overawed to request autographs.

The Sydney Ladies Swimming Club held an evening in her honour and undoubtedly there was a community celebration in Coogee, most probably at

Wylie's Baths. There were regular visitors to the house, popping in for tea and a chance to view the medal, and beachgoers at Coogee stopped to applaud as Mina walked past. If Henry had been worried about Mina's 'big head' in London, heaven knows how he felt watching the circus surrounding his daughter back in Sydney.

Amidst all the attention, Mina resumed her routine of teaching swimming and training for competition under Henry's watchful eye at Wylie's Baths. As she had publicly proclaimed herself an expert in the new crawl stroke, her most pressing concern was mastering it in time for the looming season. Certainly, she had no hope of beating the faster Durack whist she still swam the trudgen stroke. Small boys swam alongside Mina trying to keep up her pace and the recent relaxation of the laws outlawing mixed bathing meant that curious men stood amongst the women in the shallows watching her swim. She was aware of the admiring glances they threw in her direction as she climbed the wooden steps up to the boardwalk, and noted, too, the stares at her racing swimsuit from self-conscious women fixated on covering up. She cultivated an air of nonchalance—the defining attitude of the New Woman—and, despite Henry's protestations, left the Olympic cloak casually open on the few occasions she bothered to put it on. It was her father's pool, after all, she could do what she liked.

In November, Mina travelled to Adelaide to participate in club carnivals at the request of the South Australia ASA who assured her that, 'our lady members will do everything possible to make the holiday an enjoyable one.' The lady members clearly did give Mina a wonderful time in Adelaide as she sent a postcard to Harry saying, 'I am having a lovely time won't want to come home …' Being the star attraction suited Mina and she saved the poster announcing the 'Grand Swimming Carnival' which had her name emblazoned across the centre. Interestingly, a note at the foot of the poster states, 'Ladies admitted to carnival'—a departure from the 'Ladies only admitted' warning which adorned posters and programmes prior to 1912.

This notice was intended to settle any confusion amongst patrons who were not yet used to the idea of mixed competitions. As well as being billed as 'Australia's Representative at Olympic Games', Mina was also promoted as 'Champion Lady Life Saver of Australia'. Mina and Fanny Durack were the first women in Australia to obtain the Royal Life Saving Society Diploma in 1909, and, according to her later conversation with Neil Bennetts, because there was no one in Australia at the time with credentials to conduct the examination, the secretary of the Royal Life Saving Society, Sir William Henry, was brought out from England. On this occasion, Mina did outswim Durack, gaining two points more in the lifesaving examination than she did.

Whilst Mina was being entertained and shown the sights of Adelaide, trouble was brewing in Sydney and it would soon become apparent that not even Mina Wylie was exempt from the old adage concerning pride and a fall.

On her return home, she was summoned to a disciplinary meeting at the NSW LASA and, just a few days before Christmas, she was suspended from competition for one month. Her offence seems trivial in relation to the consequences: she had accepted the invitation from the South Australia ASA without first obtaining written permission from her own governing authority. Given that the South Australian ASA secretary had enclosed the relevant permission forms in the original invitation, Mina had no defence.

The regulations regarding invitations such as the one from the authority in Adelaide were clearly outlined in the NSW LASA constitution and Mina's casual flouting of the rules was not taken lightly by committee members. The month-long suspension was a humiliating rap on the knuckles and possibly intended by the stern ladies of the NSW LASA to contain Mina's growing sense of entitlement.

'It's only a medal, love,' said Florence.

'It's an Olympic medal,' corrected Mina. 'That's different.'

An incident prior to the Stockholm competition, suggests that Mina's expanding ego was not solely a result of her silver medal. In April of 1912, amidst the frantic Olympic fundraising efforts, Mina exchanged a series of high-handed letters with the secretary of the SLSC, Mrs Chambers, concerning a row between herself and another committee member. Mrs Chambers wrote to say, 'I may tell you Miss Hennebry laid a complaint to the committee of your remarks to her which she requests that you give her an explanation.'

Unfortunately, as I am by now intrigued, Mrs Chambers does not elucidate on what exactly it was that Mina had said to cause offence. Mina's reply the next day reveals a slightly petulant side to her character, 'I must emphatically say that I know of nothing that demands an apology from me to any member of the club...' and the requested explanation was not forthcoming.

The incident suggests that Mina was developing an overblown sense of her own importance which was uncharacteristic of the young woman she had been up until now. This does give a good idea of the magnitude surrounding her selection into the Olympic team, something which is difficult now to fully comprehend. These were the days when women did not appear in newspapers (except for the marriage or death notices) and, unless they were Hollywood movie stars or European Royalty, they were rarely public figures. Yet here were two young women from Sydney dominating the local, and following Stockholm, the international press.

Mina and Fanny Durack were figures that other women could admire and identify with, and their regular presence in the press sent a not-too-subtle message that not only were women capable of engaging with sport, they could be just as popular with the public as the heroic male athletes. American Trudy Ederle is credited as saying, 'it's up with the women and down with the men', during a press conference following her record-breaking Channel swim in 1926, and although Mina never made a similar public statement with regard to the battle of the sexes, her pervasive presence in the press was enough to make the point.

Women who admired Mina in the immediate years after the Olympics saw, not only a champion swimmer, but a woman who appeared to live life on her own terms. She earned her own living, she remained unmarried and she travelled the world. In other words, every time Mina appeared in the press she was, however unconsciously, redefining the unthreatening, conformist feminine ideal and offering an alternative new for women to live their lives. And a minor quarrel with a committee member of the Sydney Ladies Swimming Club would not even register on the scale of bad behaviour flaunted by celebrity athletes in contemporary popular culture.

My feeling concerning Mina's 'big head' and seemingly arrogant behaviour, is that she was finding her voice. Literally. She was no longer the quiet, unassuming young woman in white lace who agreed with her elders and unquestioningly deferred to status. She was discovering who she was and voicing how she felt. And if Rose Scott or Miss Hennebry of the SLSC were casualties of this, then so be it.

In contemporary society, sport is generally accepted as empowering for girls and young women, an antidote to the pervasive media images of sexualised waifs who comply with male heterosexual image of how women should look and behave. Numerous studies have proved that women who engage in sport when they are young have higher self-esteem and are more likely to see their bodies in terms of fitness and strength. As a consequence, they regard their ability in other areas as equal to that of men.

I believe the self-confidence that Mina displays in photographs and her apparent defiance of convention, emanated from what she was discovering about herself as a consequence of competitive swimming. She knew she was good and she saw no reason to affect an air of humility. I came across hearsay—but no evidence—that Mina was overtly demanding in the USA in 1918, and there is no denying that she was a forthright young woman who was often not prepared to compromise and had no hesitation in voicing her opinion.

In 1912, this was not the way women were supposed to behave, and any woman who dared to speak up was regarded as troublesome because she was resisting the structures of power which had a vested interest in keeping women under control. In other words, Mina was saying no, albeit in a mild tone, at a time when women were expected to do as they were told.

A photograph of Mina taken at Wylie Baths less than a year after her Stockholm medal is a good indication of the enormous affect the trip to Europe had on her perception of herself. In the picture, she wears a swimsuit which would never have passed the rigid NSW LASA regulations that were still in place. It is cut noticeably higher on the thigh than her Stockholm suit, her shoulders are no longer covered, and the neckline has been lowered dramatically. Her arms are tucked pointedly behind her back, leaving her body open to view and emphasising her shapely, womanly curves. She appears to have no qualms about the image she is projecting, and it could be suggested that she has consciously transformed her body into an exhibit to be looked at and admired. Her Olympic experience had taught her that this pose was exactly what was expected from sportswomen who willingly placed themselves in the public arena. Today we would name it as sexualisation, but Mina's willingness to present herself in this way stops me from doing so. True, the picture is audacious for the times, but she is unmistakably presenting herself as a swimmer, not as a woman inviting sex.

It is impossible to tell from the photograph if Mina, like Kellerman, was knowingly objectifying herself, or if she was, unknowingly, being sexualised by a male photographer. She is, however, undoubtedly selling herself within the context of the new commodity culture associated with modernity. If fans wanted her image, her celebrity status required her to oblige. And Mina liked being the attention and seeing photographs of herself in carnival programmes. The Coogee photograph is evidence that Mina had clear ideas concerning her image and how she wanted to be seen. Or indeed, how she saw herself. The revealing swimsuit and carefully staged 'look' established her immediately as a modern woman who eschewed Victorian puritanism. Although competition programmes in 1913 were beginning to carry images of star female competitors wearing swimsuits, the press remained under a tight rein of conservatism and would only publish images of female competitive swimmers if they were cloaked.

This contradiction is apparent in a 1914 report carried by the pictorial magazine, *Splashes Weekly*, of the Australian Ladies Amateur Swimming Championships in which the women in all six photographs (including Mina) wear full length cloaks and tuck their bare feet out of sight. Yet by this time, both Mina and Durack had posed in a swimsuit for studio photographs which appeared in carnival programmes.

The Wylie's Baths photograph gives a good idea of how rapidly attitudes towards the female body were transforming as a result of women's participation in sport, and it was not a coincidence that this shift occurred alongside a heightened demand for women's equality. Susan B. Anthony's assertion that 'bicycling had done more to emancipate women than anything in the world' was not entirely an exaggeration, as newly liberated women metaphorically shrugged off the chains which bound them to the inactive lives deemed a consequence of their frail bodies. By merely participating in sport, women challenged the ideology at the heart of male societal power which insisted that the weaker female body resulted in a natural inequality between men and women, with men, naturally, emerging superior. It also challenged the notions of chivalry and protection that defined relations between men and women i.e. women's apparent frailty required them to be dependent on men for protection (and financial security). But the women who bicycled, and then swam, rowed, played team games and even raced cars, quickly discovered that their frailty was a myth and that they too, had bodies which were designed to be active. This discovery consequently posed a fundamental challenge to the traditional gender division of society. If women could physically do what men could do, what then formed the foundation for women's omission from the structures of power?

Clothing reform was an issue which had a prominent place on the list drawn up by feminists demanding equality in the late 18th and early 19th centuries. Activists asserted that tightly laced corsets, voluminous skirts and petticoats, high necked blouses, buttoned shoes and restrictive cuffs were specifically designed to keep women inactive, literally trapped by their own bodies. One of the most common arguments put forward against women's participation in sport was the question of what they would wear in order to do so. This concern had roots in maintaining a ladylike vision of womanhood and early cyclists who dared to wear bloomers, or a divided skirt, were decried as immodest due to their improper attire.

From the late 1800s, newspapers and periodicals offered advice to women on what to wear on the golf course or tennis court, and the question of corsets—whether to wear them or not—was endlessly discussed. The anxieties (from both men and women) surrounding the abandonment of corsets appeared to reflect a larger fear, or distaste, of women's bodies in their natural shape. Corsets produced the unnatural silhouette considered the epitome of femininity, but it did so at the expense of female health, compressing vital organs and causing skeletal deformities. The medical community blamed the corset for the fainting fits and breathlessness prevalent amongst Victorian women, but the ideal of femininity was so successfully ingrained throughout society that it was often women themselves who were amongst the fiercest opponents of calls to remove the garment when engaging in exercise.

Two photographic cards sent to Mina from 'your pal Violet' in Brisbane, clearly illustrate the effect of women's engagement with sport on clothing reform. The first card, dated 1911, depicts Violet sitting on the steps of a house wearing a long white, lace dress, with a high neck and frilled sleeves. Sitting beside her, her sister wears a lace blouse and a heavy long skirt. Her tiny waist is the result of a tightly laced corset and is accentuated by a wide leather belt. The two young women embody decorative femininity, yet on the reverse of the card, Violet has written, 'Next Saturday the Excelsior Club is holding their annual dance and distribution of prizes, of which three are coming to one. At the Southport Rowing Regatta, I won a race for which I received a brooch in the shape of a pair of crossed oars and am rowing again the 19th August.'

The image on the second card, from 1913, could not be more of a contrast. Violet is pictured with four other members of a Queensland rowing team wearing smart uniforms of shorts, loose sweaters and flat, lace up brogues. Their arms are folded across their chests in a typical sporting pose, bestowing upon them an air of androgyny. The image is a startling reflection of a new femininity aligned with athleticism and modernity. Violet's second card is therefore more than a mild admonishment between friends, 'You are a lazy girl, you haven't written to me for ages'. It is evidence of how some young women of the era were actively challenging patriarchal control by rejecting the traditional restrictions on their bodies and their behaviour. The female racing cyclist hunched over her handlebars and wearing masculine clothes could not be further removed from the frail, Victorian lady whiling away an afternoon engaged in needlepoint.

With her corset free body and casual display of flesh, Mina and her friends rowing down the Brisbane river were not simple eschewing the fripperies associated with Victorian femininity, they were claiming a radical new female identity for themselves. One which was active and visible. For decades following the 1912 Olympics, the press continued to scrutinise the bodies of sportswomen searching for a tell-tale sign of masculinity and abnormal muscle development. When American swimming sensation, Ethelda Bleibtrey, visited Australia in 1921, the *Daily Telegraph* described her as 'big and bronzed' and claimed that Mina was 'frail and diminutive' standing next to the 'deep chested American'. The women were, in fact, almost the same height. The *Telegraph* article ended by reminding readers that muscular development was not appropriate for women: 'No one could miss what exercise means to girlhood. It is a means to an end, and that end is not all muscular work. Rather it is greater vitality.'[40]

Visible muscles on women were taken to indicate a desire to emulate men by cultivating a manly body, and a toned and strong female body was thus taken as a refusal by a woman to accept her inferior status. In other words, muscles were a safe prediction that this woman would not stay in her place.

*

As the Stockholm fuss and celebratory dinners abated, and once Mina had sat out her one-month suspension from competition, life returned to the familiar routine of training, competing, teaching and Wylie's Baths. Going on the evidence in the archive, Mina's social life revolved around swimming and friends associated with swimming, even the dances she attended in 1913 and 1914 were functions organised by the NSW LASA and the Royal Lifesaving Society. She frequently travelled interstate to compete and was in great demand as a swimming teacher and lifesaving instructor. As well as her duties at Wylie's Baths, for which Henry paid her a share of the 'W, H and M wages £3.15' (presumably Walter, Harry and Mina) he noted weekly in the accounts books, she taught classes at the nearby McIver's Baths (now the Coogee Women's Pool) and Woolwich Baths on the opposite side of Sydney Harbour.

I suspect there was no reconciliation with former mentor, Rose Scott, and a vision of Mina taking tea in a Woollahra home full of books and elegant furniture is not one that comes easily to mind. I do wonder, however, if she and Henry were ever invited to the home of Ernest Samuel Marks to view the two albums of photographs he created from the trip. If they were, the presence of images in the first album of naked men taking an impromptu dip in an English river would have been shielded from Mina in the interests of decency.

Marks had duplicates made of an image he took of Mina and Durack poolside in Stockholm, and he gave her one as a gift. Whilst she herself was delighted to have the souvenir, Henry might have been less than happy about the fact that images of his semi-naked daughter were circulating amongst certain sections of the Sydney community. She was an Olympic athlete, not a vaudeville act.

Mina soon discovered she had a new ally in the form of Marion McIntosh, and it was she who arranged a number of swimming exhibitions in country NSW at which Mina and Fanny Durack were the main attraction. McIntosh was passionate about women's swimming and keen to promote the sport beyond the State's capital city with a view to inspiring other young women to follow in the footsteps of her Olympian charges. No programmes from these exhibitions survive amongst Mina's possessions, but there is an uncredited photograph of Mina and Durack on a riverbank surrounded by a large crowd of attentive young girls—suggesting rural NSW was even less keen than Sydney to allow the sexes to mingle semi-naked in the water. Newspapers beyond Mina's archive confirm that she and Durack visited Lismore in late 1915, and the newspaper photograph could be from that well publicised trip.

Somewhat surprisingly, in the early days of swimming in Australia, the activity was by no means confined to the coastal cities. The desert-like climate inland made bathing in rivers, lakes and natural swimming holes a delightful way of coping with the searing temperatures. There was even a competition circuit (of sorts) for women and in 1906, Victorian swimmer Beatrice Kerr undertook an extraordinary tour of outback NSW, South Australia and Western Australia, swimming in forty-three competitions and winning five open championships. In the town of Broken Hill in the north west of NSW—a town known as the 'silver city' due to the highly productive mines—Kerr's appearance was so eagerly anticipated that the miners dug a pool especially for her to perform in.

At the conclusion of her wildly successful visit, Kerr was presented with a man's swimsuit decorated with pieces of silver donated by the appreciative miners. The silver was stitched in a pattern resembling the scales of a mermaid and despite the swimsuit weighing almost three kilograms, Kerr wore it so often it became her signature 'look'. Kerr seems to have had the confidence of Kellerman when it came to displaying her body in public, and in photographs from Broken Hill she seems unfazed at being the only woman—and wearing only a swimsuit—amongst a crowd of vigorous and slightly rough looking miners.

By 1914, Mina's friendship with Marion McIntosh was secure enough for her to be invited to the society/celebrity wedding of McIntosh's adopted daughter Lily. At the reception, Mina took her place amongst other revered sporting figures as well as stars from the Tivoli Theatre Circuit, now owned by McIntosh's husband, 'Huge Deal', who was in the midst of a scandalous and widely acknowledged affair with 'Queen of the Follies', Vera Pearce.[41] Mina's association with Marion McIntosh is the most likely explanation of a signed photograph in the archive from the outrageous and wonderfully named musical hall star, Daisy Jerome La Touche.

Arriving from England in 1913, Daisy Jerome took Australian theatre by storm with her repertoire of risqué songs accompanied by knowing winks and innuendos. She left Australia in 1916 but returned in 1922 with a French husband and 'La Touche' added to her name. Almost immediately, she became embroiled in a highly publicised court case involving her maid, whom La Touche accused of stealing her jewellery. The maid was acquitted, and the scandal only added to the popularity of the 'Electric Spark', as the stunning redhead now billed herself.

Legend has it that during one performance, a lovestruck young man in the dress circle threw himself onto the stage to demonstrate the extent of his passion. The unfortunate fan broke both his legs and injured his spine but the look of concern (or was it terror?) on the face of the object of his affection made every minute of his agony worthwhile.

Mina's photograph of Daisy La Touche is signed, 'To Miss Wylie, a dear little friend, from her new pal Daisy', and depicts La Touch posing with a silver-topped cane. Discovering that Mina had spent enough time with a woman who had the ability to make a nursery rhyme sound suggestive and that she was considered a 'new pal' delighted me. Perhaps it is the disparity between the image of the well brought up, respectable young woman from Coogee, and the headstrong, fun loving New Woman who enjoyed the company of slightly louche entertainers and, later in life, film stars.

Mina loved to socialise, and these circles filled with apparent wickedness were more fun than the Freemason's Ball in Randwick Town Hall under the watchful eyes of Florence and Henry. And mingling with theatrical personalities gave Mina a sense of Annette Kellerman's life in Hollywood, a life she continued to fantasise about creating for herself.

Two years on from Stockholm, however, it was beginning to seem to Mina that the bubble had burst. Perhaps Miss Scott had been right after all. She and Durack would be a novelty for a moment, but the spotlight would soon be redirected back onto the men. As Mina sat in the darkened auditorium of the Crystal Palace cinema on George Street watching Kellerman dive her way through 'Daughter of the Gods', she felt as if her vision of a bigger life was fading alongside the final shot. She daren't voice out loud the word 'bored', but oh, how she longed for the excitement of Stockholm. Because she had a creeping fear that her life had already peaked. That she would never see America, never go back to London, never reach the heights of Annette Kellerman. She would stay here and stagnate, and not ever become more than a young woman from Coogee who was famous for a moment. She yearned to escape into a future that was more exciting than her present. She wanted to get away from prudery and full-length cloaks and women who tutted at Annette Kellerman. And, much as she loved him, she wanted to do more than teach ten-year-olds how to swim at her father's pool.

*

In January 1914, Mina attended the NSW ASA state championships in Sydney's Domain Baths and saved the programme which included a full-page notice of the 'First appearance in Australia of the Olympic Champion, Duke Paoa-Kahanamoku'. Mina was thrilled. At last, something to look forward to.

'Look Dad. He's coming!'

'Is he now? Well, hopefully our boys will beat him this time.'

The 1914/15 tour by Kahanamoku (and fellow Hawaiians, 19-year-old George Cunha and tour manager Francis Evans) was the first visit to Australia by a reigning Olympic champion and was regarded by sporting authorities as an opportunity to consolidate the impression on international swimming that the

Australians had made in Stockholm. Australia had come second to Germany in the final medal tally of the swimming competition, but it was the Americans who were considered by Australians as their main rivals.

To have a local swimmer trounce the 'unbeatable' American champion would leave the international swimming community in no doubt that Australia was as good as any other nation when it came to sport. Cecil Healy had retired from racing but would report on proceedings through his role as reporter for *The Referee*, and Duke's greatest rivals over short distances were Billy Longworth, Mina's Stockholm team-mate, and current NSW record holder over 100yds, Albert Barry. Most eyes, however, were turned to the middle- and long-distance races where NSW swimmer Tommy Adrian might just be in with a chance of outswimming the Duke.

Duke Kahanamoku's visit to Australia is primarily remembered today for his display of surfing on Freshwater beach on Christmas Eve 1914, which is frequently credited as the birth of Australian surfing, but he came to compete as a swimmer and Sydneysiders had their first opportunity to witness the reigning Olympic champion in action at the opening carnival of the NSW State Championships at the Domain Baths on January 2nd, 1915. Such was the excitement at the presence of the American sensation that almost seven thousand spectators packed the stands around the pool, and those enthusiasts too late to gain entry climbed trees and stood on the roofs of nearby buildings, straining to see over the fence.

By the time the men lined up for the 100yds freestyle championship, the crowd had worked itself into a frenzy. But state record holder, Albert Barry, could only keep clear of the wake as the Duke powered home in a new world record of 53.8 seconds.[42] In his report of the carnival for *The Referee*, Healy repeated the assertion that the performance of the Hawaiian swimmer was 'beyond comprehension'. The rival sporting magazine *The Bulletin* concurred, describing Kahanamoku's swimming style as 'Effortless. His long arms plough through the water, and there is no splash: his vast feet revolve beneath the surface and leave it almost unmoved.'

'Well,' said Henry. 'Well…'

Because what else was there to say? The Duke had made the Australians look like beginners with their two-beat kick and thrashing arms.

'I told you,' said Mina. 'They have a better stroke than we do.'

She watched as Duke was swamped by excited men, all eager to shake the hand of the new world champion. The crowd was still on its feet, roaring approval. Albert Barry shrugged. What could he do against that?

'Do you think he'd come to Coogee?' asked Henry.

In actual fact, there is nothing in Mina's archive to prove she attended the race and she may well have been in country NSW giving exhibitions with Marion McIntosh and Fanny Durack as Duke smashed the 100yds world record. I believe if she had been at the Domain Baths that night, sitting in the VIP area with Cecil Healy and Marion and Hugh McIntosh, being recognised by the crowd as she entered, Mina would have saved a memento. Duke was headline news and she was unlikely to let such an auspicious moment pass by without an autograph, or even a photograph. Just to remind the press and onlookers of who she was.

The Australian public could not get enough of the visiting American swimmers and from the arrival reception at the Australia Hotel in Sydney, through competitions in Brisbane and Melbourne, to the farewell speeches at the Sports Club in Sydney's Hunter Street, the press pack trailed the trio, recording their every move, every word. The positive and surprisingly respectful depiction of Kahanamoku in the media was undoubtedly due to his friendship with Healy, the nation's shining example of good sportsmanship and the 'fair go'.

In a country where members of the Aboriginal population were regarded, and treated, as second-class citizens, Healy could not have been unaware of the racial issues underlying the tour (although George Cunha was white). Throughout the tour, Duke Kahanamoku made no reference at all to the Indigenous population and it is impossible to know if news of his success reached Aboriginal communities. Although I have found no evidence of racial segregation or an outright ban on Aboriginal swimmers from clubs and public pools in this era, it does not necessarily follow that non-white swimmers were either encouraged or welcome at pools such as Wylie's or the Domain Baths. In all likelihood, Aboriginal swimmers would have known to keep away from public baths or risk the humiliation of being excluded with no explanation required. Racial segregation laws were certainly in place in some public pools throughout the NSW following the Second World War, and it was not until 1965 that the pool in the northern NSW town of Mooree was forced to allow entry to Aboriginal children following the affirmative action of students from Sydney University.[43] Swimming continues to carry the dubious distinction of being a sport almost universally white at elite level in Australia, and Samantha Riley remains the only swimmer of Aboriginal descent to have won Olympic medals—a bronze in the 100m breast stroke and a silver as a member of the 4x100, medley relay team in Atlanta in 1996.

The record-breaking night at the Domain in 1915 was not the only occasion Kahanamoku swam in Sydney and there were numerous occasions where Mina might have renewed her acquaintance with him over the next six weeks. He gave surfing demonstrations on the beaches of Freshwater, South Steyne and Cronulla, and raced again at the Domain and at Drummoyne Baths. Even if she never met him in person—which I find hard to believe given the strength of the friendship three years later in the USA—she could not have missed seeing him in the papers. He was vibrant and self-assured and seemed to embody a new and modern way of being which Mina recognised from the movies. He exuded confidence without the swagger, accepting his success with a casual shrug, as if it meant little in the grand scheme of things.

Everything about Duke Kahanamoku reminded Mina how ordinary her life had become. She wanted to be extraordinary again and have adventures. She wanted to travel and see new things. Be inspired all over again. But more than anything, she and Fanny Durack wanted to beat the American girls and establish Australia as the world leaders in women's competitive swimming.

'Mr Kahanamoku told me he is going to swim at the Expo in San Francisco this year,' Mina reported to Mrs McIntosh. 'He says the sporting competition will be bigger than the Olympics in Berlin.'

'If there is an Olympics. This war...'

'Fanny and I could go to San Francisco,' Mina ventured. 'It's not as far as Europe, not as expensive. We could race the American girls there.'

Marion McIntosh paused. Then nodded.

'You could. You could both go to San Francisco.'

And wouldn't that be one in the eye for the arrogant Australian officials who continued to dismiss ladies swimming as irrelevant. Never mind what it would do for the status of the NSW Ladies Amateur Swimming Association if Mina and Durack were victorious.

'I want to send the girls to the San Francisco State Fair,' Marion announced to her husband. 'I think they could win. But they'll need you to sponsor them ...'

Visions of another Australian sporting triumph made possible by his personal generosity floated in front of Hugh McIntosh's eyes. He smiled indulgently. 'Of course, dear. Whatever you want.'

Medallists in the inaugural ladies 100m freestyle, Stockholm. L-R Fanny Durack, Mina Wylie and Jennie Fletcher (UK)

Mina exiting the pool in Hamburg, Germany, 1912.

Mina and pupils at Wylie's Baths circa 1912

Rowing team, Brisbane circa 1913. Violet is left, front.

Chapter 7

Dear Walter, we have had a swim here but don't like the water. It is 82, too warm but is the only public bath in the city. We go to the club and it is very fine. Best love from Mina.

Postcard of the Lurline Baths in San Francisco, 1918

The visit of Duke Kahanamoku to Australia in 1914/1915 was a welcome distraction from the war in Europe which was supposed to have been over by Christmas but continued its relentless toll on the Western Front into the new year. Despite the appalling casualty figures, the rush of young men signing on the dotted line and donning khaki showed no sign of abating. Many Australians regarded the Great War as their chance to prove their worth, both as a man and as a new nation, and the lust for what was sold as an 'adventure' was contagious. It is difficult to determine what effect the First World War had on Mina, as only a handful of artefacts in her archive are connected with the conflict.

One of these is a photograph of her younger brother, Harry, in military uniform, but his name appears alongside Walter's in Henry's accounts books for the pool throughout 1917 and 1918, and there is no record of him ever serving overseas. Nor, incidentally, of Walter. With both brothers safe in Coogee, Mina's war years were less traumatic than those of countless other women who lived in fear of the arrival of the black edged telegram.

Wylie's Baths remained open throughout the conflict and swimming competitions continued as normal, albeit with a collection for a hospital or the war effort as part of the proceedings. Mina could not have missed the maimed veterans haunting the city, nor been unaware of the virulent divisions in society caused by the conscription referendums of 1916 and 1917. Her former supporter, Rose Scott, was Chair of the NSW branch of the Peace Society and was frequently in the press for her pacifist views and her opposition to conscription. Mina, however, appears to have maintained the apolitical stance she had previously displayed with regard to feminist activism. Whether she was genuinely indifferent to political causes or keeping a prudent distance from anything which could tarnish her image is difficult to tell.

There is no evidence that Henry Wylie was a political firebrand or committed to a particular cause, and it is often the case that elite athletes are so entirely focused on the job at hand that their view of the wider world is somewhat blinkered. I suspect Mina was happy to offer her services to raise money for the red cross or the Australian war effort but was less inclined to engage in the raging political arguments raging concerning Australia's participation in the distant conflict, and in the conscription debate.

She corresponded with two Australian men serving in the trenches in France and a letter dated 25 May 1916, from Second Lieutenant Henry Miller Lanser, is saved amongst her belongings:

'Dear old sport Mina, It all helps to make things pleasant when mail arrives especially when it comes from an old friend and I quite agree with you this military life does get monotonous. Your welcome letter came in rather a good time as our Battalion has just come out of the trenches and are now in reserve …'

Henry Miller sailed to Egypt with the First Australian Infantry Battalion in October 1914 and survived the slaughter on the beaches at Gallipoli. His pencilled letter to Mina one year later is noteworthy more for the fact that it is surviving letter from an Australian soldier in the trenches than for the contents:

'Stir Walter along and ask him to drop me a line. So, Jim O Donnell has enlisted if he finds it as hard to take as I did he won't fall in with it at all, experience is a fine thing but frightfully expensive. After reading this hurried note you will find it comes from Your old sport Miller.'

Henry Miller Lanser was killed on 5 November 1916, and a card from his family thanking Mina for her 'kindness and sympathy in their great loss' is saved alongside his letter. [44]

Mina involved herself in fund raising efforts in support of Belgian refugees and Sydney hospitals, most notably at the lavish affairs held at Marion McIntosh's impressive Darling Point residence. At one memorable extravaganza in May 1915, guests and stars from the Tivoli circuit, including Hugh's mistress, Vera Pearce, were driven to the house in special cars which met the trams at Darling Point Road. A marquee had been erected in the garden for performances from the stars, dancing and socialising, and no one was crass enough to comment about the fact that Huge Deal was flaunting his mistress in front of his wife.

Hugh McIntosh made a point of being seen to support numerous war charities and he spared no expense on these grand charity events at 'Benoni', desirous of being seen to dip into his own pocket to support the country's war effort. Always keen to court publicity, he distributed gold passes which gave a lifetime free entry to his Tivoli theatres to Australian soldiers who were awarded the Victoria Cross.

Like Annette Kellerman and her over-the-top Red Cross aquacades during the Second World War, McIntosh's fundraising events and charitable initiatives were less about raising funds and more concerned with self-promotion and his public image. Not that Mina cared. The star-studded afternoons at Darling Point were a welcome antidote to a life which threatened to become mundane following the thrill of the visit by Duke Kahanamoku. The various dance cards present in Mina's archive from 1913 to 1915 reveal that her social life revolved around functions put on by the Sydney Ladies Swimming Club, the Royal Lifesaving Society and her father's business interests. If the annual Mason's Lodge Ball in the Randwick Town Hall was the highlight of Mina's social calendar, it was little wonder she courted invitations to 'Benoni'.

*

In June of 1914, sporting officials from around the world gathered in Paris to celebrate the twentieth anniversary of the first modern Olympics and to consolidate plans for the 1916 games to be held in Berlin. US delegate, James E. Sullivan seized the opportunity offered by the meeting to reaffirm his virulent opposition to women in sport by announcing that he would again forbid the female American swimmers and divers to compete in Germany in two years' time. Sullivan's behaviour towards women athletes at this time, both on home soil and with regard to the Olympics, was increasingly bordering on fanaticism.

Female swimmers and divers particularly incensed him but because he appeared to be unable to articulate the reason behind his extreme stance, it can only be assumed it was the brazen baring of flesh which so enraged him. Either that, or his fragile ego regarded vigorous, strong women engaging in the same activities as men as a threat to his masculinity. Ida Schnall, the high diver who had written to the *New York Times* in 1912 calling out Sullivan's misogyny, wrote again to the paper in 1913, this time referring to Sullivan as a 'narrow-minded bigot'.

Whilst her words contained more than a ring of truth, no official appeared willing to confront Sullivan over the Olympic ban or to challenge his steadfast refusal to officially recognise any form of women's sport within the USA. A few brave individuals quietly agreed in principle that incorporating women's competition as part of the activities of the AAU was not altogether a bad idea, but no one had the courage to articulate this within Sullivan's presence.

The last day of the Olympic meeting in Paris was blighted by the assassination of the heir to the Austro/Hungarian throne, Arch Duke Franz Ferdinand. Two months later, Europe was at war and the Berlin Olympics became yet another fatality on an alarmingly long list. Although the USA co-operated with the Allied forces, the nation remained neutral until 1917[45] and life, and sporting competition across the nation continued as usual.

There was, however, one unexpected event at this time which had a resoundingly positive outcome for female athletes in the USA: in September of 1914, Sullivan, aged 53, unexpectedly died. His obituary in the *New York Times* on 17 September extolled his tireless work to engage young men in sport, stating: 'There is not a schoolboy in New York who has not felt the good influence of Mr Sullivan's untiring efforts in his behalf.' No mention, naturally, was made of his unswerving opposition to young women being afforded the same opportunities.

On 18 September, the *New York Times* carried a further report entitled 'J.E. Sullivan's Funeral; 60,000 Schoolboys Will Line Route of the Procession' outlining details of the extravagant arrangements being drawn up for his farewell, including an honour guard of 200 medal and championship winners following the hearse. The article also informed readers that a subscription fund for a memorial monument to Sullivan had been established and a request was being made to city authorities to name a public playground in his honour. Ironically, the report of the deification of Sullivan as a national sporting hero was positioned in the newspaper next to a column headed, 'Mrs Barlow beats Miss Hyde at golf', a fact, and the mere reporting of it, which would have enraged the deceased.

Hopefully, the 60,000 schoolgirls who were not invited to line the funeral route alongside their male contemporaries took the afternoon off and spent it in the nearest park running, jumping, hitting and throwing balls, or at a public pool executing perfect dives led by a beaming Ida Schnall.

In lieu of the cancelled Berlin Olympics, the Panama-Pacific International Exhibition in 1915—more popularly known as the San Francisco World Fair—incorporated an extensive programme of sporting events and competitions for local and international athletes. With Sullivan out of the picture, organisers were now able to include female athletes and both swimming and diving events were scheduled for women (loud cheers from Ida Schnall!) Sullivan's obsessive determination to keep sport the preserve of men accounted for the fact that women's competitive swimming in the USA had developed at a much slower pace than in Australia.

Despite this, the sport was immensely popular amongst both participants and spectators, and Sullivan's untimely demise provided the perfect opportunity to move it into the mainstream. Huge crowds were anticipated at the world fair and a showdown between the reigning female Olympic champions and their American challengers was a dream event for promoters. In early 1915, an official invitation was extended to Mina and Fanny Durack to travel to San Francisco to compete in the biggest sporting event ever staged in the USA.

Mina's appetite for the country which had produced Kellerman's aquatic-themed block busting movies had been whetted by the recent visit of Kahanamoku. The San Francisco Expo was already shaping up to be bigger and better than any previous World's Fair—everything about the USA seemed to be bigger and better—and Mina could hardly contain herself at the prospect of attending. The designated site for the fair covered a breath-taking 2.5 square kilometres, filled with exhibition halls, gardens, a jewelled tower rising 435 feet from the ground, palaces showcasing fine arts, food, agriculture, education, industries and transportation, a branch of the Smithsonian Institute, and even a motor racing track. Nothing on this scale had been seen before.

Mina entertained glorious visions of herself and Durack being given standing ovations as they displayed their superior prowess to an adoring US crowd. Her crawl stroke had improved to the point where she felt confident she could give Durack a run for her money and, according to the few reports which had leaked out of the USA, the American women paid little attention to breast stroke as a competition stroke. No one would beat her in what had become her speciality.

In the end, however, it was not to be. The last gasp of Victorian sensibility conspired against the two Australians, as the financial assistance offered by Californian authorities did not cover the expenses of a chaperone. With the war occupying all fundraising efforts in Australia, it was impossible to raise the extra fare for something as trivial as a women's swimming race and the invitation to California had to be regrettably declined.

Mina was devastated. Her dreams of emulating Kellerman and swimming in front of thousands, dashed. It had now been three years since the Stockholm experience and she craved the stimulation of another international competition, especially one where the Australian stars could put an end to speculation concerning the flourishing ability of the American women. Marion McIntosh was equally disappointed that her protegees would not be performing in the San Francisco spotlight—she too had been entertaining visions of an Australian victory and a triumphant homecoming. Yet another point notched up against her nemesis, Rose Scott. So determined, in fact, was McIntosh to see her golden girls shine under the American sun, that in June 1916, she travelled to the USA with the express purpose of setting up a nationwide tour for Mina and Durack.

On her arrival in New York, McIntosh met Charlotte Epstein, the woman who had earned herself the title of 'the mother of women's swimming in America'.[46]

'Eppie', as she was known to her young swimming charges, had founded the National Women's Life Saving League in 1914, with the aim of preventing drowning by developing access to swimming lessons for young women and girls. She had spent years fighting with the male-governed AAU in an effort to persuade them to allow women to register for the Union's sanctioned swimming events, but had been thwarted at every turn by the virulently chauvinistic Sullivan.

Two years after his death, Eppie remained fervently committed to having women's competitive swimming officially recognised by the authorities and she saw an ally in the figure of Marion McIntosh, a woman her own age who had also fought for the right of women to compete at elite level. Eppie was a court stenographer who had been educated at the progressive Ethical Culture School, a consequence of the Ethical Culture Society which had been founded in 1876 by the visionary ethicist, Felix Adler.

Dr Adler advocated social justice for all and urged members to express their disquiet at the racial and societal inequalities rife throughout the country through moral and humane action. These then, were the radical ideas that Eppie had been exposed to as a child and a young adult. Equality was not a fanciful concept in her mind, but a human right, and the appointment 1903 of Anna Garlin Spencer as Associate Leader of the Ethical Cultural Society confirmed to the then teenage Eppie, that women had as much right to lead as men did.

Marion McIntosh may have been uneducated and a member of the New Rich, therefore dismissed as vulgar by Rose Scott, but her passion and commitment towards raising the profile of women's swimming was undeniable. Her youth and energy were valuable assets to the NSW LASA—it's hard to imagine Rose Scott making the long trip to New York to organise a swimming tour—and despite their widely different backgrounds, McIntosh and Eppie met on common ground.

Twenty years of marriage to Huge Deal had familiarised Marion McIntosh with the basics of sports promotion and she harboured a vision of a tour which would generate maximum publicity, thus ensuring maximum impact. Her role as President of the NSW LASA was to promote her swimmers, and what better platform could there be than a tour of the USA, a country believed to have more in common with Australia than class ridden, self-conscious Great Britain. The USA was, like Australia, brash and modern, full of itself, a less kind observer might have noted. The two nations were well suited.

A few days after McIntosh's arrival in New York in July 1916, the *New York Times* reported:

'Plans are being laid through William Unmack, a prominent California swimming enthusiast on one side, and Mrs Hugh D McIntosh and Mrs W Chambers, President and Secretary of the NSW LASA on the other, for a tour of the US next year by the Sydney women swimmers Miss Fanny Durack and Miss Mina Wylie, who are holders of the World's and Australasian women's records...'

The article did not sound a note of caution warning readers not to get too excited just yet because any tour by female swimmers, American or Australian, had to be endorsed by the AAU, an organisation, as we have seen, which was dominated by notoriously chauvinistic men. Regardless, serious steps were taken towards securing the women's tour with no less than twelve cities already signed up. It was a good indication of how keen the Australians were to take on the American women that McIntosh raised no objection to this arduous, possibly unrealistic, itinerary, nor raised the issue of travel and accommodation expenses. Perhaps her magnanimous husband, always keen to self-promote, had agreed in principle to fund the tour if it ever eventuated.

Brought up to speed by Eppie, Marion McIntosh was unimpressed by the male governance of women's swimming in the USA and used a second interview with the *New York Times* in August to air her views.

'I think you need a separate body to govern the sport. For the present the Amateur Athletic Union can handle it very well indeed, but in a few years the women should branch out and govern themselves.'

Easier said than done in a society even less enamoured of female athletes than even pre-Stockholm Australia.

Eppie conceded to McIntosh that women's competitive swimming was more advanced in Australia than in the USA, where the sport was, according to the *New York Times* on August 23rd, 'practically in it's infancy'.[47] The same newspaper article confidently reported:

'Practically all arrangements for the proposed invasion of the United States by the two greatest women swimmers in Australia—Miss Fanny Durack and Miss Mina Wylie—were made yesterday ...'

Two Canadian cities, Toronto and Montreal, had been added to the gruelling itinerary, and the report noted that the Australian rule requiring a female swimmer to be accompanied to competitions by a chaperone, was a rule which would appeal to the AAU, apparently still governed by the ghost of James E. Sullivan. Eppie had outlined very plainly to McIntosh the levels of hostility she would encounter amongst the men of the AAU, many of whom remained loyal to the Sullivan's ideals of sport as a male concern. Female modesty was, as ever, a prevailing concern amongst the male authorities and McIntosh expertly utilised her August interview with the *New York Times* reassure the interviewer, Frederick Rubien of the AAU, that the Australian women's swimsuits were 'regulated and cannot be immodest under our rules.'

Clearly she had not seen the photograph of Mina taken at Wylie's Baths three years previously.

As predicted by Eppie, the proposed nationwide tour by the Australian women caused a split in the AAU and prompted a stormy debate in November of 1916, during which members resolutely refused to fully sanction women's competitive swimming as a legitimate sport.

'You see?' said Eppie. 'They live in the dark ages.'

'Oh, we heard all of this in Australia four years ago. They'll back down in the end.'

And finally, after eight hours of arguing, they did. But the mania for control over women's sport instigated by Sullivan resulted in Union members insisting that the proposed swimming tour would adhere to AAU rules and not, as McIntosh had presumed to suggest, those of the NSW LASA. The Australian rules regarding neck to knee swimsuits in dark colours were, however, eagerly embraced. With Annette Kellerman's risqué film, 'Daughter of the Gods' playing to sold out houses at the nearby Lyric Theatre on Broadway, the conservative men of the AAU were anxious to avoid any suggestion of a link between the licentious image promoted by Kellerman, and any women's swimming competition sanctioned and governed by the Union.

By the end of the November AAU meeting, the visit by the Australian swimmers appeared to have been given the go ahead, but less than a month later, the Union announced the cancellation of the tour: 'Swimming Invasion Off' declared the *New York Times* dramatically in December. According to the Union, the reasons were financial: not all of the clubs involved were willing to guarantee funds to cover the expenses of the Australian women.

McIntosh's perceptive observation a few months earlier to the *New York Times* that a separate organisation free from the overbearing controls of the AAU would better suit women's competitive swimming, could not have been more clearly demonstrated. Sullivan may have gone, but the men of the AAU appeared determined to maintain their power over women's swimming, an activity many of them found distasteful in the first place. Less than a year after her first encounter with the forthright McIntosh, and completely out of patience with the men of the AAU, Eppie and a small number of likeminded women founded the Women's Swimming Association of New York (WSA).

The inaugural meeting of the Association in October 1917, was attended by more than fifty members of Eppie's National Women's Lifesaving League, and it was agreed by all present that the purpose of the WSA was to provide swimming instruction and to seek opportunities for competition for association members. With these guidelines in place, Eppie wasted no time in engaging the services of renowned swimming authority, Louis B. Handley, as head coach of the new organisation.[48] Handley was himself a former champion, having won gold medals as a member of the 4x50yd freestyle relay team at the 1904 St Louis Olympics, and as a member of the water polo team.

Eppie's engagement of Handley was a prophetic move as he had, for some time, been experimenting with improvements to the crawl stroke by introducing more beats per stroke into a continuous kicking motion. By early 1918, only a year after the instigation of the WSA, the young swimmers from New York were posting times which seriously challenged Mina and Durack's status as world champions.

Marion McIntosh was thrilled at the 1917 formation of the WSA. With women's swimming in the USA now in women's hands, it seemed the perfect time to resurrect the cancelled 1916 tour and finally bring to pass the long-anticipated Australia/USA women's showdown. McIntosh fully believed that the proclamation she had made to the *New York Times* concerning Durack and Wylie two years previously—'I don't believe there is a woman swimmer in the US who can compare with these girls'—remained the case, and Eppie was keen to put it to the test. Subsequently, an invitation was issued to Mina and Durack to come to America and race the local women on an extensive tour, again managed by swimming 'philanthropist', William Unmack (for philanthropist, read 'sponsor'). The invitation was accepted, and preparations commenced.

From the very outset, there was trouble. But this time, the difficulties came not from the men of the American Athletic Union, but from the swimmers themselves. Fanny Durack's ego appeared to be out of control, and she announced that she wanted to be the sole Australian representative on the tour. This came completely out of the blue and Durack gave no reason for it, leaving it easy to form the conclusion that she wanted all the glory for herself. How this issue was resolved is unknown—safe to say it required some sweet talking from Marion McIntosh: perhaps she used the 'you swim freestyle and she swims breast stroke' argument.

How Mina felt about the very public snub by her supposed 'close friend' is not hard to imagine. But once her presence had been reintroduced into the mix, it did not take her long to overcome whatever feelings of betrayal she may have felt and align herself with the recalcitrant Fanny Durack. Anything to secure the longed-for trip to the USA.

Despite the fact that Mina and Fanny were 27 and 28 years old respectively, it was 1918 and still unthinkable that they would travel to the USA unaccompanied. The NSW LASA selected Hon. Secretary Mrs Chambers (the same woman who had reprimanded Mina in 1912 over the row with another committee member) as the chaperone for the tour, but Fanny refused to accept this and demanded that her sister Mary be selected instead. Given that Mrs Chambers was the Rose Scott ally who had been quoted in the Sydney press in

1912 as being firmly against Mina and Fanny competing in Stockholm, this may have been payback time on Fanny's behalf towards a woman she disliked.

When the NSW LASA refused to agree to Mary Durack acting as chaperone, Fanny claimed that her sister was her trainer and it was therefore imperative that she accompany her. This, of course, was nonsense, or, at least, there is absolutely no evidence that Mary Durack had ever acted as Fanny's coach. And, as a reporter in the *Referee* pointed out, if Fanny Durack wanted the services of a trainer throughout the tour, it would be easy to find one in America keen to do the job. What seemed trivial on paper, soon mushroomed into a major stumbling block, as reported by *The Referee*, on the 8 May 1918.

'The Amateur Athletic Union of the U.S.A. has approved of Miss Durack's tour, and has asked that she be furnished from Australia with amateur credentials. These may be refused to her unless she accepts the Ladies' Association's nominee, Mrs. Chambers, as her companion during the journey.'

Without the essential amateur 'credentials', the AAU would not allow Durack to race in America. In reaction to this veiled threat, Fanny petulantly announced that she was going to the USA with her sister even if it meant she had to pay her own fares and expenses (presumably the 'philanthropist' William Unmack was standing by with an open cheque book). If the NSW LASA failed to sanction her appearance as an amateur, Fanny glibly told the *Referee* that it was her intention to join an American swimming club and swim under their name instead of representing the Australian women's association. The opinion of the *Referee* was clear:

'Miss Durack is very foolish to make such threats as these.'

Fanny Durack's attitude towards an authority which had consistently supported her for over a decade was ungracious and reminiscent of a spoiled child being denied her own way. This was not a woman finding her voice, this was someone who appeared to believe that owning the title of the 'Fastest Lady Swimmer in the World' gave a person licence to behave in whatever way they pleased.

But the NSW LASA was not merely being stubborn in insisting that their official chaperone accompany the women, their action was intrinsically tied up with the all-important view in this period of sport as an amateur concern. This meant that rules had to be rigorously applied and peevishly dismissing the wishes of the governing body, was not treated lightly: Mina had been suspended for a similar action six years previously.

In early May 1918, the committee of the NSW LASA gathered at a specially convened meeting to discuss applications from Fanny Durack and Mina to go to the USA at their own expense, but still compete as representatives of the NSW LASA. The applications were unanimously refused meaning that if Fanny and Mina went ahead under their own steam, it would be without an endorsement from their governing swimming authority, which the AAU had made very clear, was unacceptable. A column in *The Referee* warned that the AAU might now withdraw its support, subsequently putting the entire tour at risk. But Fanny and Mina either did not read it or ignored it.

It's impossible to know where Mina stood in the middle of all of this infighting (and what Florence must have made of it). On one hand, Mina was good friends with Marion McIntosh, a woman who had been extremely supportive and hospitable towards her. On the other, Mina desperately wanted to go to America and be a part of international competition again. I believe she saw this tour as a sort of comeback: her opportunity to make her mark on the world outside the narrow confines of the Sydney swimming community. If that was the case, then it was natural that she sided with Fanny Durack, the current world champion. Mina was astute enough to know that Fanny was the real draw card and that she herself was the bonus addition. Whatever Fanny did to get to America, Mina was obliged to go along with, or risk losing her place on the tour. But that thinking does give the impression that Mina was easily swayed by Durack, which I'm not convinced was the case.

A lengthy tour under the watchful eye of the Mrs Chambers was not a particularly enticing proposition. Mary Durack was much closer in age to Mina and Fanny, and she had already proved herself to be fun and amenable on an overseas trip. It is also highly possible that Mina held a similar attitude regarding her own status as the one displayed by Fanny. Henry had, after all, warned Florence about their daughter's 'big head'. She was the world record holder in breast stroke, she had a right to dictate the terms on which she would swim. Despite the warnings in the press and the freezing silence from the women of the NSW LASA, Mina and the Durack sisters packed their belongings and prepared to depart as individuals with no affiliation to any Australian association.

In her suitcase, Mina stowed the address of an American sporting promoter who had visited Wylie's Baths the previous year and watched her swim. He had assured her there was a world of opportunity awaiting her in the USA, and she fully intended to find those openings and exploit every one of them. She withdrew money from her savings account and had professional calling cards made describing the strokes and fancy aquatic tricks she could perform on demand. On the customs form Mina was required to complete before her departure from Australia she stated that she was visiting the USA for the 'purpose of fulfilling swimming engagements.' She also stated, although she was careful to hide it from her mother, that she intended to stay for 'six months abt.'

Mina and the Durack sisters left Sydney on 15 May 1918. Mina had bought a new autograph album for the trip and, as was her habit, collected a number of signatures from fellow passengers. The ship docked briefly in Hawaii where the women caught up with Duke Kahanamoku, who signed Mina's new album with the words, 'Kiu hoa aloha (dear friend) Mina, with best wishes and good luck always.'

Kahanamoku then joined the ship for the journey to San Francisco where he was to participate a swimming tour to raise funds for the Red Cross and the American war effort.

On their arrival in San Francisco, the Australian women were greeted with the news that the tour they believed they were about to undertake, had been cancelled. Perhaps they had naively assumed that the NSW LASA would accept their decision to tour as individuals and that would be the end of it. But in between the SS Sonoma leaving Hawaii and docking in San Francisco, Marion McIntosh had sent a telegram to Fredrick Rubien, secretary of the AAU, informing him that Durack and Mina were 'defying authorities' and were 'no longer in good standing'.

Just to be absolutely certain, Rubien cabled McIntosh reiterating that 'Misses Durack and Wylie cannot swim in amateur competition, US, without your sanction.' McIntosh was well aware of that, yet she informed Rubien that the sanction of the NSW LASA had been withheld. The result was the cancellation of the countrywide tour which had been touted by the *New York Times* in February as 'the feature of the year in aquatics'. An exciting itinerary had already been formalised, taking in both the west and east coasts and culminating in races at the huge 300yd Bronx pool as part of the sporting programme at the New York International Exposition. All this was now abandoned. Mina and Fanny Durack had just learned an important lesson concerning another former mentor: Marion McIntosh was not a woman to mess with.

McIntosh knew that withholding the LASA endorsement would most likely result in the cancellation of the tour, leaving the swimming duo with few choices.

They could return home with their tails between their legs and accept the rules in future—an unlikely outcome going by Fanny's recent behaviour. They could send Mary Durack home and await the arrival of Mrs Chambers, if indeed Mrs Chambers was still willing to accompany two young women who had made it very clear they did not want to travel with her. Again, unlikely. Or they could turn professional and forfeit any swimming career in Australian. It was the proverbial rock and a hard place, and an action calculated to prove to Mina and Durack that, contrary to their belief, the rules did apply to them.

The *San Francisco Chronicle* carried a report on the cancelled tour in the edition of 4 June, in which Fanny Durack is noted as laughing as she announced, 'The cancellation of our tour is news to us. When we left Sydney, there was no such talk.' After a quick consultation with William Unmack, Fanny went on to tell reporters:

'There can be no cancellation by Mrs McIntosh either as an individual or an executive of the LASA, for the reason that the ladies' body is only an affiliated branch with the Australian Swimming Association and it has no jurisdiction to issue or cancel sanctions. Mrs McIntosh has no authority to cable anyone except through the head body, that is, the Australian Swimming Union.'

It is hard to fathom what Fanny was thinking in making such a statement as she was effectively declaring war against the head of her own governing body by dismissing it as being of no consequence compared to the men's authority. Hardly the action of a united sisterhood. It was a foolhardy move, especially as the two Australians were now in serious danger of losing their amateur status. The *Chronicle* report established Fanny Durack's reputation as the outspoken, even belligerent, swimmer she became known as in the USA. Mina, on the other hand, had the sense to stay in the background and was reported in the *Chronicle* as 'rather quiet in her ways. You'd take her for a shy little person, rather than for a world record breaker.'

The Australians checked into their San Francisco hotel, in what seems to have been a spirit of high dudgeon and waited for the NSW LASA to reverse Marion McIntosh's refusal to sanction the tour. But if Fanny Durack was stubborn, she had met her match in Marion McIntosh. Negotiations stalled and without the permission of the NSW LASA to swim in the USA, Mina and the Durack sisters were stranded in San Francisco while the various swimming authorities struggled to find common ground.

As related by regular updates in the *San Francisco Chronicle*, the next few weeks were saw little progress and the stale mate quickly deteriorated into a mess of cancelled carnivals and exhibitions, and growing antagonism between the Australian and American swimmers. Fanny Durack cemented her reputation as difficult, or, as the *Chronical* put it, as 'so full of temperament as a movie star who has just bought a new car' and Mina stayed on the side-lines. The issue concerning the amateur status of the Australian swimmers moved away from their lack of official endorsement and began to question the appointment of William Unmack as tour manager as, in the eyes of the AAU, this veered perilously close to the actions of professional athletes, particularly when it was rumoured he intended to charge spectators a small fee to watch the women in practice sessions. Unmack was duly fired by Mina and Fanny, and Mary Durack assumed the responsibility of managing the, still cancelled, tour for her two charges. Whether she had the experience or ability to do this seemed irrelevant by this point.

Somewhat gleefully, the *Chronical* ran an article on June 9th quoting a Mr Rogers, the manager of the Centre Athletic Club, who was 'one mad person when it comes to talking about Fanny Durack'. Rogers asserted that Mina and Fanny had agreed to appear in a carnival organised at his athletic club but when he spoke to Fanny on the telephone she dismissed him, saying, 'We don't know anything about the Centre Club or any swimming there.' The *Chronicle* indulged Roger's rant:

'The night of her arrival I was in the restaurant and with some of our girls from the club met the Durack party. We presented them with Centre Club pins, membership cards and even sent flowers to their hotel. We discussed the programme, told Fanny Durack of spending $500 to prepare for the event and she asked what sort of bathing costume she had best wear. And now, when everything is fixed and we're right up against the night itself, I'm told that they have never even heard of the Club. Can you beat it?'

The abrupt dismissal of local man, William Unmack, was not received well in San Francisco, and a dinner which had been organised to honour the Australian women was cancelled at the insistence of a group of local female swimmers. Bearing in mind it was Unmack who had organised the honorary dinner, it is hardly surprising that Mina and Fanny were no longer welcome. The celebratory evening paid tribute instead to Duke Kahanamoku and one can only imagine how awkward he felt at being caught in the middle of the squabbling Australians and Americans.

Further bad feeling erupted when Fanny and Mina announced they were willing to race in exhibitions but would not compete against any local swimmers. In retaliation, the women of the Del Monte swimming club voted unanimously against meeting the Australians in the water. In short, the highly anticipated national tour had degenerated into petty one upmanship and bad behaviour, and no one seemed to be able, or willing, to save it.

Mina, however, was determined to salvage something from the debacle. She loved to experience new places and she was not about to mope around a hotel or give furious interviews to the press when the sparkling city of San Francisco beckoned. She saw films, or movies, as they were called in Frisco, and she socialised with new friends such as Gertrude Artelr from Neptune Beach who wished Mina, 'All kinds of good luck to you always' in her album.

The city had a surprisingly large number of theatres and dance halls, and local newspapers were reporting on a new style of music which they disparagingly referred to as 'jazz', frequently pairing it with words such as obscene, indecent or demoralising. Mina visited the site of the 1915 World Fair, where many of the buildings—most notably the stunning Palace of Fine Arts— was still standing.

She and Fanny swam in the indoor salt water Lurline Baths and the famous Sutro Baths, heralded as the world's largest indoor swimming complex and housing no less than six salt water pools and one freshwater pool. They had their photographs taken on the shores of San Francisco Bay and, despite the continuing disparaging newspaper reports, they were not short of admirers. In her postcards home, Mina made no reference to the bad feeling which now permeated the tour, or indeed of Durack's cavalier attitude towards the local swimmers and promoters. This could be taken to mean that the American press was exaggerating the situation and stirring the pot to provoke a response. Or it could indicate that Mina was smart enough to distance herself from Fanny and the ensuing bad press. Perhaps she was equally irate at the sudden cancellation of the tour by Mrs McIntosh but more aware than Fanny seemed to be of the advantages of staying silent.

On 10 July, five weeks after the women had arrived in San Francisco, the *Chronicle* carried the headline, 'Durack and Wylie want to swim at Red Cross

Show.' But before they could do so, the paper reported, there were some 'big buts' that had to be settled:

'First of all, the Durack/Wylie combination insists the meet must be held as a red cross benefit. Secondly, they declare they are willing to swim against their own records but will positively refuse to appear in competition against any of the local mermaids.'

Given that the carnival, which had been in preparation for some time, was already established as a red cross benefit, the first demand from Mina and Durack was superfluous. The second, that they would not compete against any local swimmers, was in no way driven by a fear of being beaten—Durack had previously boasted to the press how she was ready to break her own world records. It smacks of belligerence, a refusal to give the authorities, the press and the public, the showdown they desired because the tour had not been reinstated. Regardless, the Australian demands were met, and the swimming gala went ahead at the enormous Sutro Baths on 20 July. Such was the demand for tickets to see the 'Antipodean Mermaids' finally swim that a staggering $1,200 was presented to the Red Cross.

The following morning, the *San Francisco Chronicle* reported that 'Fanny Durack of Sydney, Australia, finally condescended to swim in San Francisco, and hung up a new world record for 220 yards.' Fanny's new record of 2 minutes and 37 seconds was a good two seconds faster than her previous title, causing even the cynical *Chronical* reporter to observe:

'And gentlemen of the jury, that girl can certainly swim. She used the Australian crawl and she ploughed through the water like a torpedo. She does not kick as fast or as often as the American swimmers, but she gets a lot of power in her slow kick. She has a powerful arm stroke and as she swims as straight down the tank as an arrow, she loses no time.'

Vindicated at last. Fanny Durack was still the Champion Lady Swimmer of the World. Interesting to note that the reporter from the *Chronicle* was already noticing differences between the crawl stroke of the Americans and the Australians: the influence of Louis B. Handley in New York was beginning to make its mark. Mina also triumphed at the gala and her stroke too, was analysed by the reporter.

'Mina Wylie, also from Australia, equalled her own world record of 1 minute 25 seconds for 100 yards in the breast stroke. She has a knack of doubling in the water and then fairly springing through it like a frog in a hurry to go somewhere. She made the first 50 yards in 39 seconds.'

As well as reinforcing their reputation as world class swimmers, the Red Cross gala in no small way restored the tarnished reputation of the Australian women. Previous slights were cast aside as swimming enthusiasts marvelled at the wonder of Durack and the expertise of Mina's breast stroke, a stroke not utilised in American competition at this time. The enormous publicity and press columns given over to Durack and Mina in San Francisco had made them local celebrities and three days after the gala, Mina encountered the famous film star, Fatty Arbuckle (later more known for his infamy[49]) and he willingly signed her autograph album:

'To my friend from the land of the kangaroo/ May the best of luck always follow you/ If I wasn't afraid of getting thin/ I might challenge you to take a swim. Yours truly, Roscoe "Fatty" Arbuckle, July 23rd 1918, San Francisco.'

Where she met him remains a mystery but fraternising with film stars and being feted as a celebrity was exactly what Mina had had in mind when she had pictured herself in the USA, the land of opportunity.

*

Amongst the souvenirs Mina brought back from her this USA trip was an edition of the *World Traveller* magazine, notable for a lengthy article on Annette Kellerman. The Kellerman article is entitled 'At the Traps' and opens with a large photograph of Kellerman brandishing a rifle under the caption, 'Annette Kellerman: Can she Shoot as Straight as she can Swim'. A touch inconsistent for a woman who promoted her hyper-femininity at every opportunity (and a little crass to be sporting a rifle in the same issue as a feature on returned soldiers recovering from wounds inflicted by the same weapon).

The magazine was an advance publicity stunt to promote Kellerman's new aquatic feature film, 'Queen of the Sea', which was due for release later that year. How tantalising for Mina to be in such close proximity to her idol and yet have no way of gaining her attention and it may have been the local buzz around town concerning the upcoming movie which prompted Mina to write to the Boston based journalist, Al Lippe, with plans of her own. Lippe was the sporting promoter who had met Mina on a trip to Sydney the previous year when he had become friendly with Henry through regular visits to Wylie's Baths.

Mina's initial letter to Lippe has not survived but his reply indicates that she had contacted him seeking an alternative to the stalemate which had stranded her in San Francisco with nothing to do and no way of earning an income. Perhaps the few weeks she had spent in the USA had opened her eyes to the more numerous opportunities available to women outside Australia, and her fleeting brush with the film industry in the (rotund) form of Fatty Arbuckle would certainly have fuelled any visions of Hollywood stardom. Lippe's letter is dated 25 June 1918, and suggests Mina's back up plan followed the path worn first by Kellerman. Lippe writes:

'How would a vaudeville proposition suite (sic) your friends and yourself? Say, for example, were we to secure bookings for twenty or thirty weeks in big time. In that way I feel quite certain that a goodly sum of money would be realised. With Miss Durack holding the worlds championship and you unquestionably just slightly behind her there can be no question as to the attraction. Just at present I am conferring with a man regarding such a proposition but of course will await definite word from you regarding that phase of the matter. A vaudeville act will entail the presence of a tank and other paraphernalia. Have you ladies with you a tank? … Miss Durack has received a world of publicity here in the East and I feel quite confident that the biggest booking agency in the country will be pleased to book an act in which you girls are the features.'

Lippe seemed to be under the impression that Mina and Durack were in the USA for an exhibition tour, and not to defend their Olympic honours. The idea that they would be travelling with a tank suitable for public performances is slightly bizarre as neither woman was known in the way that Kellerman was for vaudeville style appearances. But Lippe is certainly convinced that both women are highly marketable products in this new and fast-growing commodity culture. The fact that the promoter seriously believed the two women could sustain a six-month tour is indicative of the popularity of women's swimming at this time, fuelled by the craze for Kellerman's watery celluloid adventures.

Without Mina's reply, it is impossible to know how seriously she considered Lippe's offer of an exhibition tour. Her initial approach may have come out of a desire to make the best of the impasse in San Francisco and I do get the distinct impression that when Mina left Sydney in May, she had every intention of making a new life for herself in the USA. I suspect she was restless in Sydney and acutely aware of the fact that she was nothing more than a big fish in a small pond.

Mina had never lacked ambition and the success a decade earlier of Alice Cavill, an Australian swimmer who gave exhibitions in San Francisco before joining a circus troupe, was proof that an exciting career as a professional swimmer was not an unrealistic pipe dream. Mina's enduring fixation with Annette Kellerman was not merely the obsession of an adoring fan: in Kellerman, Mina saw a reflection of herself and the potential for a different life. Even if she finished up as an instructor at a prestigious swimming club in San Francisco or New York, it was still more inspiring than languishing in Sydney, a city she now regarded as little more than a country town. The letter from Al Lippe, however vague it may seem, did appear to be offering Mina the first step towards a whole new life as a performer.

'We might end up in Hollywood, Fanny. Like Annette Kellerman.'

'I don't want to dive into a stupid tank and show off like she does. That's not real swimming.'

'But they won't take me without you.'

'I want to go home, Mina.'

'Well, I don't.'

The Lippe letter clearly illustrates how women's competitive swimming was fast becoming regarded as emblematic of modernity which, in turn, was intrinsically linked to the growing commercialisation of the female body. Lippe was well aware of the insatiable public demand for Kellerman and her Perfect Body, and his vaudeville proposal was blatantly cashing in on this current craze. His letter also indicates that by 1918, the female swimmer had gone from being a shady incarnation of a certain strand of erotica, banished to the seedy halls of burlesque, to a respected and legitimate public entertainer.

When Mina first appeared in front of male spectators in Stockholm, she was, whether she was aware of it or not, engaging with modern ideas which advocated female display over invisibility. By 1918, it was clear she had more fully embraced the notion of herself as an exhibit and was open to suggestions that large amounts of money could be made from marketing her body.

In the absence of any further communication between Mina and Al Lippe, I can only speculate as to why the exhibition tour, so promisingly lucrative on paper, did not eventuate. Fanny Durack had never shown any desire to emulate Kellerman with a vaudeville type career and without Durack, Mina was possibly not considered a big enough drawcard on which sell a nationwide tour. There was also the question of the Olympics, which would undoubtedly resume once the war was over.

If Mina accepted any money at all for an exhibition appearance then her amateur status would be revoked, rendering her ineligible to compete. The memory of the 1912 glory had not dimmed, and perhaps Mina weighed up both propositions and found the prospect of Olympic competition more attractive. She could always pick up the USA vaudeville/film career later, hopefully with another medal under her belt. Perhaps too, the thought of what Florence would have to say about her only daughter embarking on a career as an aquatic showgirl was a sobering dose of reality.

*

The stumbling blocks between the Australian and American swimming authorities proved impossible to resolve and on the 3rd of August, the three Australian women boarded the RMS Ventura for the voyage home. Mina had had a tantalising glimpse of the modern marvel that was the USA but had only swum in a charity fundraiser. Her visions of record-breaking glory had not eventuated and the Hollywood career remained a fantasy.

Back in Sydney, the swimming duo refused to discuss the American experience with the press, leading to speculation and rumour concerning who was to blame. The American newspapers hinted that Durack had demanded excessive expenses for herself and her chaperone sister, and the Australian press retaliated by pointing a finger at the AAU and tour promoter, William Unmack, citing poor leadership and a lack of preparation.

There were grumblings from the NSW LASA that the American swimming authorities had communicated only with the men of the ASA in Australia, deliberately excluding the women's Association but ultimately, no one accepted responsibility for the embarrassing mess. Relations between the two swimmers and the NSW LASA were tense, but only a few days after the women arrived home, devastating news from the Western Front rendered the past differences inconsequential.

Golden Boy of Australian swimming, Cecil Healy, had enlisted in the Australian Imperial Force in September of 1915, and after service in Egypt and France, he transferred to officer training school at Trinity College in Cambridge.

He was commissioned in June 1918, and on 29 August, just two months before the end of the war, Healy joined the roll call of Doomed Youth when he was killed in France. This was a profound shock, both to those who knew him, and to the general public. Cecil Healy was the one man who should have survived—Australia needed his like as a shining example—and yet, there was something inevitable about the death of this much-loved swimmer. As if his sacrifice was the only appropriate ending to a life so faultless, so exemplary, that there could be no other outcome. This had to happen to give Australia the textbook sporting hero the country so desperately needed.

Healy's death prompted an outpouring of public grief not witnessed since the death in 1905 of teenage swimming sensation, Barney Kieran, with tributes filling endless pages of newspapers nationwide. The public was reminded of the admirable display of good sportsmanship (mistakenly) attributed to Healy at the 1912 Olympics, and he was held up as a glorious example of the laudable Australian characteristics embodied in the values of mateship and fair play.[50] There were, in fact, so many tributes and obituaries written for him, that they were compiled into a book entitled *Cecil Healy in Memoriam,* which was published in 1919.[51]

If the eulogising of Cecil Healy seemed excessive, it does give an idea of the position sport and (male) athletes now held within the national identity discourse. The Sporting Nation was a moniker the Australian population was eager to embrace but there was a tacit understanding that the 'sporting' part of 'nation' referred to (white) men and male sport. As the First World War reshaped the soldier into a national icon and claimed the beaches of Gallipoli as the place where Australia came of age, the ideal of masculinity as an essential (and defining) national characteristic was further consolidated.

Women had no real place in a national sporting discourse and war was unequivocally men's work and men's glory. By equating masculinity with a concept of national identity intrinsically linked to sport and/or war, Australian women were left with two choices. They either stayed on the side-lines and allowed themselves to be denied a place in the nationalism discourse, or they submitted to a male definition of nationhood which designated women inferior.

If they chose the latter and engaged in the Sporting Nation construct, it was as spectators of men's sport and with the full knowledge that women's sport was considered meaningless compared to the serious business of men's sport. Cecil

Healy was deified because he embodied the consummate Australian male: he was the heroic, courageous Digger and the selfless Olympian combined.

All that aside, Healy did seem to be genuinely liked and well respected amongst his colleagues and peers, and his death shattered the Sydney swimming community. He had certainly visited Wylie's Baths on more than one occasion and had an easy-going relationship with Henry, going back to the Bronte Baths days, almost two decades ago. Tributes reminded readers of his displays of surfing on Freshwater Beach with Kahanamoku in 1915, and the community at Manly, Healy's swimming club, mourned deeply. A memorial service was held at St Mary's Cathedral in Sydney and although she did not save a mass card from the service, I feel certain she, and Henry, would have attended. And mourned.

Healy had been one of the few male sporting personalities to come out in public support of Mina and Durack during the mixed bathing controversy in 1912, and photographic evidence from Stockholm suggests Mina and Healy were good friends. Certainly, judging by the E.S. Marks images, they made each other laugh. Perhaps it was the class divide that prevented their friendship from blossoming into anything more, or perhaps there was simply no desire for anything deeper from either of them. Their relationship emanated from that exclusive connection which develops between team mates, a unique bond which non-athletes cannot understand. Whatever they went on to do in life, and it was generally accepted that Cecil Healy would achieve great things, the members of the 1912 Australasian swimming team would remain forever linked by their shared experience of Stockholm.

It is impossible to know how far Mina's experience of the First World War shaped her later life, but it may have contributed to the fact that she never married. Not necessarily due to heartbreak over the death of Cecil Healy—there is nothing to suggest they were anything more than good friends. But in the years following the war, Australian women of Mina's generation encountered an empty space which had previously been filled with the vibrant young men who had escorted them on outings and filled their dance cards.

There is, of course, no reason why Mina should have married, except that in this era, it was unusual for her not to. Many returned servicemen had romanticised visions of the life they would come home to and were anxious to marry and build the security of their own family. They subsequently complained bitterly of women's new-found independence, their increased presence in the workforce as bank tellers or clerks—formerly male positions—and their reluctance to marry.

Mina was one of a growing band of women whose modern ideas concerning independence versus marriage earned them the 'bachelor girl' label, a more polite precursor to the 1980s 'career bitch' put down. Mina and her like had discovered new freedoms in this modern, permissive society, freedoms they were not about to relinquish for the drudgery of marriage and child rearing.

But did she, I wonder, take out the 1912 autograph album and lightly trace her finger over the words inscribed by Cecil Healy in Stockholm? Did she recall the poolside exchange—'It means you talk a lot, Miss Wylie'—and see again the wink he threw in her direction as she returned to her place in the crowd, clutching a red leather box. Did they compare their respective silver medals, I wonder? Perhaps she had indeed harboured a vision of attaining a more significant place in Healy's life, and his signature in her autograph album was now a poignant reminder of the space between what was, and what might have been.

Chapter 8

Dear Mum, This is a popular holiday resort and is 3 hours run in the train from New York, so we came down early this morning and are now going back. Mina.

Postcard of 'Boardwalk near Million Dollar Pier', Atlantic City, NJ, 1919

In 2008, Meredith Clarke gave the final three boxes of Mina's possessions to the Mitchell Library. The writing case and the towels from Wylie's Baths are in this collection, and there are family photographs and more postcards. What I was not prepared for, was to find items of Mina's clothing. Inexplicably, there are five silk dresses nestling amongst canvas flotation aids, Harry's shirts and Henry's Masons portraits. The first question in my mind was the obvious one: why save these particular dresses? Was there some meaning or memory held within the fabric that only Mina knew of?

We are all guilty to some extent of holding onto items of clothing out of sentiment long after we have stopped wearing them. Relegated to the back of the wardrobe, the item is so intrinsically entwined with memories of when we wore it that it is impossible to donate it to the charity shop. The school blazer. The leather jacket that asserted our rebellion. The swim suit in team colours. The T shirt that testified to our presence at Live Aid.

A former pupil of Mina's from Pymble Ladies College described how, 'in cooler weather, Miss Wylie always wore her Olympic blazer'.[52] Her reasons for this were less to do with keeping warm and more bound up with pride in her past and a desire to establish status over her young charges. Holding on to an Olympic team blazer makes perfect sense, but five silk dresses?

Like so many women before the advent of disposable ready-made clothing, Mina made her own clothes and I hazard a guess that she made four out of the five dresses herself. Not being a fashion historian, I cannot accurately date them but to my untrained eye they suggest the early 1930s. They are simple and practical day dresses, mainly in red and with variations in the style of collar and the length of the sleeves. The fifth dress, however, is a garment for a special occasion. It is made from black silk and has the dropped waist and loose tie reminiscent of the 1920s, or even the late teens.

It is elegantly unadorned, save for a row of blue buttons on the skirt of the dress and decorative buttonholes outlined in pale blue piping. The word which immediately came to mind on seeing the dress, was chic. I believe, and there is absolutely nothing in the way of a label or a diary entry to support this, that Mina purchased this dress, or had it made for her, in the USA. I imagine this because the dress appears to embody the hedonistic and modern America that had Mina in its thrall.

This stunning black creation is a lifetime away from the demure frills and lace her mother insisted she wore only a few years previously, and it was integral to Mina's emergence as a modern, independent woman. If she wanted to have a career which rivalled Annette Kellerman's, it was imperative that she looked the part. The silk dress is exactly the kind of garment that Mina's film star idols would wear on a night out in San Francisco, and perhaps she saw it as a metaphor for the life that could potentially be hers if she grabbed the opportunities offered by people such as Al Lippe.

'Your Dad will have something to say,' said Fanny, rolling her eyes. 'Spending all that money on a dress.'

The black dress may have been intended by Mina to draw attention to herself as a celebrity, but in wearing it she was also pointedly highlighting her femininity. Perhaps, like Kellerman, she was deliberately sending a message to the critics who denounced the athletic woman as masculine and unattractive to the opposite sex. I wonder if this was what she was wearing when Fatty Arbuckle signed her autograph book. Did she have it on when she went dancing in a San Francisco jazz hall? And who was it who rested their hands on her waist just above the line of decorative blue buttons?

I know she wore this dress many, many times, because the material under the arms has been replaced more than once. Perhaps it was this exact dress that accounts for the full dance cards saved alongside the theatre programmes. Photographs of Mina in later life show a small, rather stout woman, who would never have fitted into this black silk garment even if it had been a suitable outfit for an older woman to wear. Yet she held onto it.

I imagine it folded carefully in tissue paper, nestling amongst the mothballs in a black and white David Jones box underneath her bed. If Mina ever drew the box out and tentatively lifted the lid, the cacophony of music and voices and cheers and laughter threatened to burst forth and overwhelm her. There she was, the girl with shining eyes behind the shop counter ... 'Mom and I are sure excited about seeing you swim, Miss Wylie.' The young men with their endless 'yes Ma'am's', and Al Lippe with his big plans, 'Say, for example, were we to secure bookings for twenty or thirty weeks in big time ...'

This dress had symbolised what was possible and somewhere among the creases of the black silk and the fraying pale blue piping lay the remnants of the life that could have, should have, been. Fantasies of greatness entombed in the folds of material like an insect in amber.

Many years ago, my mother pressed onto me a silk and lace dress which had belonged to her in the 1960s. Perhaps, like Mina, she had made it herself as there was no label anywhere and the pale green tulle bordering the neckline had been attached by hand. I remember as a child in the seventies watching my mother pinning paper patterns onto pieces of material which would later emerge as stunning evening dresses for the formal occasions she so delighted in.

One memorable creation had gold lame sleeves which shimmered as she moved, and I saw her as a glorious multi-coloured butterfly, spreading her wings wide so the world could appreciate her magnificence. The lace dress she gave me was understated in its glory, but undeniably intended to draw attention to the wearer with a tight bodice designed to emphasise and hug every curve of a womanly body. I always intended to have it framed against a dark background edged with a thick gilt frame, creating a new item of beauty from the old. Because it was important to my mother that the dress not be thrown away.

Like Mina and the black silk, memories were obviously embedded in every stitch. In later life my mother suffered severe depression and anxiety, finally succumbing to the twilight zone of dementia. I'd like to be able to look at the dress in a frame and imagine her in her glorious prime, entering a nightclub carrying a silver handbag, a red lipstick and an air of invincibility. I'd like to know that there were nights of fun in her younger days and the later frustration and misery were not the defining characteristics of her entire life.

I'd like to have seen Mina wearing the black silk dress, dancing the cake walk in a San Francisco night club. Dreaming of Hollywood and believing the world was her oyster.

*

In November of 1918, the four-year-long bloodbath in Europe finally ended. Life, the feeling was, could go back to normal. Or at least, a different kind of normal, given that few families or communities in Australia had escaped the conflict unscathed. Limbless and shell-shocked veterans haunted the streets and a framed photograph of a young man in uniform dominated countless mantelpieces. Best to move on, was the general feeling. It's over. And Australia had acquitted herself admirably.

Despite the unadulterated slaughter, the beaches of Gallipoli were hailed by authorities as the place where Australia came of age and took her place amongst other leading nations. A new confidence began to infuse the country, a growing sense of Australia as a fully-fledged, independent nation with its own set of characteristics and national traits. The shadow of colonialism and the shame of the 'convict stain' were, at last, remnants of a past incarnation and the Australian population looked to the future with renewed self-esteem and assurance.

One score, however, remained to be settled, and only a matter of months after Mina and Fanny Durack arrived back in Sydney from the failed US tour, talks were back on concerning a second visit. Taking into account the bad feeling all round and the reported poor behaviour of Fanny Durack, it is surprising that a return visit was on the cards so quickly, especially as no individual or organisation had yet stepped up and claimed responsibility for the fiasco the first tour had become. It also seems curious that Durack was so keen to return to the USA, given her previous questionable behaviour which had been well reported in the San Francisco press.

Mina's eagerness to return is completely understandable. She wanted to be Annette Kellerman and her brief sojourn on the West Coast had whetted her appetite for the rest of the country. She longed to see New York. To stand on Fifth Avenue and look towards Central Park. To bask in the lights of the theatre marquees on Broadway. And the fact remained that the Australian women had still not proved they remained the world champions. Until they defeated Eppie's swimmers from New York, the 'unbeatable' reputation of Mina and Fanny was not secure.

That they were so keen to go back to the USA after the disastrous press which engulfed the 1918 visit, does suggest that the two Australians were utterly convinced they were invincible. Perhaps their success at the Red Cross gala at the Sutro Baths in July had given them both a false sense of security. Added to this was the fact that, thanks to the late James E. Sullivan and his searing antipathy towards women in sport, no one outside of the USA had actually seen their female swimmers compete. An air of mystery hung over the young women of Eppie's WSA. They were posting impressive races times, but Mina and Durack chose to believe the local hype regarding Australian superiority in worldwide swimming. Clearly, it never occurred to anyone in the Australian swimming community that the experiments in stroke technique by Louis B. Handley at the WSA might be effective. The general feeling amongst sporting authorities, and Mina and Durack themselves, was that the Americans needed to be reminded of who were the better swimmers. Individually, and as a nation. What no one stopped to point out, was that it was now seven years since the Olympics in Stockholm, a lifetime in terms of many sporting careers.

In June 1919, the *New York Times* carried the headline, 'Women Swimmers Coming'. The tour was on again. Who had organised this is difficult to ascertain, and the *Times* appeared uncertain as to whether this trip would involve competitions or purely exhibition appearances. The vagueness infusing the *Times* report should have rung familiar alarm bells. The reporter reminded readers of the issues dogging the first tour with regard to Mina and Durack's lack of 'credentials' and their apparent refusal to comply with AAU rules.

If that wasn't ominous enough, Sydney reporter W. F. Corbett, writing in *The Referee* on 4 June 1919, claimed that Mina and Durack were about to embark on another 'wild goose chase'. Exactly where W. F. Corbett was receiving his information from is a mystery, but he frequently peppers his reports with phrases such as 'I learn from a reliable source' and 'It has become known to me'. In his 4th June report, Corbett claims that the AAU had already made clear their disapproval of the proposed tour, due to a Mr George Dowsing being cited as tour manager: the presence of a manager, of course, implied that the swimmers were professional.

How W. F. Corbett was able to predict that the second tour would not be given AAU approval is unclear, but if he had access to that information, why did Mina and Durack not have it too? Or if they did, what possessed them to set sail given the fiasco of the previous year?

A report which appeared in the *New York Times* the following month, claimed that the AAU had officially withheld their sanction for the tour before the women left Sydney in June, and Mina and Durack were well aware of the concerns the US sporting authority had with regard to the presence of manager George Dowsing. If that was indeed the case—and again, the surviving reports contradict each other and point fingers of blame in all directions (not helped by W. F. Corbett and his 'reliable sources' in *The Referee*) it does seem a spectacularly short sighted or ill-advised move for the women to make. But make it they did, leaving Sydney bound for San Francisco on 4 June 1919.

In all the reports that I have read of the 1919 USA tour, the NSW LASA barely rates a mention and yet, as amateur Australian swimmers, Mina and Durack were still bound by the rules of their governing body. The bad publicity from the 1918 debacle may have prompted the NSW LASA to steer well clear of a second tour with the same two women—or one of them, at least—who had publicly denounced an individual and an organisation which had offered nothing less than unstinting support for almost a decade. Marion McIntosh disappears from Mina's archive after 1916, the period when they were attending theatre together and Mina was invited to the Red Cross benefits at 'Benoni', suggesting that McIntosh's refusal to sanction her own LASA swimmers in 1918 brought a decisive end to the friendship.

As head of the LASA, the organisation's dispute with Mina and Durack placed McIntosh in a difficult position. The next Olympic games would take place in Antwerp in 1920 and Durack was certain to attend, in all likelihood with Mina Wylie as team mate. If McIntosh was indeed livid at Mina and Durack for bringing the NSW LASA into disrepute with their actions in the USA, she still had to be seen to support her members. And in 1919, Mina and Fanny were still the fastest female swimmers in the world with the potential to bestow enormous glory upon the NSW LASA.

Sympathy has to lie with Florence, who had a headstrong, badly behaved daughter in one corner, and a snubbed public figure, who just happened to head the leading women's swimming authority in the country, in the other. Why couldn't Mina just swim, Florence wondered. Why was something she had loved so much increasingly accompanied by betrayals, accusations and harsh words. But hadn't Henry warned her of her daughter's 'big head' seven years ago?

Interestingly, when Mina and Durack left Sydney in 1919 bound for San Francisco, they appear to have been travelling unchaperoned, another indication that the puritanical Victorian values which had controlled women's behaviour for decades was entering the final death throes. Perhaps it was agreed all round that policing the personal lives of two women approaching thirty who were seasoned travellers and world-famous celebrities was a little insulting. Just how famous the two women swimmers were, was apparent during a brief stopover in

Hawaii where they were besieged by reporters and photographers. 'Fanny Durack and Mina Wylie Spend Day Here' trumpeted the front page of *The Honolulu Star Bulletin* on June 17th.

The women were pictured with Duke Kahanamoku on the front page of *The Pacific Commercial Advertiser* on June 18th, above an article reporting that 'Duke watched the mermaids with a critical eye and said that their strokes were as good, if not better, than ever before.' The report also made the claim that Durack had received a recent offer of '$25 000 to swim for a moving picture concern, but she has refused them all.' This may have been a complete fabrication, but in the light of Annette Kellerman's escalating stardom and the insatiable public appetite for her underwater movies, it is not inconceivable that Durack would have been approached by a film studio.

How Mina felt about this is easy to guess. If anyone was securing a Hollywood contract out of this trip, it was not Fanny Durack.

Kahanamoku joined the SS Sonoma and again sailed with the Australian swimmers to San Francisco. With the three medallists from Stockholm reunited, the absence of Cecil Healy was palpable. Where there had been four Olympic medallists, now there were three. As the ship sailed towards San Francisco, the trio shared memories of Sweden, the competition in Hamburg, Duke's visit to Australia … and the unbearable tragedy of the trenches in France.

Duke's friendship with Cecil undoubtedly had roots in Healy's magnanimous refusal to swim in the Olympic final unless the American swimmers were granted their own semi-final, and this gratitude extended to the fact that Healy accepted Duke as an equal in an era when racial hierarchies were rigidly adhered to. Undoubtedly, it was Healy's very public admiration for Duke when he visited Australia that contributed to a more respectful level of reporting in the press than would have been given to any other non-white athlete. Perhaps too, Mina and Durack had become friends with Duke purely because Healy set the standard to which the others aspired.

On arrival in San Francisco, Mina, Durack and Kahanamoku checked into the Hotel St Francis on Union Square. The media interest in the Australian duo was every bit as keen as it had been in Hawaii and a staged photoshoot of the women swimming in the bay resulted in a front page spread on the *San Francisco Call and Post*. The bad feeling from the previous year seemed to have dissipated and the impending showdown between Durack and the bright new star of the WSA, Ethelda Bleibtrey, was eagerly discussed in the local press. Mina renewed acquaintances, wrote postcards home and, I like to believe, shopped and danced. This time it would work out, she thought. This time, I'm staying.

The AAU concerns over the presence of 'manager' George Dowsing, refused to go away, not helped by Mina and Durack's insistence, according to *The New York Times* on 17 July that, 'their manager's expenses should be defrayed by the clubs where they appear'. This same article noted that Dowsing's presence and managerial role was contrary to the rules of the AAU, causing the American sporting authorities to question the eligibility of the Australian women to compete in the USA. In other words, Mina and Fanny Durack were again being accused of not adhering to the rules of amateurism by the very same authority which had invited them to compete. It was the same story, different players—a manager over a chaperone. And unbelievably, the same stalemate quickly arose.

The AAU refused to sanction the tour and Mina and Durack were stranded in San Francisco waiting for someone to sort things out. *The New York Times* did, however, report that:

'Many sportsmen have entered a protest against the Athletic Union's action declaring it to be a blot on the United States record of fair play.'

This could be taken as a veiled message to the Australian sporting authorities, as it was beginning to look as if the women were being systematically and unfairly targeted by the unwelcoming AAU which consistently projected an alternately dismissive or overbearing attitude towards the Australian women. Although it is easy to interpret this behaviour as a hangover from the late James Sullivan's pronounced revulsion towards female athletes, it may actually have had little to do with the women themselves and been tied up with a male power struggle going on across two continents. The AAU was flexing its considerable muscle and reminding the Australian authorities who held the reins of power where international sport was concerned. If the Australian women would not conform to the rules of the AAU, they would not swim in the USA. End of story.

When, at the end of July, the Canadian Amateur Swimming Association announced it would not allow Mina and Durack to swim in the prearranged carnivals in Toronto and Montreal due to concerns over their amateur status, a sense of déjà vu began to prevail. Back in Sydney, W. F. Corbett at *The Referee* claimed to be on speaking terms with the man at the centre of this year's row, George Dowsing, who was apparently 'wild at the turn things had taken.' Dowsing, according to Corbett, was unable to explain the situation clearly and so Corbett 'formed my own conclusions'. In a lengthy article on 30 July, Corbett pointed out that only the governing body of the country sending athletes abroad, in this case the ASA, or LASA, could deal with the matter of expenses for a visiting athlete.

Mina and Durack's demand that clubs hosting them in the USA should pay Dowsing's expenses was, as the AAU correctly maintained, not in accordance with accepted regulations. Corbett supported this and noted how easy it would be, if these rules were not in place, for an amateur to become what he termed a 'camouflaged professional'. What he was referring to, was an underhand way of athletes making money from their sport by channelling costs through a third party. This was an open secret in some sports, especially those where betting was involved, but it seems a stretch to infer that this was the situation here. If anyone was seeking to make money from the Wylie/Durack USA tour, it was Dowsing himself. He had already complained to Corbett that he was 'considerably out of pocket over the matter'.

On 6 August, two whole months after the women had departed Australia, W. F. Corbett was back in print in *The Referee* reporting that 'the girls' (despite being almost 30, Mina and Fanny were never referred to by the press as 'women', always 'girls'. And invariably, 'mermaids') 'are almost on the verge of turning professional in order that they may show American swimming enthusiasts they are real swimming champions'. How much of that is true is difficult to say.

Yes, the two women were incredibly frustrated at again having a tour in place, and again being told they would not be allowed to compete, but I find it hard to believe that with the Olympics only a year away, Durack would seriously consider turning professional. Mina, possibly. But only, I think, if Al Lippe or some other promoter was able to definitively offer her a deal, a tour and a lucrative contract in which she was the main attraction.

The Referee in Sydney was slightly behind with the news from the USA, where newspapers had announced a week previously that Mina and Durack had fired their manager/promoter, George Dowsing, and agreed to 'tour the US under the auspices of the Amateur Athletic Union'. [53] On a train speeding out of San Francisco on 5 August, Mina balanced her black leather writing case on her knee and wrote to Henry:

'My dear Dad, We left San Francisco this morning and are now on our way to Chicago which takes three days and three nights. We have a compartment to ourselves which is very nice and well we can do with it as we are tired out. We only got word from the AAU at 1.30 yesterday to be on the 9 am train today so we had to hurry up. As you will see by the cuttings I have sent you, Dowsing is not with us and we are travelling alone on a tour arranged by the AAU. We waited five weeks for him to try and get permission and he could not get the sanction, so the AAU asked us if we would go with them, so we would have had to return if we did not accept so we decide (sic) to make the trip. There is a chance of the AAU refunding fares to us from Australia and if we get them of course we will hand it over to Dowsing. We have had to keep ourselves for the most of the time except he has paid the hotel up till a fortnight ago but from today we get 7 dollars and 50 cents per day for board and lodgings exclusive of the travelling tickets so we should be alight from now on…'

The reassurances concerning money were welcome as Mina's trips to the USA were placing a considerable financial strain on the Wylie family coffers. In the account books for the Baths, Henry noted how much Mina's career was costing the family. In May 1918, entries read, 'Mina fare USA £20', later, 'Mina USA £3/10' and on 1 July, 'Return fare Mina £18. There was also 'Mina cable, Mina telephone', another £8. Having a sporting celebrity for a daughter was one thing, paying for it, was another.

After the 72-hour train journey, Mina and Fanny arrived in Chicago and immediately started off on the wrong foot by announcing they had never agreed to swim scratch events, i.e., races where all the competitors start at the same time. This was clearly not the case, as the Chicago press had been forecasting record-breaking swims in scratch races for well over a week. Memories from the previous year of this type of behaviour from the two Australians began to surface, and a curt telegram from Frederick Rubien of the AAU, insisting the women swim competitive races or the tour would be cancelled, swiftly terminated the argument.

Both Mina and Durack swam on the second day of the carnival and won their races comfortably, but they continued to be argumentative, with Durack complaining that the hectic tour schedule left her no time to train for championship races—an odd assertion to make given that she had been stranded in San Francisco for five whole weeks with little else to do but train for the impending tour.

The next scheduled stop on the tour was New York, and Mina and Fanny arrived on Thursday, 14 August, two days before the feverishly anticipated battle with Ethelda Bleibtrey and her WSA team mates. The two Australians were not impressed when they learned that the scheduled races at Manhattan Beach would not take place in an enclosed pool, as they had presumed, but in a course marked out in the open water. Officials from the WSA gallantly tried to make amends by offering the Australians time to train on the ocean course but Fanny, somewhat petulantly, refused, stating that she preferred to practice in an enclosed pool.

The Captain of the WSA, Mrs Muhlemberg, invited Fanny and Mina to train with the WSA women in the Association pool that evening, but again, the offer was declined. Going well above and beyond the call of duty, Mrs Muhlemberg then arranged for the Australians to have exclusive use of a public pool closest to where they were staying, in order to prepare for the carnival on the 16th. That was more to Fanny's liking.

Prior to the arrival of the women in New York, the AAU had convened in a special meeting to discuss ways to avoid a repeat of the Chicago confusion over which races the Australians would participate in. Mina and Durack were even asked to nominate which races they would prefer compete in and the programme was altered accordingly. With the tour finally underway, both the AAU and the women of the WSA were keen to do everything they could to accommodate the demanding Australians, especially as a huge crowd was expected at Manhattan Beach on Saturday. Mina and Durack, however, seemed ungrateful at best, and possessing an overblown sense of entitlement at worst.

I wonder what Eppie made of this peevish behaviour. Eppie the intellectual, the committed feminist, the leader, the inspirer, the ethicist … what did she think of the two young Australians who demanded special treatment and behaved like over indulged movie stars? Perhaps she had been forewarned by her friend Marion McIntosh as to what she might expect from the two women with their inflated egos and casual disregard of authority. I suspect Eppie wisely stayed in the background, as she is not mentioned in any newspaper reports of the races in New York, and nor does her signature appear in Mina's US album.

*

In the five years since the death of James E. Sullivan, women's swimming had established a firm foothold and a huge fan base in the USA. Sporting events were becoming so popular that the transformation of a baseball game, or cricket in Australia, from a local sideshow into mass entertainment was well underway.

What was noticeable about this transformation was the number of women now in attendance amongst the spectators. Sporting fixtures were becoming family affairs, and marketed as such, with promoters anxious to capitalise on the increased leisure time resulting from the shorter working week.

In the E. S. Marks images from 1912, women are a pervasive presence amongst the crowds at Henley regatta in England, and in the Stadion and harbour pool at Stockholm. The social interaction between the sexes at sporting events was new and exciting, and a result of the increased visibility of women in public endorsed by the modernity movement. Just as Mina had thoroughly enjoyed mingling with male swimmers on the pool deck in Sweden and Germany, so too did the rapidly growing number of women attending sporting events relish the new opportunity to interact and flirt with men in the crowd. In 1919, America was on the cusp of the jazz age and 'anything goes' was a popular mantra. Large scale sporting events, such as the looming swimming carnival on Manhattan Beach, offered the perfect opportunity for a prolonged party, the enduring hallmark of the roaring twenties. Not everyone in the crowd necessarily had an interest in women's swimming, but they did all appreciate a fun day out.

On Saturday, 16 August, Manhattan Beach was packed with crowds numbering almost ten thousand. So many spectators clambered onto the pontoons positioned at the start of the course that the floating jetties threatened to capsize. The excited buzz reached fever pitch when the female competitors lined up for the 440yds freestyle, billed as the AAU quarter-mile championship title. This was the race the American crowd had waited three years to see.

The undefeated Australian Olympic and world champion against a rumoured bright new star of their own, Ethelda Bleibtrey. Tall and blonde with the shoulders of a serious swimmer, Bleibtrey was seventeen to Durack's twenty-nine, meaning she was just hitting her stride as Fanny was nearing retirement. More significantly, Bleibtrey had been coached exclusively by Louis B. Handley.

There were four starters in the race: Eleanor Uhl from Philadephia, Charlotte Boyle and Ethelda Bleibtrey from the New York WSA, and Fanny Durack. Frenzied cheering erupted as the women hit the water and Durack had her first bitter encounter with Handley's improved freestyle stroke. The Australian crawl swum by Durack emphasised fast continuous arms with short strokes and a slow kick, but Handley's stroke reversed this, utilising a six beat continuous kick with a slower and longer overarm pull.

Durack was outclassed from the first lap as Bleibtrey, almost casually, inched ahead. In the third lap, Durack managed to almost draw level but Bleibtrey simply accelerated her stroke and pulled further away. Charlotte Boyle overtook Durack in the final lap leaving her to finish in a humiliating third place. If Fanny Durack was stunned, so too was Mina, watching on the sidelines. This was a stroke they had never encountered and Mina was astute enough to realise that this new American crawl rendered the Australian crawl, of which their nation was so proud, redundant. Amidst the wild scenes of jubilation around her, Mina had the first inkling that her dream of the spotlight and herself as a shining star may have missed its moment.

The following day, *The New York Times* described the extraordinary scenes which followed the Bleibtrey trouncing of Fanny Durack.

'With Miss Bleibtrey's convincing victory there broke forth a spontaneous volley of applause which has seldom been surpassed at a swimming meet in this country. The crowd, largely composed of women, broke out as if at a given signal and filled the air with their shouts. To an individual they were thrilled by the superiority of Miss Bleibtrey over Miss Durack—the superiority of the American girl over the foreigner. Spectators slapped each other on the back, jumped into the air with glee: fondled and hugged one another, and sometimes—in mistake or out of pure unexalted joy—the man nearest them. Women officials of the meet forgot everything in the excitement of their unleashed joy while they showered hugs and kisses unstintedly on Miss Bleibtrey. Pandemonium reigned without hindrance.'

The unrestrained rejoicing may seem a touch excessive, but it is worth remembering that the controversial Nineteenth Amendment to the U.S. Constitution, which granted women the right to vote, had only passed in the Senate two months previously, on June 4th.[54] For the women who turned out in their thousands to watch a swimming race on the blustery North Atlantic ocean, their pride was not just in the achievements of Ethelda Bleibtrey and Charlotte Boyle. It was a growing sense of pride in themselves, as women. For here was the proof that they were just as good as men. Anything and everything now seemed possible.

Mina fared little better than Durack, trailing home in fourth place in the 100yd handicap, 'An Antipodean rout', as the *New York Times* succinctly described it. Durack displayed few signs of the supposed innate Australian quality of good sportsmanship, ungraciously blaming the cold water and rough conditions for her defeat. But three days later, in the dry dock of a Brooklyn shipyard which had been filled for the occasion, and in conditions described by *The New York Times* as ideal, matters did not improve for the Australian women. Alice Lord, another Louis B. Handley swimmer, easily defeated Durack in a 250yd handicap race, and Mina was beaten in her favoured breast stroke by twins Ruth and Eleanor Smith, who dead heated for first place.

The 125yd breaststroke race was also a handicap, as requested by Mina, but the twins posted a time that even with the handicap taken into consideration, was a staggering four seconds faster than Mina's. Seven thousand employees of the Todd shipyard had been given the afternoon off to watch the women race, making the defeats doubly humiliating for the Australians. Not only did the male shipyard employees witness their own swimmers triumph, they were also treated to a display of diving by Aileen Riggin and Helen Wainwright, who went on to win gold and silver respectively in the 3m springboard at the 1920 Antwerp Olympics.[55] An afternoon of entertainment by attractive, swimsuit clad young women over four hours of riveting, chipping and welding ... no wonder the workers of the Todd shipyard cheered.

It was an unusually subdued Mina and Fanny Durack who returned to their hotel that night. The gloss of the USA which had gleamed so brightly as Mina and Durack cavorted for photographers in San Francisco Bay had well and truly worn off. The Australians were embarrassed at their poor showings and ashamed at how effortlessly they were being beaten by the WSA swimmers. The cancellation of the 1916 Olympics had allowed the Australian medallists to rest on their laurels, and to believe the press hype that they were invincible. Which perhaps accounted for their demanding behaviour and complete lack of humility.

'Mrs McIntosh will love this,' said Fanny.

And Mina suspected she was right.

*

Following the Manhattan carnival and the afternoon at the Todd shipyard, there was absolutely no doubt that the worldwide women's swimming crown now rested firmly on the head of America. To rub salt even deeper into the wound, the Australian crawl, which had caused such a sensation in Stockholm in 1912, was now obsolete, overtaken by Louis B. Handley's six beat kick. And just in case there was anyone left who hadn't noticed, *The Washington Post* crowed that 'Miss Durack's defeat evidenced the supremacy of the American crawl, which was used by Miss Bleibtrey, over the Australian crawl, used by Miss Durack.'

This was more profound than Fanny Durack being beaten by someone swimming an experimental stroke, this struck at the foundation of Australia's self-proclamation of itself as a leading nation in international swimming. America had taken something invented (allegedly) by the Australians and improved upon it. The Americans were, in effect, turning Australia's own ammunition back on itself.

How Mina felt at witnessing the crowd of ten thousand spectators thronging the Manhattan beach is a mystery as, frustratingly, she did not keep a diary. I am intrigued as to what her impressions were of the grand architecture of Chicago and the towering New York skyscrapers. And I have to keep reminding myself that, contrary to her nonchalant postcard messages home, her presence in the greatest cities of the USA was extraordinary for the time. Here were two single women from Australia travelling unaccompanied to America to swim in carnivals which attracted crowds which numbered five figures. It was only seven years, remember, since the question of women joining the Australian Olympic swimming team had divided an entire nation. Yet here she was, casually informing her mother that she had popped down to Atlantic City for the day just because she could.

I believe that the fewer postcards she sent home from USA, compared to the dozens she posted in Europe, indicate she was no longer the wide-eyed 21-year-old venturing out into the wide world for the first time. The white lace and frills had been replaced with black silk and a sleek haircut. She had a plan for a glittering future and was by no means averse to leaving Australia. What I am not so certain about, is how Durack's increasingly erratic behaviour was affecting Mina. When the press reported the various demands as coming from both swimmers, was the truth, in fact, that it was instigated by Durack, and Mina, as the lesser draw card, had little option but to go along? I suspect by the time the two women left New York, the friendship was under considerable strain.

The city of Philadelphia was next on the tour, and by this time both Mina and Durack were tired, frustrated and sulky. On the eve of the carnival scheduled for 29 August, they again declared they would not swim unless the American women were given handicaps. The AAU secretary, Frederick Rubien, who was by now at the end of his tether, threatened them both with a lifetime domestic and international ban from competition if they did not swim.

Mina and Durack duly turned up at the carnival the following day, but Durack was in a combative mood. Mina swam in an early race as scheduled and was beaten, which she took good naturedly enough, but Fanny was in no mood to be nice. First, she objected to participating in a scratch race against Ethelda Bleibtrey and Charlotte Boyle, demanding that she be allowed to give them a handicap. The organisers refused to comply, and Durack refused to swim. The crowd was growing restless, unimpressed by Durack's absence from the Bleibtrey/Boyle race. They had paid to see the reigning Olympic champion, why wasn't she in the water? She then proceeded to give her most pronounced display of what, in Australia, would be fondly termed larrikinism, but in America was regarded as belligerence.

Durack was scheduled to swim against local girl, Eleanor Uhl, in the 300yds handicap, but as she stepped up to her starting position she was loudly booed by the crowd. Without waiting for the starter's orders, Fanny dived into the pool, swam half a length and climbed out, claiming she had done what the AAU expected of her—she had appeared before the crowds, and she had swum. The Philadelphia AAU delegates immediately contacted Rubien, demanding that Durack be suspended for refusing to accept handicap rules and for failing to comply with race conditions. Rubien concurred and made the decision to cancel all further appearances of both Australian swimmers. The long-awaited US tour by Mina and Durack, was over.[56] Not only over, but Rubien was adamant that neither woman would ever compete in the USA again.

The report in the *New York Times* heralding the abrupt end of the widely publicised 'Anzac Mermaid' tour claimed that Mina and Durack were 'disappointed with the reception given them here, and object to competing in scratch races with American swimmers.'[57] It was thus easy for the American public to conclude that the issue with the scratch races was simply that the Australian women knew they would be beaten. As there are numerous differing accounts of the August evening in pool in Philadelphia, it is perhaps best left to observer Louis B. Handley to clarify what exactly was problematic about the issue of scratch racing vs handicap for Durack. Significantly, the explanation offered by Handley to Sydney sporting journal *The Referee* three months later, highlights Durack as being particularly argumentative and badly behaved, effectively exonerating Mina. On 5 November 1919, Handley's column appeared in *The Referee*:

'It is customary in this country to handicap visitors from other cities or countries on their best performance only for the first race. After that, the official handicapper erred allowances on the previous latest actual time or times. As a result, the Philadelphia handicapper naturally placed Bleibtrey and Miss Boyle on scratch and gave allowances to Misses Durack and Wylie. At this, Miss Durack became indignant, and refused to start unless permitted to give, instead of receive, time. The handicapper argued in vain that he could not possibly allow defeated contestants to conceded marks to their vanquishers. Miss Durack said with finality that it was that or nothing.'

Handley's account makes it clear that Durack was insulted at being given a handicap, and her ego prevented her from swimming. Handley also maintains that Bleibtrey and Boyle raced without Durack, who stood on the side and timed them with an official watch.

As there is no reason for Handley to make up such a story, it is clear that Fanny Durack was, by now, behaving in a shockingly high-handed and childish manner. Whether she jumped the gun due to fury at being booed by the crowd or because she was insulted when a handicap time was read out, is actually neither here nor there. She had clearly had enough of this tour and was beyond caring what anyone thought. She may have been deliberately courting suspension as she had been away for two months and was fed up, tired of being beaten and wanted to go home.

There is also the possibility that her opinion of herself and her status within the sport was so inflated that she seriously believed no official action would be taken against her. And perhaps the exaggerated significance bestowed upon athletes in Australia had contributed to an arrogance which she was unable to contain.

A reporter from the *New York Tribune* voiced his opinion that Mina and Durack had 'caused trouble for the AAU from the moment they started their first exhibition in Chicago.'[58] It was unfortunate that Mina was, by association, tarred with the same brush as Durack as she had complied with the AAU rules and swum her 100yd race in Philadelphia. Both women were held responsible for the collapse of the tour, but the more complex issue related not simply to the fact that they were women performing in a male-controlled arena, but that they were female celebrities.

Mina and Durack had dominated front pages in Hawaii and San Francisco, and the Durack/Bleibtrey face off on Manhattan Beach had been widely reported by the national press. Up until now, the lingering attitudes of the truculent James E. Sullivan had ensured that women's sport remained on the side-lines, a little reported addendum to the all-important business of 'real' i.e. male sport. Yet this tour by the two Australian swimmers had captured the nation's imagination, giving women's sport an unprecedented position of prominence.

In 1919, the female sporting celebrity was an unknown phenomenon and one which had emerged out of the new movement towards modernity. Sporting officials and governing authorities—and in the USA, these were exclusively male—had no idea how to deal with women in a position where they commanded attention and authority. The governing bodies of swimming may have believed they held the reins of power, but the thousands of women turning out to watch the female swimmers was a clear signal that female athletes were becoming increasingly influential amongst the public. They could, therefore, neither be ignored nor dismissed.

Eppie and Louis Handley appeared to instil a greater sense of discipline into their charges than Marion McIntosh managed to achieve with hers, but, if nothing else, the publicity allotted to this tour placed women's swimming in the USA on the map. In later years, particularly following their success at the 1920 and 1924 Olympics, American women swimmers and divers attained a celebrity status more akin to that of Hollywood film stars. This highly publicised tour in 1919, laid those foundations. Would Mina and Durack have been treated differently if they had been men? Impossible to know. But the issue of scratch races vs handicaps had not caused consternation when Kahanamoku visited Australia, and Durack was possibly kicking back against the excessive controlling measures placed upon the women, purely because they were women.

Back in Australia, an article in *The Sun*[59] laid the blame for the disastrous tour at the feet of the Americans, with the ousted George Dowsing referring to the taxing schedule and the lack of time allocated for the Australian women to adequately prepare as 'a conspiracy'. He was, of course, trying to paint himself in a more favourable light given that his involvement in the tour at the start had smacked of opportunism. Like Al Lippe before him, Dowsing sensed that with the right manager behind them, there was a lot of money to be made out of Mina and Durack. Money which never materialised.

A rise in anti-Americanism in Australia at this time may have been behind the fact that no newspaper in Australia appeared willing to print the fact that Mina and Durack lost because they were not as fit or as focused as their opponents, and that the Americans had developed a superior stroke. However much it rankled, it was now indisputable that Fanny Durack could no longer stake her claim on the 'fastest lady swimmer in the world' title, and that the Australians had some serious catching up to do in terms of stroke development if they were to continue to be a world ranking swimming nation.

The irony at the heart of the humiliating defeat of Mina and Durack, was that it had been their own association president who had encouraged her new friend, Charlotte Epstein, to break away from the AAU and form an American association governed by women. McIntosh had certainly not foreseen that under Eppie's efficient management and Handley's ground-breaking stroke development, the young women of the WSA would become such an unstoppable force in a remarkably short space of time. In short, it was Marion McIntosh who had inadvertently passed the baton from the Australian women to the American.

Following their unofficial debut in 1919, the women of the WSA went from strength to strength. Eppie acted as manager and chaperone for the women's swimming team at the 1920 Antwerp Games, where her swimmers won seven of the nine available medals. In 1924 in Paris, with Eppie as team manager, the American women took ten of the available fifteen medals in swimming. By 1932 in Los Angeles, the dominance of the American women had waned slightly, but the swimmers—with Eppie back once again as their manager—still managed to pick up four golds, one silver and one bronze medal.

During her twenty-two-year association with the WSA, Eppie's swimmers held fifty-one world records and produced the first woman to swim the English Channel, Gertrude Ederle, in 1926. Eppie was vehemently against American participation in the 1936 Berlin Olympics and she withdrew from the Olympic Committee in protest at Nazi policies and antisemitism. Instead, she chaired the swimming committee in charge of the selection of the teams for the second Maccabiah games in 1935, often referred to as the Jewish Olympics.

*

Infuriatingly, nothing in Mina's archive gives any clue as to how she felt about the cancellation of the tour she had waited so long to undertake. Fanny Durack left Philadelphia and began the journey back to Sydney by the end of August, but Mina stayed on in the USA for a couple of months. Where she went and with whom, is a mystery, but a postcard sent to Florence in September from Atlantic City does refer to 'we' rather than 'I', so she was not entirely without friends. Her autograph album confirms that it was November before she was back onboard ship and travelling home. She may have had a last attempt to put in motion some kind of performing career for herself in the US, but the adverse publicity hanging over her would have made it an almost impossible task.

She kept the programmes from the carnivals in Chicago, New York and Philadelphia—bitter sweet mementoes of what had been on one hand, a glorious time, on the other, a disaster. She did not obtain the signatures in her autograph album of any of the American swimmers which may hint at the, possibly self-imposed, isolation of the Australian women.

In 1922, when British swimmer Hilda James visited the USA to compete at the invitation of the WSA, she was overwhelmed by American hospitality and was taken sightseeing and socialising by her US rivals.[60] This was certainly not the case with Mina and Durack and it may have been a reflection of how they were negatively viewed by the American swimmers.

In the end, it came down to this: Mina went, she saw but she did not conquer. The dream was over. Perhaps it had never really been more than a fantasy. Rubien's announcement in *The New York Times* that neither Mina nor Fanny would ever swim in the USA again put a swift end to enthusiastic letters from Al Lippe suggesting a nationwide tour with a travelling glass tank. And her bruising brush with Louis Handley's new freestyle stroke forced Mina to re-evaluate her conviction that a second Olympic medal in 1920 was already in the bag.

Mina had reached that place where all athletes who choose not to retire at the pinnacle of their prowess inevitably end up: that final lap when they are overtaken by younger and faster versions of themselves and there is absolutely nothing they can do to stop it. The tragedy, although that is too strong a word given that her career was by no means over, is that Mina had come so close. In San Francisco in 1918 and 1919, she was within touching distance of her vision of becoming the next Annette Kellerman. But as every competitive swimmer knows, a touch is what separates gold from silver. From making the Olympic team or retiring. A touch is the space between the dream and reality.

Possibly Mina, like Alice Cavill before her, could have found a job at an exclusive athletic club on the west coast, teaching swimming to the great and the good of San Francisco and revelling in the hedonistic jazz age. But that was a long way down the ladder which she had put in position to climb to Hollywood. Her reputation in America was irrevocably tainted after the Philadelphia farce and at least, in Sydney, she could still compete. Better to let the dream go and return to Coogee.

Perhaps the black silk dress with the blue buttons was preserved as a reminder of what so nearly had come to pass. When Mina tied the ribbon just below her waist and headed off to the NSW LASA annual ball, she was once again the woman on the front page of *The San Francisco Post.* She was the swimmer surrounded by crowds after equalling her own world record at the Red Cross gala. She was the celebrity who danced with Fatty Arbuckle and caught the eye of fellow Olympians. She was, once again, a glittering package of potential, dancing the Charleston with the world at her feet.

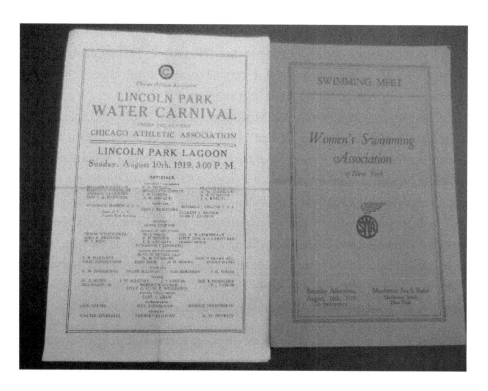

Programmes from the Wylie/Durack trip to the USA, 1919.

Chapter 9

She beat me and then I beat her and that's the way it finished up.

Mina Wylie interviewed by Neil Bennetts, 1975

By the time Mina came to be interviewed in 1975, either her memory of the 1919 USA tour was hazy, or she had deliberately reconstructed a more palatable version of events. She told Neil Bennetts that she gave exhibitions in San Francisco and Chicago and then came home. There was no mention of any competitive races, the defeat in New York or Fanny Durack's bizarre behaviour in Philadelphia which resulted in the cancellation of the remainder of the tour. It was, of course, almost sixty years since the tour had taken place, and therefore not surprising that Mina had difficulty recalling precise details. She did remember that the Americans had a faster stroke and referred to it as the 'six speed crawl'—which was close enough.

I remain unconvinced, however, that Mina's reinvention of herself and some of the omissions in the story she told of her career to Neil Bennetts, can be attributed solely to confusion or to the early stages of dementia. I believe Mina had been constructing her own version of events since 1912, when she did nothing to correct the assertions in the press that she was 14 when she was, in fact, 21. She had a keen sense of her place in Australia's sporting history and she knew what elevated a story above the commonplace. And as is patently clear from the photographs E. S. Marks took of Mina poolside in Stockholm, she was aware of the necessity of controlling her image.

I believe she exerted this control over the three boxes in the collection which contain nothing but disintegrating newspapers and uncredited press clippings. The glowing press from Hawaii is all there, but apart from W. F. Corbett *Referee* articles there is little evidence that Mina ever travelled to America, let alone twice. This strikes me as odd because Mina saved an entire newspaper even when her name appeared only in tiny print in the race results. In addition, the letter she wrote to Henry on her way to Chicago in 1919 mentions having sent him

197

newspaper clippings. Does the absence of these clippings from the archive suggest that she systematically destroyed all the press reports from both USA tours because they revealed her in a less than flattering light?

If Mina did judiciously edit her archive before hiding it in boxes, then the question concerning the absence of Fanny Durack becomes more interesting. My instinct tells me that Mina deliberately excluded Durack from the story of her career.

Possibly out of jealousy or because there was a rift in the friendship following the disastrous 1919 tour. It was undeniable that Durack's belligerence had tainted Mina's reputation and I wonder how much resentment she subsequently felt towards her former 'best friend'. A letter in one of the archive boxes does suggest that Fanny's unpredictable behaviour had surfaced well before the display in Philadelphia. There is no year on the letter which is dated 25 February and signed by the secretary of the Sydney Ladies Swimming Club, Mrs Chambers. Yes, the same Mrs Chambers who supported Rose Scott in the mixed competition debate.

'Dear Mina, I wish to thank you for your splendid effort in winning the team championship of NSW for the Club Sat last. Without your great swim we would certainly have been hopelessly out of it also for your swim in today's test race. I do not wish to say too much about Miss Durack's action. To say I am thoroughly disgusted with her unsportsmanlike action is putting it mild, but never mind Mina. You showed them a much better principal than they are ever capable of and I take this opportunity of thanking you for consenting to swim for us. I wish you success and very good luck for Saturday. From yours faithfully Mary Chambers Hon Sec.'

Intriguing as to what Fanny had done to so 'thoroughly disgust' the redoubtable Mrs Chambers. The mention of 'unsportsmanlike action' does bring to mind the image of Durack pacing the length of the Philadelphia pool with a stopwatch, timing the American swimmers. Chamber's letter and the events in the USA, imply that Mina did consistently demonstrate a greater sense of responsibility, or professionalism, than Durack. Bear in mind, however, that female athletes were (and I would argue, still are) subject to levels of scrutiny regarding their conduct that male athletes were not, and Durack may have been condemned more for behaviour that was considered unfeminine, than for the action itself.

Mina and Fanny Durack were undoubtedly close friends in the initial stages of their careers, sharing training sessions and the thrill of excelling in this new sport. They discovered Europe together and shared the adulation of their win in Stockholm. They both enjoyed celebrity status in Australia, especially in Sydney, and their rivalry was presented by the papers as a friendly one. But they clearly had their differences. According to her postcards and letters, Mina was thrilled to be back in America in 1919 and, unlike Fanny who griped continually, was thoroughly enjoying her USA experience.

The fact that the women sailed home separately suggests to me that, post Philadelphia, Mina had finally had enough of Fanny and her wayward behaviour and realised it was time to break free of the so-called partnership. The Wylie family was essentially conservative and fully prepared to conform in order to move up the social ladder. By paying for a private school education, Florence had ensured that Mina made friends with girls from decent, lower middle-class families: girls who played the piano, spoke French and had fittings with a dressmaker. Fanny Durack was the exactly the type of inner-city girl that Florence never intended Mina to meet, and nor would she have done so if it had not been for swimming.

In the 1975 Bennetts interview, Mina is quick—too quick—to point out that she defeated Fanny in the years following Stockholm, saying, 'We came back and Fanny predominated for about four years, I think, ahead of me. But I beat her at the old Domain baths in Sydney'. It strikes me as significant that nowhere in the hour-long interview does Mina refer to Fanny as a friend. In a 1996 radio documentary on Mina and Durack entitled 'Anzac Mermaids'[61], an interviewee named Doris Hyde is described as a close friend of Mina's.

Doris maintains that Mina refused to talk about Fanny Durack later in life, except to point out that she had beaten her after the Olympics. 'You wouldn't mention it', Doris says in the radio programme, laughing. Which does confirm my suspicion that Mina was well and truly fed up of being portrayed as second best to someone she outshone in terms of longevity and versatility. Again, the edited story she chose to tell in later life highlighted her defeat of Fanny Durack in 1920 and skimmed over the years of second place. It is also the version she preserved in the boxes, saving a disproportionate number of newspaper reports and photographs of the race where she out touched the reigning champion Fanny Durack.

Mina does acknowledge in the Bennetts interview that Durack was the more committed swimmer of the two, swimming three miles a day to Mina's three quarters of a mile. 'That's how she came to beat me', said Mina in 1975. 'It was too far for me. I was probably too lazy.' The latter is a telling remark, and one which may illuminate the real reason Mina came home in 1919 instead of pursuing the fantasy in America.

Maybe the fantasy proved to be simply too hard in terms of the work involved. For although Kellerman made it all appear effortless, there were months of preparation and training and dedicated commitment behind her success. And sustaining it involved strict adherence to a rigid regime of exercise, abstention and a vegetarian diet. Mina enjoyed the good things in life—more than once her brother Walter teases her on postcards about how much she eats.

And in 1975, she continued to display the take-it-or-leave-it attitude towards swimming that gave Durack the edge over her in their competitive years:

'I still go swimming … You do just as much as you feel like, you don't go doing miles a day, you just do, say, a few laps of the pool and get out and have a sun bake, and perhaps go back if it's a hot day and enjoy your life like that down by the sea.'

Maybe the real truth is, that Mina didn't want it enough. Possibly she, like the reality television stars of today, had a desire to be famous but completely underestimated the work involved and was looking for a short cut. I find it hard to believe that Mina's two month stay in the US following the collapse of the tour was completely taken up with sightseeing. Apart from anything else, Henry and Florence did not have the money to support an extended stay with no income. She may have given exhibitions or done some teaching and been paid 'in kind' with accommodation or travel expenses to ensure she kept her amateur status.

But the prospect of turning professional had already been mooted and I am certain she had conversations with theatre or sports promoters, such as Al Lippe, about the possibility of an extended exhibition tour or joining an act which already existed. Some of the grander west coast and Florida hotels were beginning to explore the possibilities of maintaining a troupe of exhibition swimmers—the Biltmore in Miami was known for this in the 1920s—but this would have required Mina to be one of many, not an individual star.

I think that although Mina desperately wanted to make a career out of exhibition swimming and harboured fantasies about Hollywood, the reality involved too many attendant sacrifices. She had an easy life in Australia. She was known and recognised, she had a loving and supportive family and however dull she may have found Sydney at times, it was an easier place to live than the teeming cities of the USA. Especially for a woman alone.

If I am correct in my supposition that there was a falling out between Mina and Fanny as a result of the Philadelphia debacle, I wonder how serious it was. Were harsh words exchanged before Fanny departed for the west coast, or did Mina take the passive aggressive route and say nothing that signalled she considered the friendship over? Fanny's personality leaps across the space of a century and although she may have been entertaining, I have an instinct she was exhausting company. She was bold and lively, and cared little what people thought of her.

Mina, the sheltered, polite, 'nice girl' may have been more enthralled with Fanny and her confidence in Europe in 1912, than she was as a self-assured woman herself seven years later. One thing I often wonder, is why Fanny never corrected the misreporting of Mina's age.

I had female friends I swam with—from Susan on the county team in high school, to Karen who first introduced me to Wylie's Baths—and it is impossible to explain the bond swimming together forges to people who don't swim. It takes the friendship to a different level, one of a visceral shared experience that is at once intimate and personal. Swimming is, by nature, a solitary sport and I believe that is part of its appeal, but I wonder how Mina adjusted to swimming laps on her own when previously she had trained with Durack?

I remember how Susan and I would try and make other laugh when we passed each other in our respective lanes and how we would nod to each other when one noticed that the other had outswum a male team member in a training session. Mina would have missed those moments she and Fanny had shared at Wylie's. But no matter how close they were, they were still rivals.

Although Fanny seemed indifferent to challenging Mina in breast stroke, Mina (and Henry) was desperate to seize the 100m and 200m freestyle. It is only hearsay that the women were 'best friends'—Mina certainly never referred to Fanny in such a way. And both women had the killer instinct when it came to touching the end of the pool in first place.

As is clear from the cards and letters Mina received in Europe, she had a circle of close friends beyond Fanny Durack. Girls whom she had gone to school with and swum with in her younger days. In Sydney there was Bridgie, Dorothy, Esme and Lily, the young women who had braved the crush on Circular Quay to press flowers and cards onto their friend. In Brisbane there were the rowing sisters, Lily and Violet, with their shorts and jerseys and admonishing postcards. There was Vera who wrote the wonderfully chatty letter describing a moonlight visit to Manly wearing her 'new coat of apricot silk, made like a cape with an imitation hood at the back'.

There were the young women who came to Coogee for tea and sat round the dining room table predicting the future with a deck of cards. If there were moments when Mina missed Fanny's exuberance and the scandalised air which invariably followed one of her wilder declarations, she would never have admitted it. Fanny didn't seem to care whether they were friends or not, and neither woman would ever confess that training with a friend was more fun than swimming endless laps on your own.

'Is that it?' asked Henry, as Mina climbed the wooden steps up to the boardwalk.

'Twenty laps,' said Mina. 'That's enough.'

'Fanny Durack wouldn't leave the water after half a mile. She'd keep going until that stroke was perfect.'

'Fanny isn't here anymore. She's gone.'

*

The debacle of the 1919 USA tour did not diminish either Mina or Durack's reputation at home and their ongoing rivalry was closely followed by the press.

On 8 February 1920, a scenario came to pass which would have been unthinkable less than a decade ago, when debates focused on whether women should engage in sport at all: women's sport, not men's dominated the front pages of Sydney newspapers. The occasion was Mina's victory the previous evening over reigning champion Durack in the 100yds freestyle at the Australian championships. *The Daily Telegraph* led with a photograph of Mina touching the rope ahead of Durack under the caption 'How Miss M Wylie gained the 100yd championship of Australia'. *The Truth* report was titled, 'Lady Amateurs: A New 100 yards Champion', *The Referee* declared, 'Mina Wylie Outstrips Fanny Durack in 100yds' and *The Sun*, 'Mina Wylie—Defeat of Durack'.

I suspect the most satisfying for Mina of all the headlines was the leader in *The Sunday News* which trumpeted, 'Fanny Durack Beaten in 100yds

Championship: Mina Wylie her Conqueror'.[62] On 11 February, *The Sportsman* gave this account of the race: [63]

'Miss Wylie took the lead from the dive and, swimming very strongly, maintained it to the finish, winning from Miss Durack by a clear length in 1min 11.4-5 secs. Miss Wylie received an ovation and was subsequently photographed by about a dozen newspaper camera fiends.'

The Sportsman reference to 'camera fiends' recalls images of the male photographers jostling for space to capture the swimmers poolside in Stockholm. Almost a decade later, women in swimsuits in public was no longer a novelty and the focus of the press attention had significantly shifted away from the body of the female swimmer to the performance of the athlete. The press coverage given to the race reflected the ongoing public appetite for women's competitive swimming, undoubtedly driven by the personalities of Mina and Durack. 1920 was, of course, an Olympic year and Mina's unexpected win was a blow to Durack who was suffering persistent health issues.

The Olympic competition was scheduled to take place over four weeks between August and September and Australian swimming fans were eager to see Mina and Durack defend their titles. For the first time, the USA was sending a team of female swimmers and divers—how Ida Schnall must have cheered—of whom almost half were WSA members. This would be the real showdown between Durack and Bleibtrey, a race held in official competition conditions without the open water of Manhattan to contend with.

Durack was eager to go and prove that Louis B. Handley's six beat crawl was not the phenomenon the women of the WSA would have everyone believe. She was selected and fund raising, always an uphill battle where women's sport was concerned, began under the ongoing NSW LASA presidency of Marion McIntosh. Only a matter of weeks after Durack's championship defeat by Mina, she was operated on for appendicitis, and then contracted typhoid fever. Unable to regain her form, she withdrew from the Olympic team shortly before departure.

It remains a mystery to me as to why Mina did not compete in the Antwerp Olympics, and nothing in the archive even hints at a reason behind her exclusion. She had beaten Durack earlier in the year, so she must have been in contention for a place on the team. And her record of more consistent behaviour than the unpredictable Durack should have made Mina an obvious choice. If the NSW LASA only managed to raise funds for one swimmer and Durack had been chosen over Mina, I'm curious as to why she was not asked to step up and take Durack's place when she withdrew after her bout of typhoid fever.

The only explanation I can come up with returns to the Wylie family finances. Florence and Henry had supported the two trips to the USA in recent years and may not have been in the financial position, or even willing, to fund another long trip. Enough was enough. And perhaps her parents silently felt that, at thirty years old, Mina's brush with competitive swimming should have been over by now.

If Mina was disappointed at not going to Antwerp, and I imagine she was, I also have the feeling she was sanguine about it. Having recently experienced the WSA swimmers and their six-beat crawl, she was under no illusion as to her medal prospects this time around, and may well have conceded that the trip was unlikely to yield the results that the Australian officials were desperate to achieve. She would undoubtedly have been a medal favourite if there had been breast stroke events for women, but the 200m and 400m breast stroke races were only on the men's programme. A 300m freestyle had been added to the women's competition since Stockholm, but there were still only three races for women compared to seven for men.

I imagine it was considered a more prudent use of the raised funds to add another man to the team than take a risk on a stand-by woman who had already been trounced by the Americans. For the Australians, the Antwerp Olympics had little to do with good sportsmanship and the thrill of taking part, it was about winning as many medals as possible to consolidate global relevance following the Great War. It was also a major opportunity to prove on a world stage that Australia was the Sporting Nation and a leader in competitive swimming. France may have prided itself on its political and artistic history, and the USA proud of its status as the leading modern, industrialised nation, but Australian authorities wanted the country to known for its sporting prowess.

With Durack's withdrawal, Australia fielded no female challengers to the US women, and Eppie's WSA swimmers dominated the competition in Antwerp. Ethelda Bleibtrey stunned spectators by taking gold medals in the 100m and 300m freestyle, and the 4x100m relay, establishing new world records in both her individual swims. The USA relay team took a staggering 40 seconds off the world record established by the British women in Stockholm, and the British team who took the silver medal in Antwerp were still an unbelievable 29 seconds behind the American women.

If ever proof was needed that Louis B. Handley had revolutionised competitive swimming, the medal table from Antwerp said it all. American women made a clean sweep of all the individual medals leaving only the silver and bronze in the relay to go to Great Britain and Sweden respectively. It was not until the Los Angeles Olympic games in 1932, twenty years after the Wylie/Durack triumph in Sweden, that Australian women had medal success in the pool with Bonnie Mealing's silver in the 100m backstroke and Clare Dennis' gold in the 200m breast stroke.

Towards the end of 1920, Mina made a monumental decision and moved to a new coach, Harry Hay, who had won silver in Antwerp a member of the 200m relay team.[64] Henry Wylie was, by now, almost sixty and ready to relinquish the responsibility of Mina's career, which showed no sign of waning, to a younger man with a superior knowledge of the developments in stroke technique. Mina was almost thirty, an age when most swimmers are contemplating retirement, but her victory over Durack earlier in the year had given her a renewed vigour.

In addition, Ethelda Bleibtrey had announced she would visit New Zealand and Australia to race local swimmers in February 1921, and Mina had no intention of repeating the humiliation of 1919. She knew that Harry Hay had experienced the six-beat crawl in Antwerp and she was hungry for his knowledge in order to put up a good showing against Bleibtrey.

Fanny Durack, however, was far from thrilled at the announcement of Bleibtrey's impending tour. She had been beset by a series of health problems throughout 1920, including a recurring bout of pneumonia, and the prospect of another trouncing at the hands of the American was not appealing. Especially on home ground. The press frenzy reporting her defeat by Mina earlier that year had been bad enough.

Not entirely unexpectedly, Durack announced her retirement from swimming due to 'ongoing health issues' in January 1921, and on the 22nd of the same month she married horse trainer Bernard Gately at St Mary's Cathedral in Sydney. If Mina was among the guests she kept no souvenir of the day. Fanny's retirement just before the arrival of Ethelda Bleibtrey could be interpreted as a convenient way of escaping the inevitable public humiliation which would result from going up against the much younger American sensation.

But Fanny was thirty-one years old and well aware that competitive swimming was a young woman's game:- three of the American women's Antwerp relay team were still in their teens. The sporting journals paid effusive tribute to Durack, expressing the regret of the swimming community at her disappearance from the competition circuit. When asked if a few months rest would give her time to recuperate and restore her form in time for the next season, Durack candidly replied:

'Next year? Why, I'll be an old woman by then, and see how many young girls are making good. No, I've finished. I'm sorry, very sorry. Nobody will ever know what a delight it was to me to win my races and hear the cheers and be shaken by hands, not only by my friends but by strangers, all of whom, I know, wished me good luck.'

Mina attended a dinner and dance at the Wentworth Hotel in Sydney to mark Fanny's retirement and nodded respectfully as the achievements of her former team mate were read out and toasts raised to her good health. Any lingering bad feeling between them was laid to rest as Mina, hand on heart, wished Fanny well in her retirement. The press and Fanny's adoring fans may have been distraught to see her go, but Mina was not. Now the spotlight shone fully on her, and her alone.

*

The saturated press coverage of Ethelda Bleibtrey's 1921 visit to Australia was every bit as intense as the reporting of the 1914/15 visit by Duke Kahanamoku and George Cunha had been.

There was frenzied excitement at the prospect of seeing this unbeatable woman swim, so much so that on 9 February, *The Referee* pronounced Bleibtrey's first appearance at the NSW ladies championships as 'the greatest day in the history of the NSW LASA'. The reporter also paid tribute where tribute was due, noting that:

'The great risks in these visits are financial and this visit has only been made possible by the sportsmanship and generosity of the Hon Hugh D McIntosh, on behalf of the Referee, in guaranteeing the £400 expenses incurred in bringing the celebrated American girl to this country.'

Naturally, Huge Deal would be involved with a visit from the most talked about female swimmer since Fanny Durack, and naturally he would be credited in the press for making the visit happen, even if it had been his wife's idea. £400 was a small, yet very smart investment for Hugh McIntosh, as well as a great boost to the reputation of the NSW LASA and the social standing of his upwardly mobile wife.

Ethelda Bleibtrey's visit had been timed to coincide with the NSW state championship carnivals and the Australasian championships in Brisbane. She had also agreed to visit Melbourne at the end of March before leaving for home. There were three carnivals scheduled for the NSW championships, on Saturday 12th, Wednesday 16th and Saturday 19th of February. Bleibtrey was expected to swim at the opening competition but was delayed in New Zealand and sent word that she would arrive in time for the midweek meeting.

The carnival programme for Saturday 12th continued as planned, and the subsequent report of proceedings in *The Sun* on Tuesday 15th, reassured readers that the feted American would not find the Australians a complete pushover, stating; 'Mina Wylie swam the fastest quarter-mile she has done yet, and had Miss Bleibtrey competed, a ding dong battle would have ensued.' *The Referee* also gave a good indication of the pressure now on Mina to uphold Australian glory with a report written by Mina's Olympic team mate Billy Longworth, entitled, 'Miss Wylie's splendid form'.

'Miss Mina Wylie once again forcibly demonstrated how much superior she is to her opponents in the mother state. In the quarter mile championship of NSW, she took the lead immediately and swimming a clean and pretty stroke, soon opened up a fair margin from the others, winning by 40 yards in the splendid time of 6min 44 2.5 sec.

Although not approaching Miss Durack's best time, this shows that Miss Wylie has a decidedly good chance of extending Miss Bleibtrey...'

Longworth, at least, was under no illusion that Mina would beat the American star, conceding that the best she could do would be to push Bleibtrey to a faster time. He acknowledged too, that the American swimmers were now more advanced in stroke technique than the Australians.

'Miss Wylie has evidently picked up something from the American champions who have come this way, her arm movements—slow, methodical, powerful—in this race reminding one of Norman Ross.'

To be compared to Norman Ross, an American who had toured Australia in 1920 prior to the Olympics where he had taken home three gold medals[65] was an enormous compliment, not least because he was a male swimmer. Longworth was effectively saying that men and women had similar ability in the pool. His report ends with the slightly alarming statement that, 'Mrs Gately (Miss Fanny

Durack) was a keen spectator at the Carnival and hinted that she was not finished with competitive swimming ...'

Any second thoughts Durack may have been having about retirement at this stage, however, were outweighed by her reluctance to face Bleibtrey again. For now, Durack positioned herself safely in the spectator stand where she, in a somewhat superior manner, announced to the press that she was 'very pleased with the form shown by Miss Mina Wylie.'

Ethelda Bleibtrey arrived with her mother in Sydney on Wednesday 16th, just in time for the competition that evening. Her arrival at Circular Quay was reported in detail the following day in *The Daily Telegraph*[66] and the similarities with Annette Kellerman were hard to miss as Bleibtrey gushed:

'Look what swimming has done for me'... Would you believe that three years ago I was almost an invalid? Why, I was a weakling. I suffered from curvature of the spine. Three years ago, I could not swim a stroke. But I was keen and I learned to dog-paddle.'

Incredible to believe, and a testament to the skill of Handley (who received no remuneration for coaching the WSA team) that Bleibtrey had gone from dog paddle to Olympic gold medallist in the space of three years.

Bleibtrey's party was whisked from Circular Quay to an official civic reception in the Lady Mayoress's rooms in the Sydney Town Hall, where scarlet hibiscus and red roses dominated and the Lady Mayoress wore 'a becoming two-piece frock, combining a figured sea-green ninon jumper with an accordion-pleated navy georgette skirt'. Bleibtrey, the guest of honour, 'looked fetching in a simple navy satin-de-soie frock worn with a jaunty stone coloured tam o shanter perched on the side of her head.'[67] Had the press shared such thrilling details of Kahanamoku's attire following his official welcome in the Australia Hotel?

Guests of the Lady Mayoress included Mina, Marion McIntosh ('three tiers to her knife-pleated skirt, and the long-waisted bodice was richly embroidered') Fanny Durack and a handful of NSW LASA swimmers who would be competing that evening against the 'sunburned white haired' American. That afternoon, Marion McIntosh hosted a garden party for Bleibtrey at her new, even grander house, 'Belhaven', but if it was an attempt to wear her out before the competition that evening, it did not work. Although clearly tired, Bleibtrey won the 220yd NSW Championship easily, a good six yards clear of Mina.

The press coverage the following day once again placed women's sport on the front pages of national newspapers, but any sense of empowerment female readers gained from this was swiftly undermined by a reporter from the *Daily Telegraph* who dredged up the tedious tutting about femininity and women athletes, insinuating that active women were only acceptable when their 'girlhood' was not compromised by strength or muscles.

'On the starting board, Miss Bleibtrey fairly eclipsed her Australian opponents. She looked big and bronzed and beside her Miss Mina Wylie, in whom swimming Australia reposes her faith now that Miss Fanny Durack is no longer active, looked frail and diminutive. No one could miss what exercise means to girlhood. It is a means to an end, and that end is not all muscular work. Rather it is greater vitality. The American girl is deep chested and of medium height and built on loosely set but well-developed lines.'

Far from towering over the 'frail and diminutive' Miss Wylie, newspaper images of the competition prove that the two women were almost the same height and of a similar build. Perhaps a point was being made about the less attractive and Amazonian American, compared to the more feminine 'Australian Girl'. The *Referee* reporter, displaying a touch of the nascent anti-American sentiment brewing throughout the country, credited Bleibtrey for her lack of 'yankeeisms', although he did not elaborate on what exactly those might be.

At the final carnival of the NSW competition on Saturday February 19th, Bleibtrey beat her own world record in the 100yds freestyle, swimming a time of 1min 4.2/5 sec. Mina managed second place and recorded a personal best time. A race which generated just as much excitement as the 100yds championship was a novelty mixed handicap in which a male and female swimmer were paired for a 220yd race, each swimming 110yds. Mina was paired with her coach Harry Hay, Bleibtrey with Olympian Keith Kirkland, and Stockholm veterans Billy Longworth and Les Boardman raced with Lottie Fevyer, the former NSW schoolgirl champion, and Lily Robertson, who had taken third place in the 100yds freestyle championship.

The women led off the first 110yds with the men bringing home the second, resulting in a finish described by *The Sunday Times* as 'one of the best thrillers seen for years. It was a case of touch and touch in favour of Hay, who managed a wonderful sprint.' The result meant that Mina could truthfully say in later years that she had beaten Ethelda Bleibtrey. Even if it was a handicap race.[68]

The conclusion of Bleibtrey's visit to Sydney caused the swimming correspondents for both *The Referee* and *The Sportsman* to muse on the superiority of the coaching methods in the USA. Underlying their opinions, was, of course, the fear that Australia was losing its place as a leading nation in competitive swimming and could not match the improvements introduced by the coach of the WSA. Billy Longworth wrote in *The Referee*:[69]

'Some few issues ago I emphasised the idea of introducing a coaching system for our young swimmers. The necessity of this is shown by the wonderful swimming of Miss Bleibtrey, who states that her great prowess in the water is due solely to the American coach Mr L B de Hanley of the NY Athletic Club. Miss Bleibtrey states that Mr Handley has under his instruction some very fine junior swimmers who are expected to do very well next year. Miss Mina Wylie is also an example of a great improvement due to coaching. Until this season she has been only capable of covering 100 yards in and around 1.11, but this year, under tuition from Harry Hay, she has done 1.6 and may do even better with a little more practise on the American methods.'

The admission that the American swimmers had now advanced so far beyond the Australians that the latter were copying their techniques, was not an easy one for the local community to make. But the evidence was in plain sight. Australian swimmers (male and female) were no longer the force to be reckoned with that they had been a decade previously.

A loose and uncredited clipping amongst Mina's papers bemoans the fact that local swimmers were being sold short by Australia's out of date coaching methods and that 'Australia would go a long way towards regaining her lost swimming laurels if young swimmers...were trained and coached like the American girls.' Poor coaching standards affected young women more than young men as there were few women who had the credentials, or ability, to coach potential champions. The handful of male coaches who were familiar with the new six beat crawl, such as Harry Hay, were more likely to be interested in coaching male swimmers as they had a better chance of going to international competition than female swimmers did.

Hay's coaching of Mina was an exception as she already had an international reputation and, following her retirement, Hay exclusively coached men. Mina and Fanny Durack taught swimming to girls after giving up their racing careers but neither of them coached any young women for international competition. They may have had little interest in coaching or felt they lacked the requisite skills, but I suspect the field was so male dominated that both Mina and Fanny realised there was little point trying to break through the barred door.

The Bleibtrey circus, with a handful of NSW LASA swimmers (including Mina) and officials in tow, arrived in Brisbane on February 23rd. Another civic reception was held in another Town Hall at which the Mayor, on behalf of the Queensland LASA, welcomed the swimmers to the city. *The Daily Standard* repeated the Mayor's observation that this gathering was, 'somewhat different from other receptions. Instead of being surrounded by a galaxy of beauty, he was generally surrounded by a lot of hard-faced men.' Tinkles of feminine laughter around the room. In a display of cutting-edge journalism worthy of any thinking nation, the reporter from *The Brisbane Daily Mail* noted that:

'The swimming girl is purely feminine. Bleibtrey is of medium height with a sun-browned face—the effects of sunbathing. She has blue eyes and flaxen hair, and although only 19 years of age, weighs 11 stone.'

Readers were left wildly anticipating what Bleibtrey would weigh at 20 years of age.

In her speech of thanks, Bleibtrey proved to be both gracious and modest, and praised Mina's 100yd Sydney swim saying, 'If it was not for her splendid performance, I would not have been able to put up a record'. NSW LASA secretary, Mrs Mary Chambers (yes, the same Mrs Chambers) returned thanks on behalf of the Association and agreed that Mina was a world class swimmer.

However, she ended her speech by saying, 'Miss Wylie has been swimming for years against Miss Durack and she showed great determination in keeping going when she knew she could only be second to Miss Durack'. This provoked a round of applause from the assembled swimming sorority. Given that it was only a year since Mina made national headlines with her 100yd win over Durack, I wager she was silently seething.

At the Australasian Ladies Championships at the South Brisbane Baths, Bleibtrey continued to outswim all in her path, breaking the world record for 220yd freestyle and touching a good twenty yards clear of Mina in second place. Whilst Mina shaved six seconds from her personal best time over this distance, it still left her trailing Bleibtrey-the-invincible by a remarkable eight seconds. The informal nature of the Brisbane competition is apparent in a handful of photographs in Mina's archive in which she features with Bleibtrey and other competitors. The photographs show various groups of women swimmers and female officials (more hats!) sitting on what looks like a roughly constructed bank of seating made from wooden slats and with wild grass growing in between the tiers. Presumably this was the reason the Mayor of Brisbane had used his welcome speech to Bleibtrey as an opportunity to rally support for a new 'up to date' swimming pool in the city.

Comparing the 1921 image of the swimmers in Brisbane with the photograph of Rose Scott and her swimming group outside the Town Hall circa 1906, it is hard to believe that only fifteen years have passed. To being with, the swimmers in 1921 are photographed actually wearing the uniform of their sport instead of trussed up in white gloves and high collars. They are relaxed, casual even—a young woman seated on the ground leans against Bleibtrey in the row above, and drapes her arms over her knees in affection. The officials are smartly dressed but there is a distinct absence of the flowers, fake fruit and cascading gauzes which adorned the headgear in the earlier image.

One woman—and I can hear the tutting emanating from Scott's Woollahra home miles away in Sydney—is holding a baby. Even stranger is the presence of an older man dressed in work clothes of an open shirt, canvas trousers, a cloth cap and no shoes, standing in the back row and grinning at the camera. Who is this man and why is he in a photograph with female swimmers and officials?

Hazarding a guess, I'd say he is the swimming pool equivalent of the groundsman, maybe even the pool manager—it is Brisbane in 1921, after all. Whoever he is, he is clearly delighted at being included. The noticeable thing about the Brisbane photograph is the informality and the sense of democracy pervading the grouping. The working man, the woman with the baby, and the fact that neither Ethelda, nor Mina, has commandeered the central position of authority, as Rose Scott did in the Town Hall picture, creates an impression of a group free from hierarchy and embedded in an atmosphere of mutual respect.

There is something quite beautiful about the Brisbane images, the same wistfulness I detected in the E. S. Marks photographs of the rowers onboard ship and in the changing tent at Henley. It is the sense of innocence I pick up on, the unworldliness of the of the young women around the pool with the wild grass and makeshift seats. None of the pressures of sponsorship or drug testing or a worldwide television audience. Just a handful of smiling young women, proud of their involvement in the carnival and enjoying each other's company.

I like how the images clearly depict a group of 'new' women who casually assume a modern and liberated femininity. None of these swimmers are ashamed of their bodies or self-conscious about displaying themselves to a photographer, and their confidence in inhabiting the sporting space speaks volumes about how far women and swimming has come since 1912. But the biggest contrast compared to the photograph of Rose Scott and her swimming ladies outside the Town Hall, is that all of the women in 1921, competitors and officials, are having fun. Their smiles are genuine and there is no one to impress.

In another photograph, an older (fully clothed) woman is flanked by Mina, Ethelda and three unidentified swimmers. I'm curious as to who she is (Mrs Chambers, perhaps?) and why she displays an awkwardness which is only highlighted by the laid-back attitude of the swimmers beside her. Mina has her arms casually folded in what has, by 1921, become a recognised sporting gesture and her body language is almost nonchalant as she stretches her legs out in front of her like a cat in a shaft of sunlight.

It is worth remembering that this was the first major competition Mina had swum in without the shadow of Durack looming either in the next lane or in the spectator stands pronouncing on her form. Perhaps it is Durack's absence that accounts for Mina's air of insouciance. That, and the fact that all Australian eyes are currently focused on her as the nation's leading female swimmer and she is mentioned in the same breath as a woman with three gold Olympic medals.

After Brisbane, Mina returned to Sydney and Bleibtrey travelled to Melbourne where she won the 400yds championship of Victoria, touching the side of the City Baths a full 30yards (more than a length of the pool) ahead of her nearest contender, Mina's friend, Lily Beaurepaire.

Melbourne was also where Bleibtrey encountered her only bit of bad publicity for the entire tour, when the press reported that she had refused to swim in a race at a carnival event at the City Baths. This was not the full story and Bleibtrey was upset enough by the misinterpretation of events to offer an explanation to *The Argus* on 19 March. She did this through an intermediary, none other than the NSW LASA secretary, Mrs Chambers, who had assumed managerial responsibilities for Bleibtrey's tour. Chambers told the reporter that on the evening in question, Bleibtrey had competed in the 220yds championship and given a backstroke demonstration, followed by an exhibition of fancy swimming and a then a diving exhibition.

'She was very tired after this exertion and did not feel well enough to start in the handicap event. The following announcement was made through the megaphone: 'This event has been especially put on for Miss Bleibtrey. But she has refused to swim and has left the baths.' ... Miss Bleibtrey said today that the

Melbourne public recognised that she had done her full share, but it was the officials who had caused an unpleasant incident.'

Shades of the USA in 1919.

Before she departed Australia, Bleibtrey agreed to a farewell appearance at the Coogee Aquarium Baths where she would swim handicap races and give exhibitions of strokes and diving. As this event had not been on the original schedule, I suspect it came about due to her blossoming friendship with Mina. Why else would the wildly popular Bleibtrey be farewelling her adoring public in the 25 metre Coogee 'acca' instead of the much larger Domain Baths? I find it impossible to believe that Mina would have persuaded 'Thel' to come all the way to Coogee and not taken the opportunity to show her Wylie's Baths. In 1921, Henry's pool was still thriving, and Harry had joined his father as a full-time employee.

I picture Ethelda on the wooden boardwalk, looking down at the pool and marvelling how entrancing it all was. Compared to the forbidding, grey Manhattan ocean back home, this was like something out of an Annette Kellerman fantasy. I see Henry blush as Thel exclaims over the underwater swimming certificate hanging on the wall of the rickety office. I see Florence smile at Mrs Bleibtrey in wholehearted approval of her unaffected and well-mannered daughter. I notice Harry try to catch her eye. I hear the applause of the onlookers as Thel and Mina flit out of the changing hut and down the wooden steps to the edge of the pool.

Swimmers stare in stunned wonder as the champion lady swimmer of Australia grins at the champion lady swimmer of the world and they dive in, sending a rush of waves across the wall and out towards Wedding Cake Island. Thel whoops and laughs and floats in the sun.

'It's so beautiful,' she exclaims. And Mina smiles.

'I know.'

Mina's friendship with Bleibtrey could only have come about in the absence of Fanny Durack. Mina was under no illusion that she could beat Bleibtrey and so was less inclined to view the American as The Enemy, which Durack would have done. With Durack out of the way, Mina was the most senior female swimmer in Australia in terms of achievement, and so it was perfectly natural that she and Bleibtrey would be thrown together at functions and official dinners.

Fortunately, they hit it off and a genuine friendship seems to have developed. Bleibtrey had a sense of mischief about her that appealed to Mina—in 1925 she was arrested for swimming in Central Park reservoir to raise awareness at the lack of public swimming facilities in New York—and her friendship with Duke Kahanamoku was another source of common ground. And who wouldn't like Thel, with her jaunty hats and sailor dresses, her newly bobbed hair and her ease with officialdom and the press? She was unaffected, charming and generous with her time, even attending the Girls' High School carnival in Sydney where she demonstrated the WSA crawl to eager young freestylers.

The visit of Ethelda Bleibtrey to Australia proved beyond the shadow of a doubt, that she was the greatest female swimmer the world had ever seen. Durack was now a memory, and Mina was back on the map and re-established in the press and public favour.

With promises to keep in touch, Bleibtrey sailed for the USA at the end of March. On her arrival home in New York, the WSA gave a welcome home celebratory dinner for their brightest star and announced to the triumphant assembled company that:

'Australia saw, Ethelda conquered and Australia was satisfied, and she now sings the praises of our unbeaten champion.'[70]

Oh, if only James E. Sullivan had lived to see the women swimmers he so despised claim the world crown. Even in 1920, success was the best response to the bullying AAU, which continued to refuse to relinquish any control over women's sport. Unbelievably, when the first New York City marathon was held in 1970, the AAU still had rules in place which banned women from entering road races. The NYC marathon officials ignored the rules and opened the race to women, but the AAU regulations meant that the times posted by the finishing women would not be official. The Amateur Sports Act of 1978 finally removed the authority of the AAU to set and maintain rules in women's sport.

The Referee lamented the departure of Bleibtrey from Sydney, noting:

'Although it seems too much to expect, Sydney ladies who have met her and the hundreds who have seen her wonderful displays in the water, are hopeful that she may one day determine to come this way again to gather in fresh laurels and perhaps be tested by a generation of girls now rising to their best in swimming.'

Alas, it was not to be. Ethelda Bleibtrey turned professional the following year and became a successful coach and teacher in New York and Atlantic City.

When Mina was inducted into the International Hall of Fame in Florida in 1975, Bleibtrey, then in her seventies, was living 45 miles up the coast in West Palm Beach. I like to think they spent an afternoon at the pool together, and at some point, Mina withdrew from her sturdy handbag a photograph, carefully wrapped in tissue paper. There she was, the beautiful, laughing young woman in a swimsuit, instantly recognisable by her shock of sun-bleached hair.

'To Mina, With bestest love always, Thel'.

US 1920 Olympic champion, swimmer, Ethelda Bleibtrey on her 1921 visit to Australia

Brisbane swimming carnival 1921. Mina is centre of the third row, standing behind Bleibtrey.

Chapter 10

Two references are required before pupils are admitted to the school. These must satisfy the principal who reserves the right to refuse admission. Parents to whom this regulation may seem unnecessary are courteously reminded that the application of this rule to all proves a safeguard to their own daughter.

Prospectus for Pymble Ladies College, 1930

Fanny Durack had been thirty-one years old when she hung up her swimming goggles in 1921. One year later, Mina was now the same age but far from showing any sign of retiring, she was going from strength to strength. At the beginning of March, *The Referee* recorded her world record in the 50yds backstroke and her victories in the Australian championships in the 100yds, 220yds and 440yds, noting that:

'Miss Wylie now holds the highest place among the Australian lady swimmers and possesses every title in freestyle event, both state and Australian, except the 50yds in which she had to strike her colours to Miss Lilly Robertson.'

And it was not just in her own country that Mina's continuing success inspired awe. In the USA, the WSA spring newsletter of 1922 included a lengthy article which referred to Mina as the 'all round swimming champion of her own country' and noted that:

'The world's greatest swimmers of our sex are very young girls at present. Yet here is a champion who was in the racing circuit before some of the topnotchers today were born, and who has managed to keep abreast of the times, maintaining steady improvement throughout the last season when she swam 100yds in 1min 6, the fastest time ever she made at the distance. An achievement which stamped her as one of the leading sprinters in the international ranks.'

The same newsletter also reported the unexpected return of Fanny Durack to competition after a two-year absence. Unexpected, because she had already been given a retirement dinner by the NSW LASA the previous year and been farewelled by the press in effusive column inches. Two years out of competition is an almost impossible obstacle to overcome (just ask Ian Thorpe) as Durack discovered in Melbourne, where she was defeated in the 440yds Australian championship by none other than Mina Wylie.

Mina's new coach, Harry Hay, proved to be either more inspirational than Henry, or a harder taskmaster (or both) and in the winter months between the 1922 swimming seasons he kept Mina in better shape than she had ever been. Henry had always allowed Mina to slacken off her training regime in the colder weather, but Hay was less indulgent and moved their sessions from Wylie's Baths to the indoor pool at the Coogee Aquarium. As well as improving her six-beat crawl, Mina and Hay made the decision to move away from the sprint races, typically dominated by younger swimmers, and focus on middle- and long-distance races.

Although Mina had never been an endurance swimmer, her new and improved stroke technique enabled her to keep a steady pace over a longer distance without tiring. Defeating Durack in March had given Mina renewed vigour and throughout the southern hemisphere winter she diligently stuck to Hay's intense distance workouts and continued to improve her stroke technique. The work paid off and in December Billy Longworth was writing in glowing terms in *The Referee* of Mina's victory in the 880yds Ladies Championship Carnival in Melbourne.

'At last this girl's remarkable courage and perseverance have been rewarded, as she now stands supreme in this country and is putting up even better performances than in the past.'[71]

This victory in Mina's first foray into distance racing was even more impressive given the fact that on 22 July that year, Mina's beloved mother Florence had died at home, aged fifty-six. The condolence letter from a neighbour acknowledges that Florence had been ill and in pain for a long time, in which case Mina's initial response may have been one of relief that it was now over. But the quietly refined, unambitious woman who had been the recipient of so many of Mina's postcards was now gone.

In 1909, Florence had taken up her pen at an interstate swimming carnival in Queensland and written in her teenage daughter's autograph album, 'All's well that ends well.' Did it end well for Florence, I wonder? She never saw Ireland or France, or the magnificent royal palace at Drottningholm in Sweden. But she did see her daughter become 'one of the first.' Perhaps that was enough.

*

In March 1923, Mina and the ubiquitous Mrs Chambers travelled to New Zealand to participate in 'Joy Week'—not as scandalous as it sounds, merely the Auckland Summer Carnival. Festivities included a naval and military tattoo, a torchlight procession, floral fete, a revue company and a swimming competition at which Mina was billed as the star attraction. The swimming events were held in Calliope dry dock which was part of the Devonport Naval Base on Auckland's north shore. When the dock had been built in 1888, it was the largest facility in the Southern hemisphere and when filled with water, just like Todd's shipyard in Brooklyn, it made the perfect competition pool.

Mina's first race was the 100yds freestyle on the 20th March, when she went up against five local swimmers including Pauline Hoeft, the current New Zealand record holder with a time of 66.2 seconds. This time equalled Mina's personal best but was still almost 2 seconds away from Bleibtrey's current world record.

Despite it being eleven years since her Olympic triumph, Mina could still draw a crowd and almost four thousand spectators crammed the seats around the dock to see the local champion and the Australian legend go head to head. The audience was not disappointed as Mina and Hoeft gave them a thrilling race which ended in dead heat which was timed at 69 seconds. After much deliberation, the first place was awarded to Hoeft, a decision later queried by the New Zealand Aquatic Magazine which suggested that the judges at the carnival were not senior enough, and therefore not equipped with the knowledge to make the correct decision.[72]

By the time Mina swam at the carnival at the Tepid Baths in Auckland a week later, she had been joined by Queensland champion, Elsie Venning. Nine years Mina's junior, Venning wrote regular updates of the tour, an early form of blogging, which were published in the Brisbane Courier. On the 6th April, her column discussed the dead heat between Mina and Hoeft. 'Somehow or other they gave the decision to Pauline Hoeft', Venning pronounced, 'but everyone here says that Mina should have got it.' Mina did beat Hoeft over 100yds in the Tepid Baths carnival on 26 March, in a time of 68 seconds which was described by Venning, who came fourth, as a 'very popular win'.

She also recorded in the same column that Hoeft, who had a German father and a Samoan mother was, 'a very big girl. We thought Ethelda Bleibtrey was huge, but this girl beats her.' There is a Pathe newsreel clip of Annette Kellerman congratulating Pauline Hoeft in New Zealand in 1922, and she doesn't strike me as the giant Venning would have her readers believe.[73] But, as every woman knows, jibes concerning weight or appearance are designed to undermine, and maybe this was Venning's attempt at payback for the unjust victory in Auckland.

Mina and Venning swam in Mount Eden, a suburb of Auckland, then spent a week at the thermal spa town of Rotorua where they presumably relaxed and enjoyed the geothermal pools, as there is no record of any carnival or races.

In the Mitchell Library archive there are three small black and white photographs of Mina standing outside the main bathhouse in Rotorua. She is wearing a sailor jumper, a dark skirt and an unremarkable hat, and she looks neither fashionable nor particularly feminine—the antithesis of Annette Kellerman. She looks, in fact, like a slightly overweight, middle-aged woman, and not the reigning Australian champion. But Mina had always been more interested in how she swam rather than how she looked, and she was still swimming well. Leaving Rotorua, the Australian party travelled to Wellington where Mina and Venning swam in a carnival at the Te Aro women's baths, a harbour pool described in the 1897 *Cyclopaedia of New Zealand (Wellington Provincial District)* as being 165 feet long and 73 feet wide and 'securely protected from the visits of sea monsters'.

In a letter Mina received from Henry, he assures her that the family business is thriving in her absence, 'We had a very warm Good Friday the glass at the ladies showing 95 and as you understand "Biz" was good the Ladies getting within 14/- of the record for that day.' Clearly, his preoccupation with finances and 'the work' had not diminished over the decades.

At the start of the 1923/24 swimming season, the committee of the NSW LASA agreed that a rematch between Mina and Hoeft would raise the profile and popularity of the NSW championships at the end of the season. Accordingly, in November 1923, an invitation was extended to Pauline Hoeft to compete in Australia at the beginning of 1924. As required, the NSW LASA informed the male executive of the Australian Swimming Union (ASU) of their plans and thought no more of it—the ASU had never been particularly interested in the comings and goings of women's swimming.

But the familiar power struggle raised its tiresome head, and on 13 December 1923, the *Evening News* reported 'considerable pouting and ruffling of feathers among our girl swimmers'. The male executive of the ASU, to which the NSW LASA was affiliated, had responded to Hoeft's invitation with a typically haughty letter in which the women of the NSW LASA committee were informed that the Union had:

'... considered this matter and has decided to place same before the associations of Victoria and Queensland for an expression of opinion. Before doing so, it would like to know the reasons which have actuated the Ladies Association in singling out Miss Pauline Hoeft for a special invitation, and if this information is forthcoming it will be sent along to the other associations, together with arrangements for the tour for their consideration.'

It was a letter worthy of James E. Sullivan, and it provoked a furious response from the women of the NSW LASA who deemed it an 'insult'. What had Queensland to do with their own tour, they asked. More to the point, why was the male union dictating to the women's swimming authority what they could, and could not, do? Particularly as the NSW LASA was merely seeking consent, not funding. But again, why was the women's authority having to ask consent from the men's authority? Had the ASA sought permission from the LASA before inviting American Norman Ross to visit Australia in 1920? Or Kahanamoku in 1914?

The Sydney Sportsman carried an article reporting that Mina Wylie 'was ready and willing to meet the New Zealand champion ...' but the seething committee members of the NSW LASA responded to the male Union by swiftly cancelling Hoeft's invitation. While the response did come across as petty— cutting off one's nose to spite one's face—it was, in fact, a bold gesture intended to undermine the power exerted by the male authority over women's swimming. Why the men of the Australian Swimming Union felt the need to interfere in the proposed visit of Pauline Hoeft is anyone's guess. It may have been a flexing of male muscle to remind the women of the LASA who controlled sport in Australia, or irritation at the higher profile and higher gate takings of women's swimming than men's. It did smack of an unnecessary wielding of power just for the sake of it. And it denied swimming fans a race which would have been worth seeing.

The *Sydney Sportsman* article from December 1923 regarding Mina and Pauline Hoeft, ends, curiously, on this note:

'I, for one, was under the impression that Mina Wylie had definitely announced her retirement from the game last season, but she informs me that I was mistaken. I am glad of it for swimming can hardly afford to lose her yet awhile.'

The (anonymous) journalist is inferring that Mina had finally called it a day at the end of the 1922/23 season, that is, on her return from New Zealand. But the NSW LASA issued the invitation to Pauline Hoeft specifically to bring about a rematch between the New Zealand champion and Mina. Regardless, there were obviously rumours floating about that Mina might be coming to the end of her career. In February 1924, she travelled to Brisbane as NSW representative at the Australian national championships, but she became unwell and was unable to swim. She returned to Sydney where she was swiftly admitted to the Wootton private hospital in Darlinghurst and operated on for appendicitis. By the time the season ended a month later, Mina had quietly announced her retirement.

There were no effusive press columns and no farewell dinners, and there is nothing in her archive which even hints at the reasons behind her decision. She was, however, 32 years old and may have felt that to retire unbeaten was more dignified than a protracted farewell involving not qualifying for a final or a series of fourth places in races she used to win. Perhaps her decision had something to do with Henry, now a widower and requiring more of her time and attention. With Florence gone, it is probable that Mina had assumed most of the domestic burden—cooking, cleaning, being attentive to the men of the house—and perhaps Henry had even encouraged her retirement.

Mina had never been under any illusion concerning the finite career of an elite athlete, but for someone who had been in the public spotlight for over a decade, a return to being no one was a sobering thought. Mina's identity was so completely wrapped up in that of a champion swimmer, and had been for so long, that the removal of this definition challenged her sense of self. Who was she if she was not 'Lady Champion Swimmer Mina Wylie'? A redefinition was necessary. But as what? Employment was unlikely to yield an answer as Mina had never been part of the workforce and it was a touch late now to start training for a new career. She did consider clerical options and purchased a book of teach yourself shorthand exercises, and perhaps she really could envisage herself as one of the hundreds of modern women working as stenographers in various city institutions. Or even as a journalist reporting on swimming events throughout the country.

In the USA, Mina had encountered the wildly popular 'stunt girls', female reporters who both participated in, and wrote about sport. These daredevil women such as Nellie Bly and Mary Bostwick covered aviation and racing car competitions, as well as traditional sports such as baseball, football and even

223

boxing, often disguising themselves as men in order to gain access to the inner circle and locker rooms. The idea of Mina infiltrating such bastions of masculinity as the surf lifesaving club or the dressing rooms of the NSW Australian Football Association for a post-match interview does make me smile, but I think it's highly unlikely that she saw herself in that role. More realistically, where employment was concerned, Mina had her father's business on her doorstep and she continued to teach swimming at Wylie's and at McIvers Baths, a few minutes' walk away.

By the early 1920s, Walter had married and moved from Coogee to the North Shore, and at some point after the death of Florence, the remaining Wylie family moved from Carr Street to the house on Neptune Street. Neptune Street ran between the green spaces of Grant and Trenerry Reserves on the southern headland of Coogee Bay, and was two minutes away from Wylie's Baths. The house at number 13 was a large family home, newly built when the Wylie family took possession, suggesting the move had been planned for some time. In March 1924, Mina's life became centred more on the house in Neptune Street, and less on Wylie's Baths. She still taught and swam there, but there was no longer any need for the intensive daily training sessions with Harry Hay.

1924 was an Olympic year but Australia sent no women to the swimming competition, which was again dominated by the Americans who won ten out of the fifteen medals on offer in women's events. Mina's life settled into an easy routine, looking after Henry and teaching swimming and lifesaving to little girls at McIver's on a Saturday morning. If she missed the training sessions and the talk of the forthcoming season, she kept the thought to herself. Until, that is, November 1924, when the news broke of the impending visit of another American champion, the improbably named Mariechen Wehselau from Hawaii. At the recent summer Olympics in Paris, Wehselau had won silver in the 100m freestyle (her team mates Ethel Lackie and Gertrude Ederle took gold and bronze respectively) and gold as part of the 4x100m freestyle relay team. Still smarting from the Pauline Hoeft rebuke, the LASA invited Wehselau to swim in the 1925 state championships and this time the ASU raised no objection, probably due to the fact that Samuel Kahanamoku, brother to the much-loved Duke and bronze medallist in the 100m freestyle in Paris, was also coming.[74]

The temptation proved too much for Mina and in January 1925, the *Singleton Argus* reported that 'Miss Wylie has been training for some weeks at her father's Coogee Baths, and is confident of being able to reproduce all her old dash in the sprints.' Unfortunately, (again, ask Ian Thorpe) a few weeks training will not make up for twelve months of relative inactivity and Mina was reduced to being 'among others' in *The Sun* report of the NSW Ladies championships at the Domain Baths on 31 January. The 'many-colored frocks' of the women spectators (who, it was noted, far outnumbered the men) received more press attention than Mina did.

*

After convincing victories in Brisbane and Melbourne, Wehselau returned to Hawaii and Mina to Coogee. The only evidence in her archive of her activities in 1926 is a theatre programme for 'Keep Smiling' which she saw at the Palace Theatre in Sydney on April 17th. Other than that, how she passed her days is a mystery. She was no longer racing and her form was no longer the subject of speculation amongst Sydney reporters or the swimming fraternity, which was currently fixated on Andrew 'Boy' Charlton, and the thought of what he might achieve at the 1928 Olympics in Amsterdam. Charlton had brought home two medals from Paris, bronze for the 400m freestyle and gold for the 1500m, and when Frank Beaurepaire's bronze in the 1500m freestyle was added to this, the Australian men were beginning to establish a solid reputation as distance swimmers.

It was generally acknowledged that the Americans were unbeatable in the sprints but if Australian swimmers focused their attention on middle and long distances, it was a discipline in which the country could dominate. That thinking, naturally, did not include women, as the longest distance on offer to them in the 1928 Olympics would be the 400m freestyle. It was not until 1968, a staggering four decade later, that the 800m freestyle for women was introduced into Olympic competition.[75]

The thinking behind attitudes which deemed the female body incapable of swimming a race of 800m was literally blown out of the water in the (European) summer of 1926, when, on 6 August, a nineteen-year-old American named Gertrude Ederle became the first woman to swim the English Channel. Her time of 14 hours and 34 minutes was two hours faster than the existing record established in 1923 by Italian, Enrico Tiraboschi, thus re-igniting the well-worn debate concerning physical fitness and the female body. Feminists on both sides of the Atlantic were ecstatic at the news that a woman had conquered the Channel and newspaper column inches discussed this indisputable proof that women should now be considered as good as, if not better, than men when it came to physical prowess.

The feminists from the late 1800s who had vigorously campaigned for dress reform had been proved correct: liberating the female body was inexorably linked with liberating women full stop. Ederle, who was one of Eppie's WSA swimmers, fanned these flames when she announced, 'It's up with the women and down with the men' during a packed press conference in Dover the morning after her extraordinary swim. The press in the USA focused on the swim as an American triumph, and feminists saw it as a victory for women, proving that not much had changed since the Durack/Wylie triumph in 1912 when Australian nationalists and feminists battled to claim the success as their own.

The reports of Ederle's swim in the Australian press played down both her nationality and sex and tended to focus on the technicalities of the swim itself, concentrating on weather conditions, wind speed and the fact that Ederle swam Handley's six beat crawl. On 11 August, *The Referee* described an inspiring scene as fires were lit along the cliffs and beaches of the Kentish coast to guide Ederle through the dark, and the report in the Adelaide *Mail* gave the impression of an entertaining few hours at sea with Pop Ederle playing jazz records on a gramophone and Trudy singing along as she swam. The article also reported that Trudy's sister, Margaret, occasionally jumped in to swim alongside her sister and when Trudy showed signs of flagging, held up a sign with the words, 'Think of Mother!' in bold letters. Probably an exaggeration but a wonderful scene for the film version.

Two years later, in March 1928, Mina and Fanny Durack were reunited when they swam in a fun event at the NSW ASA Championships at the Domain baths. All funds raised at the championships were to be put towards the Olympic travel fund, and the programme for the carnival featured a full-length picture of Boy Charlton, the swimmer on whom Australians pinned their hopes.[76] Mina and Fanny raced in an event billed as the 50 yards Old Olympians Race which was open to:

'... all bona fide amateurs who have at any time represented Australia at the Olympic Games. Time limit: one hour. Any competitors who have not completed the distance within the time limit will be ejected from the water. Ambulance in attendance outside baths.'

Without a doubt, the star of the carnival was the impressive six foot tall, 20-year-old, Boy Charlton. Charlton had been raised in Manly and was a member of the North Steyne Life Saving Club, co-incidentally Cecil Healy's former club. It was therefore fitting that it was Charlton who won the Cecil Healy memorial trophy at the 1928 ASA championships. As he moved to the podium to collect the trophy, Mina recalled the gentle teasing, the guiding hand under her elbow, the hand on her shoulder as the group posed for a photograph during the cruise on the archipelago. A whole decade since the country had mourned Cecil Healy. Could that be possible?

'I was sweet on him,' said Mina, smiling at the memory.

'You were. I remember,' said Fanny.

Charlton held the trophy in one hand and waved to the crowd with the other.

'And that young man never even met him.'

'Couple of old relics, Mina,' said Fanny. 'That's what we are now. Faded photographs and names in history books.'

Fanny took Mina's arm as they walked out into the Botanic Gardens.

'But we're still the first,' said Mina.

It might have been Mina's participation in this fun event which led to her one last moment in the competitive swimming spotlight. On 9 April 1928, *The Daily Guardian* carried a short report entitled, 'Mina Wylie was surprise in Coogee Swim'.

'Miss Mina Wylie, ex-Australian champion over all distances, who retired undefeated in 1924, caused a sensation at Coogee Aquarium on Saturday by winning Randwick and Coogee Ladies Club 100yds handicap from scratch in 72 secs. Miss Wylie won by over four yards and could easily have knocked a couple of seconds off her time had she been extended.'

Admittedly, it was a handicap race, and she swam six seconds slower than her time at retirement, but how thrilling to be back in competition and to bask in the atmosphere, the camaraderie, the cheers, the adrenalin. And the victory, of course. Like Fanny Durack before her, the lure of competition had proved too enticing (or too familiar) for Mina to resist. But ultimately, she knew the time had come to let go. The win at the Coogee Aquarium was the last race Mina swam.

In the black hardback account books for Wylie's Baths, Henry's diligent recording of the daily facts and figures continues until April 1929, when the meticulous columns in cursive script, stop. A month later, on May 29th, at his home in Neptune Street, Henry died. His death certificate gave his age as 68, and the cause of death as cardiac failure and hepatitis.

In Mina's archive, Henry's possessions are in separate boxes from Mina's swimming memorabilia, suggesting that an attempt was made to sort the contents into some semblance of order before they were stored under the house. If it was Mina who did this, then the presence of Henry's underwater swimming certificate from 1897, his Masonic lodge programmes and photographs, and finally, his death certificate, have an agonising poignancy about them.

By holding onto the tangible reminders of Henry, Mina kept her father close. It had been Henry, after all, who had stood beside her on the deck of RMS Malwa as the ship sailed through Sydney Harbour heads in 1912, and watched her come back from fourth place to second to become Australia's first female Olympic silver medallist. It was Henry who gave Mina her career. Her identity.

And on his death, he gave her the house in Neptune Street.

*

With the death of Henry in 1929, Mina's archive ostensibly ends. There is the photograph of her with Neil Pickard at the Sydney passport office in 1975, and one undated newspaper article in which Mina is asked by a reporter what she thinks of Australia's medal chances in the 1932 Olympic games. A random form requesting an increase in her petrol ration, presumably from the Second World War, and a note on Pymble Ladies College writing paper are the sole relics of a life beyond the death of Henry. That's it. The life Mina was intent on preserving was one where the leading lady was a local and international celebrity, the archetypal 'Australian Girl', daughter of the owner of an ocean pool and a product of the new Australian beach culture. She was The First. And that's the story Mina wanted remembered and passed on.

So here it is then. Thirteen boxes of evidence from this ground-breaking life. Thirteen boxes for 93 years. That's roughly one small cardboard carton for every seven years of life. It's not much really, when you think about it. And what did Mina choose to save? Swimming programmes, medals and autograph albums with signatures of school friends, her mother, long dead Olympic athletes and a disgraced film star. Photographs of a scandalous music hall singer, an unbeatable American and the woman who epitomised modernity with her black leotards and her Perfect Body. Postcards from Europe and the USA and the folding leather case on which they were written. Newspaper articles which carried her name or image. Travel brochures from Marseilles, New Zealand, Ceylon and San Francisco. A London bus timetable. Accounts books and towels from her father's pool. A letter from a soldier killed in the muddy battlefields of France. Sewing patterns and five silk dresses. Dance cards with the pencils still attached. A postcard of a female rowing team and a French phrase book. The theatre programme from a matinee of 'Undine'. A souvenir brochure of the 1909 visit of the American Fleet, cards containing get well wishes, school books, cinema tickets, season cards for Sydney Ladies Swimming Club, a lifesaving certificate, a tram ticket from Wellington, a diary, labels recording various undated wins, letters, a photograph of Rose Scott surrounded by women in big hats, an essay on the benefits of swimming, Professional calling cards and a letter promising to make her a star ... An Olympic silver medal depicting a naked athlete being crowned with a laurel wreath and the words 'Olympiska Spelen Stockholm 1912'. Like I said, not much really, when you think about it. Just things.

Whenever I picture Mina sorting through her mementoes and deciding which to keep and which to throw away, I always come back to the same question:- who did she think would find this collection? And what did she expect them to do with it? I could be wrong when I suggest that she had given no thought beyond the action of actually packing the boxes: she may have known exactly what she was doing when she locked the lid of the metal chest and walked away.

Perhaps her intention was always that someone would find it and offer the collection to a museum where it would be preserved. If that was indeed the case, then I imagine Mina hovering somewhere, watching as I lift each box onto a table in the Special Collections Room at the Mitchell Library. I am aware of her impatience as I linger too long on family photographs, struggling to assign a name to a face.

'Leave that, it's not important. Look at this one...'

And onto box 2, with the Olympic programmes and the elegant Sydney Ladies Swimming Club rule books spilling out of the boxes within the box. This packaging of Mina's life, fascinates me. The metal chest with the thirteen boxes inside. The subsequent separation of Mina's effects into even smaller boxes within the bigger ones by museum staff. Little white birthday presents tied with ribbons and laces. Each holding another exquisite gift. I hear Mina smile as I hold the daring 1913 portrait of her standing in front of the rocks at Wylie's Baths.

'There now. Isn't that something?'

It is indeed.

'And all these people I met. See…?'

The autograph albums and the voices of athletes in their glorious prime calling across the space of the years. Did Vera in Redfern ever imagine how her letter with news of her first dance and her new beau, Lionel, would delight a century later? Could Al Lippe have foreseen the images his letter with references to vaudeville and a glass tank and a nation-wide exhibition tour would conjure up? And the writing case … That old and battered box of faux leather with all those written words still encased inside.

I wonder if the things that Mina considered important or significant were the same objects as I did. I lingered on Henry's underwater diving certificate because I too, was a woman who adored her father. The image of Mina's two brothers rowing out into Sydney Harbour to wave to her made me weep. Because I have two sisters.

The theatre programme for Kellerman's star turn 'Undine' fascinated me, not purely because the idea of an aquatic show onstage intrigues me, but because I once worked backstage at the Palace Theatre in London where Kellerman performed. Mina's archive, to me, was sheer delight. It reminded me of the fun of the carnivals in my teens, the camaraderie, the thrill of competition. Time and time again, I found my younger self in Mina's archive. I have kept some of the things she had kept:- swimming medals, a special dress, signed programmes. I think we would have been friends.

While it is relatively easy to piece together Mina's life when she was a competitive swimmer by utilising the clues she stashed in the hidden boxes, it becomes significantly more difficult to find her beyond her retirement from the swimming circuit. Without a doubt, part of that difficulty stems from the innate male bias throughout the sporting discourse but, in fairness, what is there left to say about an athlete who is no longer competing? At her peak, an Olympian is a glorious, awe-inspiring example of the human body at its fittest, strongest and fastest. When age begins to knock flaws into this perfection, we look elsewhere. We want to gaze upon the victorious in all their magnificent splendour, not weep over the has-beens.

But I wanted to find Mina Wylie beyond what she had allowed me to see. My interest in her life post-competition stemmed from a desire to know what becomes of a person who has been a significant someone and is then a no one. Is

Annette Kellerman, the swimmer who could not cope with a life out of the spotlight and ploughed all her savings into maintaining her own celebrity, the norm? A Norma Desmond grotesque, clinging onto faded youth? I had a good idea that this was not Mina, purely because she disappeared from the press until the Florida controversy in 1975. So where was she for all those decades? And what did she do? More to the point, where would I have to go to find her beyond the Mitchell Library?

*

Mina was 38 years old when Henry died. She had never lived away from home and she had never had a full-time job. She was now the sole owner of the house at Neptune Street but was adamant she would not sell. It was a two-minute walk from Wylie's Baths, where Harry now assumed all managerial duties, and it was an integral part of Henry's memory. Mina had lived in Coogee since she was a child and her identity as a champion swimmer and the outdoors loving 'Australian Girl' had been formed by Coogee and Wylie's Baths. There was no question of moving away.

And certainly not when the suburb continued to thrive as visitors flocked to the Palace Aquarium and to the amusement pier, opened in 1928, which stretched 180 metres out to sea and housed a theatre, ballroom, restaurant and penny arcades. The family business was secure, but even before Henry's death, Mina had been astute enough to realise that she needed to find a position of her own. Not purely for the additional income, but to maintain an individual identity beyond Henry and the baths. Mina had been an independent woman since she strolled the streets of London arm in arm with Jennie Fletcher in 1912. She was not someone who could go from 'champion lady swimmer' to 'daughter of' in one short step.

There are two clues in Mina's collection as to where she went to establish her individual identity beyond the swimming circuit. The first is an undated note which reads:

'Dear Miss Wylie, As there will be no teacher down at the pool this afternoon I am leaving it in charge of two girls. Would you mind just keeping your weather eye open in case anyone wants to get drowned.'

The note carries the crest of Pymble Ladies College. And hidden amongst Henry's Masonic rule books and programmes in box 9, is a card with a poem on the facing side: 'Deep peace of the Running Wave to you/ Deep Peace of the Flowing Air to you/ Deep Peace of the Quiet Earth to you/ Deep Peace of the Shining Stars to you/ Deep Peace of the Son of Peace to you'. Inside the card is a mass of signatures and best wishes surrounding the sentence, 'To our dear Miss Wylic, love from the many generations of girls and staff. 6 July, 1970'.

The occasion for the card is not clear but I'm hazarding a guess and saying it is a belated birthday card (Mina's birthday was the 27th of June) from the staff and pupils at Pymble Ladies College (PLC). Something about the choice of poem on the card and the numerous signatures inside touched me. It felt genuine. A card signed by a group of people who chose to do so, not because they felt obligated. Four years after Mina had retired from this particular job, she was still receiving cards from her former colleagues.

The year before Henry died, Mina was engaged by Pymble Ladies College on Sydney's North Shore to teach swimming and lifesaving. The school had been founded in February 1916 as a branch of Presbyterian Ladies College, Croydon, and had started humbly enough with sixty pupils, but grew rapidly, almost doubling the intake in the first year of operation. By the time Mina joined the staff in 1928, the school had a roll of over four hundred girls, a quarter of whom were boarders.

How she secured this impressive position is unclear, but her name still carried a certain kudos and she held the all-important Royal life-saving diploma enabling her to teach those skills. The partnership was beneficial to both parties: Mina brought status to the swimming programme at the College, and in turn, the College gave Mina employment in her own right at a well-respected educational institution. The emerging philosophy of a healthy body and a healthy mind was reflected in the PLC curriculum which advocated the unconventional view that sports activities were just as important for girls as boys, and an integral part of a well-rounded education.

In 1926, amidst much pomp and ceremony, a swimming pool within the college grounds had been opened by the Governor-General, Lord Stonehaven. In order to equal the excellent standards already in place in the academic curriculum, a teacher of high status was required by the college to oversee and teach the swimming programme. In late 1928, Mina took up the position she held for the next forty years.

By the late 1920s, Australia was continuing to strive to construct a unique and recognisable national identity which was both free of the increasingly pervasive 'Americanism' and which severed, once and for all, the lingering vestiges of Colonialism. This perceptible 'Australian-ness' was evident in the arts where novelists such as Miles Franklin and Katherine Susannah Prichard, and artists May Vale and Clarice Beckett were building reputations on works which were defined by their Australian environment and landscape. Middle- and upper-class educational establishments, however, remained heavily influenced by the recent colonial past, reproducing both the architecture and ideals of the great schools and universities of England. The main hall and elegant arched colonnade of PLC were reminiscent of an Oxbridge College and deliberately styled to enforce class distinction and allegiance.

When Mina stepped through the college gates in 1928, she entered an ordered world of manicured lawns and girls in hats and white gloves, the future wives of the men who would lead the nation. PLC was the embodiment of upper-class English nationalism and a secluded sanctuary for the privileged few. It was only when I visited the college in search of Mina in the school archives that I realised how prestigious her position at PLC would have been in the interwar years.

I knew she had taught there for many years and I had jumped to a conclusion which featured the words 'mighty' and 'fallen'. How depressing, I had thought, to spend four decades supervising the frog kicks of cossetted little girls who would never make state finals, never mind an Olympic trial. How frustrating. Yet as I walked alongside the main oval and saw the imposing red brick buildings rising up elegantly in front of me, I realised why Mina stayed here for forty years.

It matched her status as 'one of the first'. These little girls might well be the daughters of the privileged elite, but they were lucky to have her. And Mina knew it.

From the very start of her time at the school, Mina's skills were in great demand. The 'Swimming Notes' section of the 1929 college magazine records, 'Miss Mina Wylie, who was the examiner of the life-saving candidates, had a very busy time as there was a large number of entries.' On 30th May, 1930, a report in *The Sydney Morning Herald* on the annual presentation by the Royal Lifesaving Society, noted that the Ekland Cup for the girl's school gaining most points in competition was awarded to Presbyterian Ladies College, Pymble— Mina was already proving her worth. Strangely, she does not appear in the annual school photographs with other members of staff, which suggests her position may have been part time and classed as coach rather than teacher, the latter definition belonging to the new breed of full-time sports mistress(es) populating private schools. Whatever her classification, PLC offered Wylie a financial lifeline during the economically depressed 1930s when jobs for women, particularly women approaching forty, were extremely rare.

What struck me most when I visited PLC, was how the surroundings and the atmosphere were the antithesis of Wylie's Baths. Henry Wylie had utilised the natural geography to create an unrestricted space for leisure quintessentially Australian in character and environment, but the architects of PLC had unashamedly reinvented the Australian landscape to create a 'little England'. In addition, Wylie's epitomised an emerging Australian identity in which sport, the beach and a disregard for class hierarchy were core values. PLC, with its laws of exclusivity, discipline and conformity, was its polar opposite.

Photographs held in the school archives of swimming lessons call to mind the great Busby Berkeley musicals, with identical girls forming geometric patterns in large bodies of water—a larger scale version of the Wylie family aquatic act. Girls in black regulation swimsuits and matching caps hang onto the side of the pool or stand, poised, on the edge. In the water they swim in perfect formation, no head lower or higher than anyone else, no girl faster than the swimmer next to them. They even float in a flawless straight line. They are an unidentifiable mass of conformity. No one stands out or calls attention to herself.

On the playing field, a shot of seven rows of twenty girls dressed in identical gymslips, white blouses, stockings and gym shoes, with their arms raised above their heads in an exercise routine, is so far removed from the barely controlled bedlam within the space of Wylie's Baths as to belong to another time, another country. Boisterous boys dominated Wylie's Baths with their shouting, dive bombing, splashing, mischief making and showing off. They wore borrowed swimsuits which didn't fit and were never washed, and with no spare money available for lessons, they learned to swim by watching others. The popularity of Henry's ocean pool meant that swimming an entire length was nigh impossible without some sort of collision with an over excited child. At PLC, the pupils swam dignified laps in peace. Here, just like the women in the first decade of the twentieth century, here they could become good, confident swimmers without having to adapt their behaviour either to please, or to accommodate men.

Photographs of PLC pool show what I assume are Mina's lifesaving classes, although she is not present in any of the images. A line of frowning girls firmly holding fellow students under the arms while the latter submits to the 'rescue'. A 'drowned' student prone on the pool side while the life saver presses down on her lower back to expel the water from the lungs of the victim. The rapt concentration is a reminder that this is serious business. The images of life at PLC beyond the pool show girls in white tunics performing what looks like Rudolf Laban interpretive dance in the woods. The hockey team. The tennis team. End of year prize day.

It is an idyllic world far removed from the rioting on Sydney streets during the post-war depression and the furious agitation of the growing communist party. Here was a side of the 'classless Australia', the 'working man's paradise', that the nationalists preferred not to acknowledge. For the myth of a modern nation built on egalitarianism and 'the fair go' might be proven to be exactly that. A myth.

The fact that Mina appears to have straddled the two vastly contrasting spaces and social situations of Pymble Ladies College and Wylie's Baths with relative ease suggests a personality able to adapt. She herself had been privately educated, admittedly at a much less impressive institution, but still, she was not completely unfamiliar with the class of person she was now mixing with on the north shore. And I believe she enjoyed this rarefied atmosphere. Maybe it brought back memories of the formidable Rose Scott and the attention she had so graciously bestowed upon the teenage Mina. She certainly entered into the spirit of the school and the college magazine of June 1933 notes that: 'Miss Wylie gave an exhibition of swimming strokes old and new.'

Walking about the grounds of Pymble Ladies College, it occurred to me that I was overlooking the most obvious connection between Mina's past and this inspiring school.

It was a female only space, a concept Mina had been extremely familiar with in her younger days. Just like the NSW LASA, the structures of power within PLC were in the hands of women, and perhaps this was, in some way, reassuring to Mina, endowing her with a sense of security. A quick glance at the staff directories over the decades reveals that she was, by no means, the only woman with the prefix, Miss. I suspect it was a relief not to have to be constantly made aware of her unmarried state, or indeed her independent lifestyle. At PLC, Mina was surrounded by educated, forward thinking women committed to the education of girls and the pursuit of a life as an autonomous woman. How liberating that must have been.

With only scant evidence of Mina's time at the school it is difficult to build an accurate picture of how she fitted in to the daily college life. Did she attend evening functions, I wonder? The sixth form Shakespeare production, the annual dance. Her past would have given her a certain kudos amongst Hollywood obsessed teenagers …

'Did you really meet film stars, Miss Wylie?'

'I did. And I swam on Manhattan Beach in New York in front of ten thousand people…'

And she had already made the trip 'home', an adventure high on the priority list of ambitious, young Australian women.

'Did you see the Queen, Miss Wylie?'

'No. But I met the Crown Prince of Sweden.'

I wonder if she ate her lunch in the staff room and chatted with the full-time teachers? It was sixteen years since the 1912 storm over the all-male swimming team and undoubtedly, there were members of staff who clearly remembered the national debate concerning Mina and Durack's participation. Perhaps one or two women had even been amongst the crowd welcoming Mina and her medal back home at Circular Quay. Amongst all those university educated women, there had to be a handful who had engaged in sport as students. Sydney University, for example, had a long history of women's sporting clubs: the women's tennis club was founded in 1887, the boat club in 1896, hockey in 1908, and 1910 saw the formation of the Sydney University Women's Sports Association. Mina, therefore, already had the respect of many staff members who were duly impressed with her success in sport as a woman.

For Mina, a coaching position within such a highly regarded educational establishment offered the perfect opportunity to reinvent herself within the swimming community and the wider public. She had not turned her back on the sport and become a stenographer or a mother but had taken a practical side step into another division of the same whole. Psychologically, this would have had a positive influence on any feelings of loss she may have felt at losing her competitive career. I like to think she occasionally took the red box holding the silver medal to show her most promising pupils what was possible.

Twenty years after Mina joined the staff of PLC, she presented two trophies to the school to be awarded to the junior and senior breast stroke champion. Perhaps this was tied up with her ego, she wanted to ensure an enduring legacy, or perhaps she genuinely wanted to give the girls something to strive for. It is certainly not the action of someone who felt that teaching the six-beat crawl to ten-year-olds was beneath her. And suddenly—again, how could I overlook what was so glaringly obvious—I realised that although Mina's contemporaries had been dead for decades, there were generations of swimmers who had passed through Mina's hands who were still alive. And who were, as I discovered, eager to share their memories of the bright eyed, forthright swimming teacher who 'missed nothing' and 'stood for no nonsense'.

One former pupil painted this lovely image of, 'Miss Wylie in her brightly coloured cotton button-through dress over her black swimming costume, mannish brown sandals and wide-brimmed straw hat.' Others noted that, she could be fun—'I do seem to smile when thinking of her, so I think there was a sense of humour there', and that, 'her legs, arms and face were all dark brown, rather leather-beaten, no doubt after goodness knows how many years of being pool-side.' And proof that old champions never lose their technique:

'We were always delighted when she came into the pool with us to correct arms movements and we always wanted her to demonstrate by swimming a length or two. She had a wonderful stroke and just seemed to glide through the water so effortlessly'.

A PLC Old Girl described Mina as 'part of the institution' and another cited Mina as an inspiration: 'I wanted to follow in her footsteps swimming breaststroke and after leaving school I continued training with her by going out to Coogee.' She was remembered as 'a rather distant, private person, but we were all aware that she was an Olympian.' Probably because she wore the official team blazer just to remind them. And, my favourite, 'She had a nice smile, although we didn't see it very often. I liked her.' [77]

*

With Mina established at PLC and Harry running Wylie's Baths, the siblings settled into a new existence without Henry, their lives revolving, as they had always done, around swimming and Coogee. The fact that neither of the siblings married is curious and leads me to wonder if they inadvertently fell into relationship that was verging on co-dependent. Harry remained single out of loyalty to Mina—what would become of her if he left Neptune Street? Mina stayed single out of loyalty to Harry—the house may have been in her name, but she could hardly turn him out in favour of a husband.

Perhaps they simply enjoyed the life they had fashioned for themselves and had no desire to be married. They had companionship, an income and a home in a prime position filled with memories of Henry. In later years, when indoor pools and more up to date facilities challenged the popularity of Wylie's Baths, I wonder if Harry viewed the family business as a burden. But Wylie's was the last remaining link with Henry and their childhood. His legacy was their legacy, and to give it away would have been a betrayal of everything he had worked so hard to achieve.

Mina's income from teaching would not have supported them both for any length of time and the pool was all Harry knew in terms of employment. They may both, at times, have considered themselves trapped in a situation that, although not unpleasant, allowed no space for alternatives. Equally, they may well have considered themselves extremely fortunate to have both a secure home and a business, particularly when neither Mina nor Harry would have found it easy at their age to secure employment anywhere else.

Evidence of Mina throughout the PLC decades is difficult to find. To all intents and purposes, she disappeared. She lived quietly with Harry in the house that still displayed a postcard from Stockholm on the mantlepiece—'I am having a ripping time…'—but the days of being recognised in department stores or attending charity galas at Darling Point mansions were long gone. The bitter sweet curse of celebrity—that the star shines brightest just before it fades—had caught up with her. She played tennis at White City courts in Paddington and invited friends to Neptune Street for a hand of poker. She sewed her own dresses and played the piano. She saw movies at the Randwick Ritz and walked around the cliffs to lay flowers on the grave of Florence and Henry. But other than that, there is little information on which to build a composite image of how Mina filled her time.

Mina remained on the staff at Pymble Ladies College until 1970, an unbelievable 42 years of service. I don't believe she pined for her lost glory years, I think she was too pragmatic for that. She had a job she enjoyed in a highly reputable educational establishment, surrounded by women who respected her, and, in later years, I suspect, were very kind to her. I like the fact that she retained a link with swimming after she retired. It feels apt, somehow. The woman I think I have found is not someone who would have been the right fit for a stenographer pool or the shop floor of David Jones. Mina was perfect for PLC and the institution proved ideal for her. What a pity Florence did not live to see it. How proud she would have been.

'Looking back now, I think Miss Wylie would have been a lot of fun to be with when she wasn't "on duty", but with us she was business-like, correcting our swimming strokes while walking up and down the side of the 25m pool and wearing one of her more or less shapeless cotton dresses.'

I love that image.

A lifesaving class at Pymble Ladies College, undated.

Chapter 11

Coogee was like living in the bush, in the country when we came here. You could hardly see a house or anything. Today you couldn't see a vacant piece of land, that's how the world has changed in my time. Of course, probably I've lived too long now…

Mina Wylie interviewed by Neil Bennetts, 1975

If it had not been for the fact that Mina was selected as an honoree by the International Swimming Hall of Fame in 1974, it is highly likely that she would have disappeared from national cultural memory. With every death of a contemporary, Mina would have slipped a little more into obscurity until she resided in oblivion, surrounded by all the other female athletes The Sporting Nation had no need for anymore. I was surprised at how quickly Mina, as far as the press and the public were concerned, ceased to exist.

Apparently, the day she retired from competitive swimming was the day she stopped having any cultural or national relevance. When I stopped relying purely on Mina's archival boxes for information, however, I discovered that she may have been unknown to new generations of swimming fans and sports reporters, but the swimming community remained very much aware of who she was and where she fitted within the context of Australian sporting history. The years missing from her archive, those decades between Henry's death in 1929 and her visit to Florida in 1975, were not, as I had initially imagined, Mina's 'wilderness years'. She had been visible and had left imprints of herself in various places over the decades, she just hadn't taken the time to save the evidence.

If I wanted to find out what became of Mina after her swimming career, it would involve stepping outside the hushed sanctuary of the Special Collections room of the Mitchell Library and venturing to Pymble and Mosman on Sydney's north shore, to Coogee, to Melbourne, to Stockholm and even to Fort Lauderdale in Florida. Chasing a vision that was always one lap ahead.

1956 was an enormously significant year for the Australian populace as Melbourne was due to host the Olympic games. These 'Games of the XVI Olympiad' would be the first to be staged in the Southern Hemisphere involving a shift from the usual July/August timescale to November/December to accommodate the different seasons. At the beginning of the year, Mina and Fanny Durack received invitations to attend the opening ceremony and the swimming competition as VIP guests. Forty-four years on, here was proof that 'the firsts' were far from forgotten and were still able to command a certain level of respect.

When the new school year started at PLC, the girls in their black regulation swimsuits and identical swimming caps looked at Miss Wylie with a new level of awe. Many, many years before they were even born, their own swimming teacher had not only competed in the very same competition that was coming to Melbourne, she had brought back a medal. And here she was, standing poolside demonstrating the perfect breast stroke arm recovery. Eyes watched a little more keenly, legs kicked that extra bit harder.

In March 1956, however, newspapers reported the death of 'the world's greatest woman swimmer of her time'[78], Fanny Durack. At sixty-six her death was unexpected and the result of a heart attack. Durack had maintained her involvement with women's competitive swimming as an official and the day before her death she had been timekeeping at a Sydney competition. With Durack's death, the original team of nine Australasian swimmers who competed in 1912, was reduced to six. Cecil Healy had been gone for four decades and Malcom Eadie Champion, the only New Zealander in the team, had died in Auckland in 1939.

There is no evidence that Mina attended Fanny Durack's funeral but unless it was a private affair, I find it hard to imagine that she did not. Perhaps she sat with her former team mates Billy Longworth and Harold Hardwick and smiled as she remembered Durack laughing when Mrs McIntosh challenged Rose Scott at the Town Hall meeting, and raising an eye brow when Mina held up the black silk dressed edged with pale blue piping.

'Your Dad will have something to say. Spending all that money on a dress...'

Did Mina weep, I wonder. For her best friend and the battles in the pool and their lost shared youth. Had Mina moved on from the Philadelphia fiasco and consigned it, along with the Chicago and Manhattan Beach carnival programmes and city map of Stockholm, to a box in the attic? There is always the possibility that Fanny Durack and Mina Wylie had not spoken for years. Whatever the case, Mina was now the only one left of the celebrated duo. And the Olympic Games were only a matter of months away.

Despite the tag of the 'Friendly Games', the 1956 Melbourne Olympics came at a difficult time in international politics, and Egypt, Iraq and Lebanon announced they would not participate in protest at the Suez Crisis.[79] In addition, at the beginning of November, the Soviet authorities brutally crushed the Hungarian Revolution, an uprising initiated by students which spread nationwide, against the communist government of the Hungarian People's Republic. The presence of the Soviet Union at the Olympics subsequently caused the Netherlands, Cambodia, Spain and Switzerland to withdraw their teams.[80]

Two weeks before the opening ceremony on November 22nd, the People's Republic of China announced their withdrawal from the event due to the presence of a team representing the Republic of China. Boycotts aside, Melbourne eagerly anticipated hosting nations from all over the world and regarded the competition as an opportunity to promote the city and Australia to a global audience.

In November, Mina travelled to Melbourne and took her seat with the other VIP guests to witness the opening ceremony and the competition in the swimming pool. It couldn't have been a more resounding success with the Australian team finishing at the top of the swimming medal table (a feat never since repeated) with a total of fourteen medals, three clear of the nearest contender, the USA. Dawn Fraser, Lorraine Crapp and Faith Leech took gold, silver and bronze respectively in the 100m freestyle, and in the 200m freestyle it was Lorraine Crapp who won gold, with Dawn Fraser taking silver. The Australian women rounded off their competition with a new world record in the 4x100m freestyle relay, winning gold for Fraser, Crapp, Leech and Sandra Morgan.[81]

How did Mina feel watching these women follow in the path that she and Durack had carved out for them? Elated, undoubtedly, and proud of her countrywomen. Perhaps, however, there was a bitter sweet tinge to the experience. Not because her time had passed but because what she and Fanny Durack had debuted, was now commonplace. Women unashamedly inhabiting sporting space and displaying their physical prowess and their bodies, was no longer extraordinary. And the games as an event was so far removed from the competition she had experienced that it was difficult to draw a clear connecting line. Television cameras, banks of journalists, sixty-seven competing nations, commercialisation, political tensions ... the Olympic Games had become both big business and a diplomatic tool. I wish Mina had saved evidence of her presence at the 1956 Melbourne games. She must have mingled with the victorious swimmers at official functions—the oldest and the newest. What a pity no one took a photograph.

I may be joining tenuous dots, but I'm confident in saying that it was at the Melbourne Olympics where Mina first encountered a sporting official from Sydney by the name of Vivian Chalwin. Chalwin was a wealthy engineer who had arrived in Australia from England in 1951 and had quickly established himself as a leading behind-the-scenes figure in sporting circles. As a recent arrival to Australian, Chalwin may have been unaware of the significance of Mina Wylie to Australian swimming before meeting her in Melbourne.

He may even have wondered who this beaming sixty-five-year-old wearing a frayed green team blazer and surrounded by people who wanted to shake her hand, was. Once he found out, he was intrigued. He had seen the photographs, of course, read the names in the historical accounts of Australian swimming, but here was someone who had actually been there.

'It wasn't a real pool like the Domain. Just the harbour. It was so muddy we couldn't see the bottom.'

Chalwin was entranced. How had he never met this woman before? And why had he never been to Wylie's Baths?

'My father was the first person to allow mixed bathing in his pool. Dual bathing, they called it then. Families used to come and stay the whole day—there was nowhere else they could swim together ...'

One year later, when the Melbourne Olympics had been and gone, Vivian Chalwin issued an invitation to Mina to visit his home in Cremorne on Sydney's north shore. But this was not a simple join-us-for-a-cup-of-tea-and-slice-of-cake invitation, this was a unique fundraising event billed as a 'Cavalcade of Olympic Swimming Champions 1900-1956'. And Vivian Chalwin's home was no ordinary house. Over the six years he had been in Sydney, Chalwin had transformed a conventional house on the North Shore into his version of an Italianate castle, complete with crenelated parapets, square towers, a ball room, a theatre, stone lions guarding the entrance and a swimming pool.

On 24 March 1957, Chalwin opened this thirty-roomed residence to the public for an event intended to establish a scholarship in physiology at the

University of Sydney in memory of Australian swimmer Frank Cotton. Cotton had been a keen swimmer, narrowly missing selection for the 1920 Olympic Games, and his scientific research primarily focused on muscle physiology and the effect of athletic exercise on the heart and circulation. The fundraising event at Chalwin Castle was the perfect tribute to Cotton, and a veritable who's who of Australian swimming.

Australia's first ever Olympic medallist, Freddie Lane, was present, and Mina, Harold Hardwick and Billy Longworth from Stockholm. Boy Charlton and Moss Christie (Paris, 1924), Bonnie Mealing (Amsterdam, 1928, Los Angeles 1932), Clare Dennis (1932) and members of the triumphant 1956 Melbourne team, including Murray Rose, John Henricks and Lorraine Crapp. For the serious swimming fan, this was the stuff dreams that were made of.

Even more extraordinary is the fact that the 'Cavalcade of Olympic Swimming Champions' was preserved on film. Someone recognised the momentousness of this occasion and ensured the afternoon was preserved for posterity. Mina told Neil Bennetts twenty years later:

'I was invited over to Mr Chalwin's pool at Shellbank Avenue in Cremorne and they asked me to give an exhibition. Freddie Lane was present but he said to me, he said, 'No I'm too old now, I'm not (going to) give an exhibition.' He said, 'it's too much for me.' So, I went in and did it and they put the screen on and they evidently took it up.'

I engaged in a burst of online sleuthing and discovered a couple of short films on YouTube featuring Chalwin Castle. One was of particular personal interest as it featured the 300-seat theatre which Chalwin had built to promote the arts in Sydney and which he offered free to recognised drama, opera and classical music companies. Incredible as it now seems, this private theatre had played host to Glenda Jackson, Joan Sutherland, Joan Carden, Roger Woodward and Yehudi Menuhin, amongst many others. But my search was for Mina, and a few clicks and two messages later I was in touch with Jo Thompson, Vivian Chalwin's daughter, now living in Mosman. She remembered Mina coming to the Cremorne house and informed me that she had a number of items which 'might be useful'.

The very next day, I sat in front of a TV screen as Jo inserted a DVD into a player.

'You'll like this,' she said.

Which was the understatement of the decade. The DVD held the footage filmed that March afternoon in 1957 at the 'Cavalcade of Olympic Swimming Champions.'[82] The parade of smiling black and white ghosts, diving and swimming laps in the slightly surreal setting, was utterly spellbinding.

'Oh, there she is,' said Jo. 'There's Mina.'

Sixty-six years old, grinning and relaxed in the pool. There she is. Alive and swimming.

It's hard to articulate why I felt so emotional at this, my first sight of Mina. Maybe because I had already been looking for her for so long it had never occurred to me that she might still exist somewhere on film.

Because looking at a photograph is one thing and hearing her speak on an old recording, another. But seeing a person move and smile and chat … the missing pieces are filled in. The photograph moves. The voice has an animated face. And it was only as I watched the footage of Mina in the pool that it dawned on me how important it was to me, another swimmer, to actually see her swim. We swimmers often maintain that the personality of the swimmer can be deduced from their stroke. Slow and methodical—someone reliable, unlikely to offer any surprises. Lots of splashing down the centre of the lane—an aggressive narcissist.

Mina's stroke on the DVD is strong and unhurried, sure of itself. She often lifts her head mid-stroke to look forward—a throwback to the days before the invention of goggles. She breathes every second stroke, favouring the left side, and employs a fast kick. She has not taken on the developments in breathing technique or arm recovery, and her body sits much higher in the water than that of the younger swimmers. Her stroke dates her, and the awkward turn at the end of the first lap brings the distance between 1912 and 1957 into clear focus.

It is two whole lifetimes away from the insouciant tumble turn of the dazzling Murray Rose, whose entry dive takes him almost the full length of the pool. But if physicality is the embodiment of character, then Mina's strength in the water immediately defines her. Her physicality is that of a woman ten, even twenty years younger. She is strong and resilient and her eagerness to display her skills alongside the present Olympic champions suggests that in the thirty-three years since her retirement from competition, Mina had lost none of the self-confidence so evident in the E. S. Marks photographs from Stockholm.[83]

The fact that there is no sound with the footage adds to the ghostly, almost ethereal feel. The picture is sometimes of poor quality, flickering in and out like a snatched memory, but the images are compelling. The hushed crowd is seated under graceful arches lining the Italianate pool with the terrazzo floor. Chalwin, in his Olympic blazer, hovers in the background. The divers launching themselves into flight with twists and turns often enter the water feet first, mindful of the insufficient depth of the chocolate box pool.

Occasionally, the action of the swimmer has been slowed down on film, adding to the already other-worldly feeling of the footage. There is a middle-class formality hanging over the strangely subdued audience that is an odd juxtaposition with the grinning nonchalance of the champions. There is Freddie Lane, almost eighty, recounting anecdotes whilst the bronze horse he received in place of a medal in 1908 stands on a table beside him. There is the teenage Murray Rose, three times gold medallist in 1956, resplendent in the full glory of youth. Moss Christie being patted on the back by Chalwin. Bonnie Mealing demonstrating her backstroke prowess. And there is Mina. Wearing a plain white bathing cap and smiling up at the camera from the shallow end.

In a post-swimming shot later in the film, Mina poses with Murray Rose, Boy Charlton and Freddie Lane:- the oldest, the newest, and two notables in between. She appears to have dressed for the occasion, augmenting her lace collared outfit with a string of pearls. It is clear she is thrilled to be included in this high-profile event and I suspect—I hope—a good deal of fuss was made over her.

I wonder if Harry went with her to Cremorne that Sunday, leaving the pool in someone else's capable hands. They would have driven over the harbour bridge, following Chalwin's careful instructions, and parked in the space he had set aside for them. Harry would have shaken Billy Longworth's hand and they would have briefly reminisced about Henry. He would have watched Murry Rose with astonishment and asked Mina to introduce him to the great Boy Charlton. And when Mina stood in the line-up for an official photograph, Harry would have beamed with the same pride Florence had been unable to contain when the Wylie Family Aquatic Act had their portraits taken in Brand's Studio on Park Street at the end of the last century.

*

Harry might have been a year younger than Mina, but he lacked her energy and stamina and was eager to retire as soon as it was possible. In 1959, the three

Wylie siblings sold the Baths to Desmond Selby, who renamed the business the 'Sunstrip Pool'. Mina still used the pool for her daily laps and continued to teach there, so, apart from Harry being at home all day, selling the family business did not mark a great upheaval in her life. She and Harry continued to live at 13 Neptune Street, in the large house with rooms dominated by Henry's ghostly presence and windows which overlooked his second greatest triumph. In the dusty and fraying rooms, Mina and Harry were like the Stockholm postcard still propped up on the mantelpiece: residue from another era which had been in the same place for so long that to remove it would leave a space that nothing else could possibly fill.

In 1970, aged seventy-nine, Mina finally left PLC for good. The journey from Coogee was simply too much and even Mina had to admit she was beginning to flag. She still had her little girls at McIvers Baths on a Saturday morning where, even more than she had been at PLC, Mina was part of the institution. She had, after all, been a committee member of the Randwick and Coogee Ladies Amateur Swimming Club since 1923, the year the club took over the lease and management of the ladies only pool.

She had voted in favour of the 1923 proposal to offer free swimming classes to girls and women at the pool on a Saturday morning, and she had volunteered her time and skills ever since.[84] With her retirement from PLC, Mina and her friend Doris had more time to sit in the shade between swims eating sandwiches and playing cards. Swapping detective novels and discussing the news. It was a fine life, Mina mused, enjoying life down at the sea with friends. Not a bad way to live. Not at all.

But in 1974, just as she had settled into a quiet routine and resigned herself to ending her days in relative obscurity, Mina was invited back to the Italianate castle in Cremore by Vivian Chalwin. This time the invitation was to a reception welcoming Buck Dawson, the Executive Director of the International Swimming Hall of Fame (ISHOF) to Sydney.

Dawson had been the driving force behind the Hall of Fame complex which had been officially dedicated in Fort Lauderdale on 27 December 1965, and unbeknownst to Mina, Vivian Chalwin and Buck Dawson had been exchanging letters for years discussing the prospect of Mina becoming an ISHOF Honoree. Her invitation to Dawson's reception was a chance for Chalwin to subtly assess Mina's physical and mental condition before issuing the invitation to travel to Florida.

The reception for Buck Dawson took place at Chalwin Castle on Sunday February 10th, and again, someone associated with the occasion had the foresight to record it for the history books. In the photograph of the hundred or so assembled guests taken, Mina has been placed (or placed herself) at the front of the group. A stocky figure, dressed up for the occasion with the ubiquitous set of pearls and white shoes to match her handbag, she radiates pride as she takes her place amongst swimming royalty. Mina's beaming smile confirms she is having a wonderful afternoon and her bright, sharp eyes are shining.

I imagine a conversation between the octogenarian Mina and the seventeen-year-old Shane Gould, star of the 1972 Munich Olympics where she had won an incredible five medals, including three gold.[85] Sixty years separated their respective competitions, yet their connection came down to the same thing: both had won Olympic medals. I like to think Shane Gould was honoured to meet Mina and told her so. I like to think Mina felt that was exactly as it should be. Ironically, the group in the photograph taken on that summer afternoon in 1974, is standing on what was the swimming pool of Chalwin Castle but had since been filled in and converted into a tennis court.

On the evidence of that Sunday afternoon, Chalwin deemed Mina fit enough to travel and cope with the publicity of an inauguration ceremony, and in April of 1974, Mina received an official letter from Dawson inviting her to become an Honoree of his famed museum. By this time Mina, Les Boardman and Theodore Tartakover were the only surviving swimmers from the 1912 Olympic swimming team:- Harold Hardwick, Billy Longworth and Frank Schryver were now, like Healy, Champion and Fanny Durack, faded ink in Mina's autograph album. To be awarded this honour just when it seemed her time had passed was not simply reassurance that her achievements were remembered, but that she herself had not been forgotten.

*

By the time Mina boarded her flight to the USA at Sydney airport on 15 May 15 1975, there could not have been many newspaper readers left in NSW who were not aware of who she was and why she was headed to Florida. MP Neil Pickard's public appeal for funds to send Mina to her inauguration ceremony had clearly touched a nerve with the Sydney public, and the sense that a serious wrong had now been righted accompanied Mina up the aircraft steps. So too did the loyal Harry, who sat next to her for the entire trip, and her advocate, Vivian Chalwin. This was not the first time Chalwin had officially accompanied a swimmer to the ISHOF, he had travelled with Dawn Fraser for her belated inauguration ceremony in 1972.[86] But even Fraser, the greatest female swimmer of her time (many would argue, of all time) had not been surrounded by the publicity and front-page headlines which had circulated around Mina in the last week.

Owing to concerns about Mina's health, she and Harry were put up in Buck Dawson's home in Fort Lauderdale, rather than a hotel. Judging from a handful of photographs taken at the pool complex in which Mina looks to be in vigorous physical health, the concerns focussed on her mental health and increasing confusion. It is entirely possible that Harry had been included on the trip to offer stability to Mina and give a sense of the familiar, although in the photographs from her time in Florida she is beaming and clearly having a wonderful time. She attended a celebratory dinner and dance for inductees aboard a riverboat, and placed her hands in wet cement, freezing her prints for eternity beside previous inductees. She joked with film star and former Olympic medallist, Buster Crabbe, who was known for his portrayals of Tarzan, Flash Gordon and Buck Rogers on the silver screen.[87]

She grinned and nodded as Buck Dawson read out her unequalled achievements—an Australian championship title for twenty consecutive years, world records in freestyle, breast stroke and backstroke, three times Australian champion in all three strokes—and repeated her story of the 4x100m relay event in Stockholm: 'We wanted to swim twice, but they wouldn't let us do it.' She posed in her Olympic blazer beside a picture of her younger self and shook hands with curious well-wishers. In short, she had a ball.

And if she, at times, was not entirely sure of where she was or what was going on, did it really matter? Harry was beside her, Vivian Chalwin was attentive and caring, and Henry and Florence hovered on the edges of memory. In my version, she had the silver medal from Stockholm in her pocket, a tangible keepsake bestowed upon the long gone twenty-one-year-old who this crowd had gathered to honour. The space between the decades vanished and the circle was complete.

Having seen the ghostly apparitions in the sports stadium in Stockholm, I knew I had to travel to Fort Lauderdale and visit the International Swimming Hall of Fame. This I mistakenly did in August, and my first thought on exiting the Florida airport was how on earth Mina had coped with the humidity. I was aware before I arrived that Buck Dawson and the ISHOF had played a major role in the revitalisation of the Fort Lauderdale beach area, and images on display at the museum verified that the complex had once been a thriving and important venue to both the city, and US swimming.

With accommodation for 4,500 spectators, the competition pools had earned the complex the reputation as the finest swimming stadium on the entire east coast, and had hosted national and international swimming, diving, water polo and synchronised swimming competitions. With Dawson's death in 2008, however, the place had slipped into decline—perhaps it had slowly been doing so since his retirement in 1986. Fifty years after its inauguration, there was a sad air of neglect clinging to the complex in 2015. The pools were still operational but barely used—I swam laps alone—and graffiti adorned the lockers in the changing rooms. Even the Walk of Fame where luminaries such as Esther Williams, Johnny Weissmuller, Dawn Fraser and Mina had fixed their handprints in cement had been dug up and destroyed.

But the passion behind the Hall of Fame was palpable, and it was still staffed by people who loved swimming and swimming history and had a genuine desire to hear Mina's story. And although the storage of archival material was haphazard, the librarian in charge (a woman in her nineties who remembered Mina's inauguration) knew exactly where everything was and how it related. She had even taken the time to set aside files of Mina's contemporaries that she thought I should see: Ethelda, Duke, Eppie and Fanny Durack.

Here was the complete catalogue of WSA newsletters and pictures of Fanny Durack as a child. A photograph of Duke and Mina on a beach in Hawaii, and the San Francisco newspaper reports of Fanny's dismissive attitude to the local swimmers. Here was an entire box devoted to Annette Kellerman, and another to the famous aquacades at the Biltmore Hotel in Miami, a forty-minute drive away. I was in heaven.

I even found the tired museum with its outmoded methods of presentation and worn exhibits, completely exhilarating. And I was not the only person who had made the pilgrimage to Florida specifically to visit this national shrine to swimming:- I encountered an immaculately dressed, petite, white haired woman who had performed in aquacades in California the 1950s, searching the display cabinets for a glimpse of her younger self. In one case I marvelled at Annette Kellerman's sequined jacket and leggings from 1915, and in another, a tiny bottle of brown water taken from the harbour pool in Stockholm. Had Mina seen that, I wondered. And did she laugh?

There was an entire corner dedicated to Dawn Fraser, and a separate case held the two-piece swimsuit worn by Gertrude Ederle (adorned with the badge of Eppie's WSA) when she made her record-breaking Channel swim in 1926. Mina would have seen this too, I thought. She would have stood right here. Or maybe here. I pictured her in the great hall, wearing a shapeless flowery dress and holding her silver medal in her blazer pocket.

Annette Kellerman was inducted into the Hall of Fame in the same year as Mina, but Kellerman, then living in Australia, was not well enough to undertake the journey to Florida. On one hand, Mina missed out on meeting (again?) the woman who had been her idol throughout her youth, but on the other, if Kellerman had been there, she would undoubtedly have pulled the focus away from Mina. Annette Kellerman, I was told by the all-knowing librarian, had been no stranger to Florida and had actually filmed sequences for her aquatic movies in a pool in Miami. This pool was the Venetian Pool in the Coral Cables district, a 'must visit' attraction for anyone interested in the history of swimming.

I dutifully boarded a train to Miami and made my way to Coral Gables, a suburb so named because of the decorative coral adorning many of the buildings in the district. All roads in the suburb appeared to lead to the pool and as I approached the railings of what is still the largest pool in USA, I suspected I was in for a special treat.

Created by the wonderfully named architect Phineas Paist, and designed by Denman Fink, the Venetian Pool was constructed in a reconfigured quarry and opened in 1924. It is a spectacular riot of camp with waterfalls, tropical foliage, plaster grottoes and Italianate architecture, including a replica of a Venetian bridge. When the pool was first in operation, it was drained regularly to allow the Miami Symphony Orchestra to perform in the resulting perfect acoustic bowl. In later years, there were gondolas on the water, musicians strategically positioned on balconies and famous singers to serenade the poolside dancers well into the night. On the walls of the pool entrance building, there were numerous photographs of Kellerman filming in the Venetian pool and I swam into nooks and crannies, trying to pinpoint the exact location where she posed as a mermaid among fake pink coral.

I pictured Kellerman bossing the cameraman as they filmed in the grotto and water filled caves. How did they get the lights in there without electrocuting everyone? And could that possibly be the very waterfall which features in the iconic image of Kellerman, seemingly nude, her long hair strategically placed over her breasts, leaning back into the cascade? Was it at this pool that she donned the gold sequined swimsuit and matching hat and performed underwater ballet for the camera? In these slightly surreal surroundings, nothing would surprise me. And it occurred to me that if ever there was the perfect example of two wildly opposing extremes built for the same purpose, it is the Venetian Pool in Miami and Wylie's Baths in Coogee.

*

I believe that Mina's legacy as the plucky young woman who battled misogyny and took on the men of the Australasian Olympic selection committee was a myth first introduced during the Florida fares controversy of 1975. In fact, the ideal time to ignite a debate about women, sport and history would have been in 1956, in the context of the first Australian Olympics. An enterprising reporter could have interviewed Mina and Dawn Fraser together and opened up a discussion about how things had changed, or not, for women swimmers since their first Olympic appearance. But the issue of discrimination against women in sport was laughed off in 1956, and it was not something that many reporters would have been interested in pursuing.

Twenty years later, however, in the context of a political climate of women's protest marches and renewed calls for equal rights, the issue could neither be ignored, nor dismissed. And 1975 was, after all, the International Year of Women. Mina was the perfect 'poster girl' for the Women's Liberation Movement and living proof that nothing had changed for women in over sixty years.

Six months after Mina's triumphant return from Florida, Neil Bennetts came to 13 Neptune Street to record her for his sound archive. She was an old hand at these interviews by now, they all wanted to know the same thing:- tell me about Stockholm in 1912, and why wouldn't the men let you go? None of the reporters who interviewed Mina in 1975 at the height of the controversy engaged in fact checking, and it was this oversight which enabled the myth of sexual discrimination amongst the male sporting officials in 1912 to take hold and embed itself in Mina's story. Not that I am saying there was no prejudice—it cannot be denied that Mina and Durack were not initially offered places on the team due to issues concerning their sex. When the additional cost was raised as justification for excluding the two women, no official suggested that two male swimmers who were not medal contenders give up their places on the team in favour of Mina and Durack, who were. But within two minutes of the Bennetts interview, it is clear that the tale of discrimination that Mina had been agreeing with for the last six months, is now something she has come to whole heartedly believe.

'When we went to the games in 1912 the men hadn't anything to do with ladies' swimming and they didn't think it was right that women should be sent from Australia to Stockholm. After a long fight with them we were allowed … given permission to go, and both Fanny and myself went to Stockholm at our own expense.'

She doesn't take the time to clarify that the women's branch of the ASA had to give permission for herself and Durack to compete before the male Olympic selection committee could offer them places on the team, and at no point in the interview does she bring up the Rose Scott/Marion McIntosh fray over the segregation rule. She then tells Bennett, 'When the Australian flag went up for one, two in Stockholm, of course, Australia sort of took the credit for it, for which they weren't really due, I don't think.' Mina seemed to be conflating a wider authority, which she refers to as 'Australia', with the male sporting officials whom she had come to regard as being against her inclusion in the team.

It is an odd statement, because who else other than 'Australia' would take credit for two Olympic medals won by Australians? I think she was attempting to separate the male authorities, who she was now painting as unsupportive, from the female authorities i.e. the LASA committee, who she had recast in her mind as supportive. But this was overlooking the fact that eight women on the governing committee voted against allowing Mina and Durack to swim in Stockholm.

Like the journalists who reported on the Florida fares controversy and Pickard's public fund, Bennetts had not done the research which would have enabled him to introduce Rose Scott and the segregation rule into the conversation and it was his deference to Mina's version of events that allowed her to present it as fact. But the Bennetts interview was never intended to be broadcast, although Mina may not have known that at the time. It was purely for archival purposes—Bennetts' hobby in retirement—so there was no real reason to check any of her claims.

Nonetheless, the fiction that Mina and Fanny Durack had been refused places on the Olympic team by men who did not want to include women in sport, took root and flourished, and it is difficult to find a contemporary recording of Mina which does not repeat the myth. It is, of course, a better story, and perhaps Mina was well aware of that in 1975. She was someone, remember, who had never taken the time to correct the ongoing mistake concerning her age. In a feature on Mina in *The Canberra Times* in 1976, reporter Jeff Turnbull not only asserted that, 'Mina Wylie, 77, had to overcome male chauvinism before she could become one of Australia's first women Olympians', he maintained that she did so when she was only thirteen.[88]

Mina corroborates this in the radio documentary, 'Anzac Mermaids', claiming, 'I was too young to go alone.'[89] Perhaps, by now, the image of herself as an extraordinary child prodigy had come to form part of her identity, resonating, as it did, with the success of Shane Gould, who had won five medals at the 1972 Olympics in Munich at the age of fifteen. In the same radio documentary, Mina repeated another falsehood which she appeared to have come to believe regarding the male swimmers:

'The government paid their fare, or the association, but nobody paid our fare. Dad paid mine and Fanny Durack's people paid hers.'

It is possibly an indication of her mental state at the time of the interview—which, in the lack of any evidence, I am taking to be post 1975—that she had completely forgotten Marion McIntosh's public appeal fund. In the burst of publicity surrounding Mina's rediscovery in 1975, the fact that the women had to pay their own fares was repeated in a number of newspaper reports, without a qualification that this was also a requirement of the male swimmers. It was another strand of the discrimination myth which journalists were eager to tell, and readers equally keen to read. Mina was the 'against-the-odds' heroine, who had defeated prejudice at every turn and deserved our applause and our thanks.

Although the media campaign had a positive outcome for Mina and re-established her a figure of national significance, the row concerning her expenses overshadowed the Florida event itself. NSW newspapers carried stories and images of Mina (and Pickard's) campaign for her to attend her inauguration ceremony, comparing it to her and Durack's 'battle' to swim in Stockholm, but no Australian newspaper actually covered the ceremony in Florida, or printed images of the ceremony and celebrations. Which does raise the question as to what it was exactly the media was interested in where Mina and this story was concerned.

With so few female athletes given heroic status within the Sporting Nation, Mina as a figure in 1975, undoubtedly appealed to the female populace, engrossed, as many of them were, with the question of women's place in society. Mina's version of events told the triumphant story of victim to victor that many women wanted, even needed, to hear at the time. But when her statements are examined in any depth, Mina in 1975, reveals herself as an unreliable witness. The enduring question, of course, is whether the myth of Mina Wylie, the reshaping of the events of 1912 and her role in them, is a more beneficial legacy in the context of women and sport within Australia, than no legacy at all.

*

There are enough hints concerning Mina's mental health in 1975 to suggest that she was in the early stages of Alzheimer's disease. As this is a progressive illness, her symptoms would have worsened over time and the words 'care home' would have been gently introduced into conversations concerning the future. I think, however, that Mina retained enough control over her faculties to be acutely aware of her legacy, or at least, her memorabilia. She donated ten photographs to the Mitchell Library in 1976, and it was this act which pushed the matter of her swimming archive to the top of her priority list.

If the Mitchell Library had initially turned down the offer of the collection, Mina may have tried other archives such as the National Museum in Canberra, or any number of sporting institutions. But the real reason the artefacts ended up concealed in the basement of Mina's house could actually be quite simple: no one else wanted them. Who, after all, has the space to store thirteen boxes of items belonging to an elderly relative?

Whatever the circumstances, by the late 1970s Mina was taking stock, probably in the knowledge that a move into full time care was inevitable. It may have been the recent media focus on her Olympic participation that caused her to set aside items associated with the 1912 competition, yet throw away souvenirs of the 1956 Olympics her forty years at PLC.

Perhaps she had come to believe that the image the press had created, the plucky girl who fought against authoritative men and triumphed, was indeed the most relevant figure of a life filled with many different incarnations. She was also canny enough to realise that the Olympics and her supposed 'battle for inclusion' was all the reporters seemed interested in. Few press reports on Mina in 1975/6 made mention of the fact that competing in the Olympics was only one part of a much greater sporting life and that her greatest achievements in swimming came after her return from Stockholm when she learned the new crawl stroke. She may have felt, not incorrectly, that 1912 was her best chance being remembered. Or even, that it was the only thing a nation which regarded sporting success as an international calling card, would consider as worth remembering.

At some point in the late 1970s, Harry and Mina left the house that they had called home for some fifty years and took up residence in the nearby Daintrey nursing home. By this time, they were so welded to each other's company that separation was never discussed. The house, still in Mina's name, could not be sold without her permission and this was not forthcoming. It lay there empty, unlived in yet undisturbed, just as Mina and Harry had left it, for almost a decade. A Great Expectations shroud of dust sheets and cobwebs but without the presiding Miss Haversham.

On 6 July 1984, Mina died at the care home, aged ninety-three. She had outlived both her brothers and all her 1912 Olympic team mates. *The Australian* carried a three-column tribute illustrated with an early image of Mina[90], but the *Sydney Morning Herald* could only manage a three-sentence footnote and the *Weekly Courier* repeated the error regarding her age. She was buried in a private ceremony at Randwick general cemetery where, according to her wishes, she was laid to rest in the same plot as Florence and Henry. Amongst the mourners was Jeanette Buckham, principal of Pymble Ladies College, who later noted in the school magazine that Mina had been 'the best teacher of breaststroke that I have ever seen.'[91]

*

Individuals today (other than swimming enthusiasts or historians) who are aware of Mina Wylie, are most likely to be those who swim at Wylie's Baths, now classified by the National Trust of Australia. After a period of closure following severe storm damage in 1978, the Sunstrip Pool was taken over by Randwick Council, and the day to day running of the pool was handed over to a community management committee.

The original name of Wylie's Baths was reinstated, a decision which was undoubtedly influenced by the rediscovery of Mina three years previously and her inauguration into the ISHOF. The Wylie of the original Wylie's Baths may have been Henry, but in 1978 it could just have easily referred to Mina and the council was aligning itself, and the suburb, with a local figure who now had national and international recognition.

The renaming of the pool was a deliberate move by council members to create a site of historical significance which gave residents a sense of their community as important within Australian sporting history. This symbolic transformation of Wylie's Baths from a site of recreation into a site of history does assume that sport is so central to Australian identity that sporting venues have cultural and historical significance. Yet Wylie's was not a significant sporting venue in the way that Randwick Racecourse or the Sydney Cricket Ground was, and the lack of spectator accommodation meant that the pool had not played the same role in the nation's swimming history as the Domain Baths or Bronte pool in the early days. The significance of Wylie's which justified a major 1994 restoration project, derived from the existence of the original wooden boardwalk and the association of the baths with the now rediscovered Mina Wylie.

In 2001, Mina's significance to the pool and to the suburb was underlined even further with the creation of a three-sided bronze sculpture of Mina by local artist Eileen Slarke. Monuments to female (or non-white) athletes are rare (not only in Australia) and are almost always the result of either community action or a related association such as a sporting club. Dawn Fraser and Fanny Durack have swimming pools named in their honour, but Mina is only one of a handful of Australian female athletes to be commemorated in monument form and this is undoubtedly due to the tenacity of her supporters on the Wylie's Baths Trust who were the driving force behind the statue. Beside Mina's statue at the entrance to the pool is a plaque which reads:

'Wilhelmina (Mina) Wylie, a silver medallist at the VI Olympiad, Stockholm, has the distinction of being one of the first female swimmers to represent Australia at an Olympic Games. A Coogee resident, Mina was taught to swim at Wylie's Baths by her father, Henry Wylie, who established the pool in 1907.'

Mina learned to swim in Bronte Baths and had been competing for five years by the time Henry opened his pool, but the facts matter less than function they are performing i.e. linking this particular pool, and suburb, with an Olympic legend. But the statue does more than draw an association between the site and a seminal moment in Australian sporting history, it contradicts the notion that only male athletes are worthy of memorialisation in the form of a monument, and it challenges the view that only men are capable of the feats that will earn them legendary status. Metaphorically then, the statue claims a place for women in a wider sporting context, and the positioning of the monument at the entrance to the pool irrefutably claims the space as Mina's.

Mina's enduring value to sport in Australia is her status as 'one of the first'. Ironically however, this again reinforces the view of sport as a male concern and female athletes as exceptions to the rule:- any success they have is notable because they are women, not because they are exceptional in their chosen discipline. The accumulation of misinformation surrounding Mina's memory suggests that her position in Australian sporting history is tenuous. She is included as a pioneer, but her secondary status as a woman in the field of sport ensures that any attention is superficial, and the facts are unresearched. She is used, just as she was in 1912, to tick the inclusion box.

*

Mina's story is not straightforward and there are as many versions of her life as there are versions of Mina herself. In one version, she was a feminist advocate who, for decades, gave free swimming lessons to little girls at McIver's Ladies Baths in Coogee. In another, she deliberately constructed a version of her own story that inflated her heroism and significance in the history of women and sport in Australia.

In yet another, she lied about her age and, possibly conveniently, forgot it was the segregation rule that rendered her ineligible for selection onto the Olympic team. On the two most notable occasions when Mina dominated the front pages of Sydney newspapers—the 1912 mixed bathing debate and the 1975 Florida controversy—her ability as a swimmer was of secondary importance within the wider contexts of gender and nationalism. And on both occasions, this context had emerged from enormous social upheaval concerning the place of women in society. Perhaps this is why she has acquired the reputation of a crusading feminist.

There is no question that Mina was the personification of modernity and an independent and confident woman who inspired other Australian women to view themselves in a new light. She travelled to the jazz-age USA and kept dubious company. She remained single and financially independent. She was headline news at a time when women were kept resolutely in the private sphere. Mina captured the imagination of the public both in 1912 and sixty years later in a way that, arguably, no other female athlete has done since. And what remains indisputable, is that no other female swimmer, worldwide, has equalled her achievements and longevity in the sport.

There are three sides to Eileen Slarke's statue of Mina: one greets the visitor as she arrives, one watches over the swimmers in the pool, and one looks towards Randwick cemetery where Mina is buried. The bronze reproduces the pose Mina adopted in the E S Marks photograph of the three medallists. Shoulders back, head high, arms by her sides. Even the bangles on her wrists are visible. It tells the viewer that this is someone of note. Someone worth remembering. And if anyone is looking for Mina Wylie, they will find her here. At Wylie's Baths.

Many pieces. One whole.

Three sides. One person.

I look again at the E. S. Marks photograph of the three medallists in the inaugural 100m freestyle for women in Stockholm. I look at it for a long time. Mina's defiance makes me smile. I bet she looked up at the crowd as the trio walked back down the boardwalk to the waiting photographers. I bet she smiled.

See? Told you.

In the photograph, there is a space between Mina and Fanny Durack. I walk along the edge of the murky pool with the towering diving platform. I push past the eager men and their bulky cameras and I place myself into that space. Fanny shifts slightly to make room. Mina and I exchange smiles. I congratulate her. We turn to the camera, shoulders back, heads up. We're Olympic medallists. No one will tell us what to do.

Reception at Chalwin Castle for Buck Dawson (front, wearing eye patch) 1974. Mina, front row with handbag. Vivian Chalwin is front row left, wearing a blazer. Dawn Fraser, far left with Boy Charlton. Shane Gould, right, arm around an unidentified man.

Mina at her inauguration into the International Swimming Hall of Fame, Florida, 1975.

Epilogue

My search for Mina Wylie began and ended at Wylie's Baths. It was some twenty-five years ago that my friend, Karen, with her raucous laugh and red and black Holden Menaro, first took me to swim there. I was too entranced with the wooden boardwalk, the rickety steps and the tabby cat enthroned in the women's changing rooms to concern myself with who had built this haven of tranquillity. I swam blissful laps watching black and white striped fish and luxuriating in the waves breaking the sea wall and caressing my back. Stretched out on the warm concrete, Karen and I spent an entire summer at Wylie's in the early 90s, earnestly discussing the films she would make and the stories I would write.

Our futures were the shining shells we reached out to touch on the floor of the pool as we glided past. Two decades later, after a long sojourn overseas, I returned to the restored pool and was intrigued by the three-sided bronze statue which greeted me at the entrance. How had I never heard of this woman? Why did I not know that she had trained at this pool for a career which outlasted all her contemporaries? And thus began my search.

As I leafed through water-stained carnival programmes and deciphered faded messages in autograph albums, I became obsessed with Mina Wylie. Bit by bit I came to believe that she wanted to be found within the scraps of information she had so carefully preserved. She wanted her story to be told. She demanded it. And so I scrutinised the contents of her boxes of memorabilia and pored over photograph albums, determined to make connections which would bring me closer to her.

I visited places she had been and convinced myself I felt her presence. I touched her dresses and read private correspondence. I held her Olympic medal and marvelled at the weight of it. I gave her a romantic interest and a dream of Hollywood stardom. I heard her speak and I saw her swim. And finally, I came to realise that some of her statements were simply not true and that she had a gift for exaggeration. I also cursed her for not finishing her 1912 diary or saving photographs from the Melbourne Olympics. But I did find her. Or at least, a version of her. The version she allowed me to construct through the objects she left behind.

With each object I lifted from a box in the Mitchell Library, I was acutely aware that she had placed it there for a reason. Perhaps she wasn't fully aware of the magnitude of her actions because she was old and confused and knew only that her tangible memories must be preserved.

But there is the possibility that she knew exactly what she was doing when she knelt in the dim and airless void underneath her house and methodically packed her life out of sight. Hoping that someone might find it, and might, just might, understand. And although the space between her action and her hope being realised stretched to forty years, it did happen. She was right. Her life was worth something. And as I engaged in this delicate act of decoupage, I believe I came to know her. Sometimes, I even believed I was there with her, closing the gap as we both sprinted to the finishing rope. I see you, I whispered. I'll catch you.

Throughout this process, I have often wondered who Mina would have become if Henry had not recognised her potential and encouraged her into competition. Most likely she would have married in her early twenties, settled in a lower middle-class suburb and produced children who would have been taught to swim by their grandfather in the pool that still bears the family name. She may have eschewed marriage for life as a modern woman – a stenographer or teacher—she had the education behind her. But Mina Wylie realised she was good at something, really good, and she had the audacity and the support to pursue it.

It brought her fame, international travel, recognition and financial security. I look at the photograph of Mina at Wylie's in 1913, her swimsuit cut too high on the thigh, her hands resting confidently on her hips and her shoulders thrown back in a gesture of defiance. Just try and stop me, she says. Just try. And I want to sit down with her and say, you don't have to tell me. I know exactly what you mean.

I think Mina and I would have got on well. We would have paced each other on bright days at Wylie's—she could have corrected my breast stroke. We would talk about New York and theatre and Annette Kellerman and how our respective worlds are still governed by bullish men who jealously guard their turf. I'd show her the photographs of me in my royal blue and white swimsuit in the front row of the County team. She would confide her crush on Cecil Healy. I would go to her house for tea and sing 'By the Light of the Silvery Moon' round the piano in the front room. We would play duets then go to the movies at the Randwick Ritz. Oh yes, Mina and I would have been great friends.

The thing is, at some point in all of our lives, the past needs to be packed into boxes and stored underneath the house out of sight. The dresses, the rings from childhood, the charm necklace, the medals. Not because they have no relevance, but because the person in the pictures with the curling edges has long gone.

It is not you, or her, or me anymore. It was a moment in time, a breath snatched in between strokes. In order to keep swimming, it is necessary to exhale.

I go to Wylie's Baths and lower myself in at the northern end. I nod to the statue watching over the swimmers and I push off. My stroke is strong and steady and not something that will diminish in the final lap. I do what I have done since I was five years old. The one thing that has given me strength and made me who I am.

I swim.

I swim with the black and white fish and the waves on my back, and the shells beneath me open up to reveal perfect shining pearls. I turn my head to take a breath and there she is, almost on my shoulder so intent is she to take her place. Gold bangles on each wrist and her hair flowing out behind her, Mina Wylie matches my freestyle, stroke for stroke. We lock eyes, and we understand.

The sky darkens, and green and pink flashes of light crackle amongst the stars. Delicate fairy lights twinkle on the surface of the water. All the breaths and all the strokes have been leading to this moment.

A wave lifts us up and carries us over the sea wall into the ocean. And the group of women pulled on by the shining moon gets bigger and bigger with every memory, every photograph, every delicate pressed flower removed from the dusty pages of an unopened book. Mina leads us on. Because she is both the moon and the sun, the sea and the turning tide. She is the streak of light skimming the breaking waves.

Mina swims towards the silver moon.

And I swim with her.

Notes

Introduction
[1] MLMSS 5078 Wilhelmina (Mina) Wylie – papers, 1872-1938.
[2] By sculptor Eileen Slarke. The memorial was erected on the site in 2001.

Chapter one

[3] Quoted in 'Swim star, 77, to get her trip to America' *Daily Mirror*, 13 May 1975.
[4] 'No help for fares' *The Canberra Times,* 15 May 1975.
[5] The care home has since been demolished so the exact dates of Mina and Harry's residence are impossible to confirm.
[6] Wylie, Mina & Bennetts, Neil. (Interviewer) 1975, Mina Wylie interviewed by Neil Bennetts. http://trove.nla.gov.au/work/22932421
[7] The 86 oral history interviews recorded by Bennetts were purchased by the National Library of Australia between 1975 and 1995.
[8] 'How Miss M Wylie gained the 100 yards championship of Australia' *The Daily Telegraph*, 9 February 1920.
[9] Despite his open misogyny, Sullivan was, in fact, married.
[10] 1912 was the last time Australia and New Zealand fielded a combined team under the titled Australasia. From 1920, New Zealand competed as a separate nation.
[11] See Ramsland, J., 2007. Barney Kieran, the Legendary 'Sobraon Boy': From the Mean Streets to 'Champion of the World'. Sport in History 27(2), pp.241-259

Chapter Two

[12] Renamed the Dawn Fraser baths in 1964.
[13] Throughout her career, Kellerman was often spelt Kellermann. Whether this was a deliberate change, possibly to Anglicise the name during the First World War, or a recurring mistake, is unclear as there is no consistency in the spelling at any given period.

[14] On her return to New York, Trudy Ederle was presented with the coveted red roadster by *The Daily News* amidst scenes of pandemonium as the huge crowds amassing for her honour parade brought the city to a standstill.

[15] Australian Dress Register ID: 549

Chapter Three

[16] Kellerman's performance at the New York Hippodrome in 1907 is often credited as the birth of what is now known as synchronised swimming.

[17] Released in 1952, 'Million Dollar Mermaid' was a musical film retelling the life of Annette Kellerman. Directed by Mervyn LeRoy, the film starred Esther Williams.

[18] The difference between the strokes was in the number of kicks per arm rotation. Australian crawl had four, but the early American crawl refined the stroke to incorporate six, thereby increasing speed.

[19] Kellerman, A. (1918). How To Swim. New York, George H. Doran Company.

[20] Kellerman, A. (1919). Physical Beauty - How To Keep It. London, William Heinemann.

[21] Reginald Leslie "Snowy" Baker (1884 – 1953) was an Australian athlete, sports promoter, and actor.

[22] Written by Manuel Nklein and directed by James R Sullivan.

[23] Sculptor Eileen Slarke included the bangles in her 2001 bronze rendition of Mina which stands at the entrance to Wylie's Baths.

[24] Australian States granted women the right to vote at different times. South Australia in 1895, Western Australia in 1899, NSW in 1902, Tasmania in 1903, Queensland in 1905 and Victoria in 1908.

Chapter Four

[25] 'Honour goes to Coogee race-winner' *The Canberra Times*, 11 January 1976.

[26] Healy did, in fact, go on to win a silver medal in the 100m freestyle, and a gold medal as part of the men's 200m freestyle relay team.

[27] In 1916, McIntosh bought the *Sunday Times* newspaper and associated weeklies *The Arrow* and *The Referee*.

[28] 'Lady Swimmers, Will They Go? E. S. Marks Says Yes', *The Sun*, 18 March 1912.

[29] The E.S. Marks Athletics Field in Sydney's Centennial Park is named in his honour.

[30] The irate Schnall transferred her talents to baseball and by 1913 she was Captain of the New York Giants female team.

[31] The misreporting of Wylie's age continued throughout her life and upon her death, various obituaries gave her age as either 86 or 93.

[32] Producers Wendy Carlisle and Michelle Rayner. Broadcast 18 February 1996.

[33] Lily de Beaurepaire and her brother Frank became the first Australian siblings to compete in the same Olympics in 1920. Lily did not advance to the finals of the 100m and 400m freestyle, but Frank won bronze in the 1500m and silver as a member of the 4x200m relay team. Frank had previously won a silver medal in 400m freestyle and a bronze in the 1500m in 1908, and went on to win a third bronze medal for the 1500m and a third silver medal for his part in the 4x200m relay in 1924. Both Frank and Lily dropped the 'de' from their surname in later years.

Chapter Five

[34] Collection of photographs relating to the 1912 Olympic games, Stockholm, from the E.S. Marks Sporting Collection. E.S. Marks/Q85-86.

[35] At Henley, the Australian rowers won the Grand Challenge Cup.

[36] Mina's blazer is held in the Bowen Library in Randwick.

[37] A compilation of this footage can be viewed online at https://www.olympic.org/stockholm-1912

Chapter Six

[38] 'A Lady Swimmer Back in Australia – Miss Wylie's Victories' *The Herald*, 4 October 1912.

[39] Hugh McIntosh bought the Tivoli theatre business in September 1912, although the terms did not include the five theatres in Sydney, Melbourne, Adelaide, Perth and Kalgoorlie which he leased for varying terms.

[40] 'Arrival of Miss Bleibtrey' *The Daily Telegraph*, 17 February 1921.

[41] Vera Pearce was the Aunt of future Australian Prime Minister Harold Holt (1966-1967) who disappeared whilst swimming off Cheviot Beach in Victoria on 17 December 1967. His body was never found.

[42] The current world record for men's 100m freestyle stands at 46.9 seconds and was set in July 2009 by Cesar Cielo of Brazil, at the FINA world championships in Rome. Cielo was wearing a polyurethane body suit, subsequently banned by FINA from January 2010.

[43] See Curthoys, A. 2002. *Freedom Ride: A Freedom Rider Remembers*, Allen and Unwin, Sydney.

[44] While stationed at Mena Camp in Cairo, Henry Miller recorded a Christmas message which was sent back to his family in Sydney. The message remains the only known recording of an Australian soldier serving in the First World War and can be heard at:
https://www.nfsa.gov.au/about/our-mission/sounds-australia

[45] US Congress voted to declare war on Germany on 6 April 1917.

[46] For further information on Charlotte Epstein, see her entry in the encyclopedia section in the Jewish Women's Archive:
https://jwa.org/encyclopedia/article/epstein-charlotte

[47] Australians to try for all US titles' *New York Times*, 23 August 1916.

[48] Handley remained in this voluntary role with the WSA until 1952.

[49] Arbuckle (1887–1933) was one of the most popular and highest paid silent screen stars of the early 1900s. Between November 1921 and April 1922, he was the defendant in three trials for the rape and manslaughter of actress Virginia Rappe. Arbuckle was acquitted in the third trial and received a formal written statement of apology from the jury.

[50] On the 100th anniversary of Healy's death, the Australian Olympic Committee announced that an award bearing his name would be presented at the Olympic Games to the Australian athlete who best demonstrates exceptional sportsmanship.

[51] Andrew, J. 1919. *Cecil Healy: In Memoriam*, John Andrew, Sydney.

Chapter Eight

[52] Email correspondence with P. Ross, 23 October 2011. The blazer is now the property of Randwick District and Historical Society. Australian Dress Register ID: 548.

[53] Uncredited clipping in box 5 of Mina Wylie's archive, dated 30 July, 1919.

[54] The election of 1920 was the first US Presidential election in which women in every state were permitted to vote. Republican candidate Warren G. Harding was victorious

[55] At the Paris Olympics in 1924, Aileen Riggin won silver in the 3m springboard event and bronze in the 100m ladies backstroke. Helen Wainwright won silver in 1924 in the 400m ladies freestyle.

[56] For a more comprehensive analysis of the 1919 USA tour, see Lucas, J. A. and I. Jobling (1995). "Troubled Waters: Fanny Durack's 1919 Swimming Tour of

America Amid Transnational Amateur Athletic Prudery and Bureaucracy."
OLYMPIKA-LONDON ONTARIO- **4**: 93-112.

[57] 'Anzac Mermaids Cancel Their Tour' *The New York Times*, 30 August 1919,

[58] 'Foreign Mermaids bring their tour to a sudden end' *The New York Tribune*, 30 August 1919,

[59] 'Girl Swimmers: Miss Durack and Miss Wylie Treatment in America' *The Sun*, 8 October 1919.

[60] Described in detail in McAllister, I. H. (2013). The Hilda James Story: Lost Olympics. UK, emp3books Ltd.

Chapter Nine

[61] Carlisle, W. & Rayner, M. 1996. *Anzac Mermaids*, radio programme, ABC Radio National, broadcast 18 February. 1996. A recording of this programme is available in the library of the Maritime Museum in Sydney.

[62] 'A New 100 Yards Champion' *The Sportsman,* 11 February 1920, 'Mina Wylie – defeat of Fanny Durack' *The Sun*, 8 February 1920, 'Lady Amateurs: A new 100 yards champion', *The Truth,* 8 February 1920, 'Mina Wylie outstrips Fanny Durack in 100 yards' *The Referee*, 11 February 1920, 'Fanny Durack Beaten in 100yds championship: Mina Wylie her Conqueror', *The Sunday News*, 8 February 1920.

[63] 'A New 100 Yards Champion' *The Sportsman,* 11 February 1920.

[64] Harry Hay coached Boy Charlton to a 1500m gold medal in the Paris Olympics in 1924.

[65] Ross won gold medals in the 400m freestyle, the 1500m freestyle and as a member of the 4x200m freestyle relay team.

[66] 'Arrival of Miss Bleibtrey' *Daily Telegraph,* 17 February 1921.

[67] 'Swimmer's Civic Reception: Glad to Tell You Anything' *The Sun,* 17 February 1921.

68 A mixed 4 x100m medley relay was contested at the delayed Tokyo Olympic Games in 2021

[69] 'Coaching System Necessary' *The Referee,* 23 February 1921.

[70] WSA spring newsletter, 1921.

Chapter Ten

[71] 'Miss Wylie comes into her own: Wins 880 yards championship ladies carnival in Melbourne' *The Referee*, 15 December 1922.

[72] 'A Great Evening with the Swimmers: Misses Hoeft and Wylie's great contest' *The New Zealand Aquatic Magazine*, 23 March 1923.

[73] https://www.britishpathe.com/video/miss-annette-kellermans-congratulations

[74] Duke Kahanamoku won the silver medal in the 100m freestyle in Paris, to Johnny Weissmuller's gold.

[75] A women's 1500m freestyle race was contested for the first time at the delayed Tokyo Olympic Games in 2021.

[76] Charlton won silver in the 1500m freestyle and silver in the 400m freestyle at the 1928 Amsterdam Olympics.

[77] With thanks to Elizabeth Penfold, Janet Halliday, Ann Windeyer, Elspeth Browne, Kate Macpherson, Leith Toll, Gabrielle Hogan, Trish Butterworth, Cynthia Norley and Pat Ross.

Chapter Eleven

[78] 'Fanny Durack Dies at 64' *The Canberra Times*, 22 March 1956. (Durack was 66 on her death)

[79] Egypt nationalised the Suez Canal, resulting in the invasion of the country by Israel, France and the United Kingdom.

[80] A water polo match between the Soviet Union and Hungary on 6 December became known as the 'Blood in the Water' match after a Hungarian player, Ervin Zador left the water with blood pouring from his face after being punched by Soviet player Valentin Prokopov.

[81] Australian men repeated the clean sweep of the 100m freestyle with Murray Rose (gold), John Devitt (silver) and Gary Chapman (bronze).

[82] The footage can now be viewed on You Tube at: https://youtu.be/rgjzchzkV6E

[83] The film footage of Chalwin's Cavalcade of Olympic Champions is the only known footage of Mina and early Olympic swimmers who competed before the advent of television.

[84] This tradition of free Saturday morning lessons continues at the pool today.

[85] Gould's gold medals came in the 200m and 400m freestyle, and the 200m individual medley. She set world records with these three victories. She won silver in the 800m freestyle and bronze in the 100m freestyle.

[86] Fraser was elected to the Hall of Fame in 1965 but, owing to her 10-year suspension by the Australian Swimming Union, she was unable to attend her induction ceremony and a second ceremony was held in her honour in 1972.

[87] Buster Crabbe won bronze in the 1500m freestyle in the 1928 Olympics, and gold in the 400m freestyle in 1932.

[88] 'Honour goes to Coogee race-winner' *The Canberra Times*, 11 January 1976.

[89] The documentary was broadcast in 1996, but Mina died in 1984 and there is no clarification as to when the interview with Mina had taken place.

[90] 'Swimmer has completed her longest race' *The Australian*, 16 July 1984.

[91] *The Magazine of the Pymble Ladies' College, Sydney*, December 1984. Number LXXIII. PLC archives.

Ingram Content Group UK Ltd.
Milton Keynes UK
UKHW020612160323
418667UK00008B/732